STOIC WARRIORS

Stoic Warriors

THE ANCIENT PHILOSOPHY
BEHIND THE MILITARY MIND

——

NANCY SHERMAN

OXFORD
UNIVERSITY PRESS

2005

OXFORD
UNIVERSITY PRESS

Oxford University Press, Inc., publishes works that further
Oxford University's objective of excellence
in research, scholarship, and education.

Oxford   New York
Auckland   Cape Town   Dar es Salaam   Hong Kong   Karachi
Kuala Lumpur   Madrid   Melbourne   Mexico City   Nairobi
New Delhi   Shanghai   Taipei   Toronto

With offices in
Argentina   Austria   Brazil   Chile   Czech Republic   France   Greece
Guatemala   Hungary   Italy   Japan   Poland   Portugal   Singapore
South Korea   Switzerland   Thailand   Turkey   Ukraine   Vietnam

Copyright © 2005 by Oxford University Press, Inc.

Published by Oxford University Press, Inc.
198 Madison Avenue, New York, New York 10016
www.oup.com

Oxford is a registered trademark of Oxford University Press

Library of Congress Cataloging-in-Publication Data
Sherman, Nancy, 1951–
Stoic warriors : the ancient philosophy
behind the military mind / Nancy Sherman.
p. cm.   Includes bibliographical references and index.
ISBN-13: 978-0-19-515216-6
ISBN-10: 0-19-515216-6
1. Stoics. 2. Psychology, Military. I. Title.
B528.S299   2005
188—dc22   2004065476

1 3 5 7 9 8 6 4 2

Printed in the United States of America
on acid-free paper

For my parents,
Beatrice and Seymour Sherman,
and my aunt,
Anna Cohen

Like the inner wall of a house
that after wars and destruction becomes
an outer one—
that's how I found myself suddenly,
too soon in life. I've almost forgotten what it means
to be inside. It no longer hurts;
I no longer love. Far or near—
they're both very far from me,
equally far.

I'd never imagined what happens to colors.
The same as with human beings: a bright blue drowses
inside the memory of dark blue and night,
a paleness sighs
out of a crimson dream. A breeze
carries odors from far away
but itself has no odor. The leaves of the squill die
long before its white flower,
which never knows
the greenness of spring and dark love.

I lift my eyes to the hills. Now I understand
what it means to lift up the eyes, what a heavy burden
it is. But these violent longings, this pain of
never-again-to-be-inside.

—Yehuda Amichai,
"Like the Inner Wall of a House"
(trans. Chana Bloch)

Contents

Preface and Acknowledgments

This book is about "sucking it up." In politer terms, it is about being stoic as part of military bearing. The issue could not be more pressing, given the U.S. Army's expansion of "stop-loss" orders to keep soldiers from leaving the service and the general malaise of a war in Iraq that has turned into street fights with insurgents. As war turns uglier and deadlier, the need to be stoic in war seems ever more urgent. The question that preoccupies me is what light ancient Stoic theory can shed on our contemporary notions of what it means to be stoic. In particular, how can tensions internal to the ancient debate itself instruct us about the attractions and dangers of austere self-control and discipline? These questions grew out of a stint at the United States Naval Academy, where I held the Distinguished Chair in Ethics from 1997 to 1999. Popularized notions of being stoic resonated with young and older officers alike, but so too did the readings of actual Stoic philosophers such as Epictetus. The idea that one's happiness could depend solely on one's own virtue and that one's agency and control might be bulletproof appealed to them. But few had thought seriously about the costs of being stoic. Personal psychological costs may be the most obvious. Critical, but little noticed, are diminished capacity for moral reasoning and reduced ability to lead others in difficult and deadly circumstances.

As this book goes to press, thousands of U.S. combat troops are in Iraq and Afghanistan. Some will never return. Others have returned or will return ravaged by war. Some will suffer from psychological trauma but think that not being able to tough it out is a sure sign of moral weakness. Others know better but worry about the stigma of seeking psychological help; they worry about the shame of not bearing up in a culture in which unflappable strength is always expected. Others worry that if all who suffer psychological pain or impairment do seek help, the Veteran's Administration may not be able to provide treatment for them. (A recent study from Walter Reed Army Institute of Research indicated that 17 percent of those returning from Iraq suffer from symptoms related to post-traumatic stress disorder three months after their return. Other studies predict that the number will be higher later on, as assessments are made not just three months after return from combat, but one or two years later.) As one soldier candidly put it, comparing Iraq to Vietnam, "Emotional, mental and psychological problems will be the Agent Orange of this war."[1] In the pages ahead I look at the idea of "toughing it out" or being stoic as both a blessing and a curse for military men and women—a blessing in that it girds them for facing the horrors of war, a curse in that it promises a kind of invulnerability that it cannot deliver and that leads to the undoing of mind. Surprisingly, some ancient Stoics voiced similar worries about the costs of being too stoic. In the end, I argue for a gentle Stoicism that can still, in Seneca's terms, "cultivate humanity."[2]

I have written this book in a way that I hope makes elements of Stoic doctrine accessible to a wide audience. In the course of doing so, I have necessarily been selective in my choice of texts and my overall coverage of debates in the sources and commentaries. Some purists may be disappointed by this; nonspecialists may be relieved. My own hope is that I offer enough to each camp to think about and reflect on.

By and large I paint a portrait of Stoicism drawn from Roman Stoics. A distinctive emphasis in Roman writers, such as Seneca, and not as much in the earlier Greek Stoics, is the notion of decorum and the aspects of outer comportment that are under one's control. This focus is instructive for the military where the uniform, the gaze in one's eyes, and the attitude conveyed in voice can be all-important for showing solidarity and leadership. Still, a focus on comportment, while empowering, can also seem shallow and superficial, at odds with what rests deeper in one's character. The Stoics themselves take up this tension in the story that follows.

I should also note that the book focuses largely on the morality involved in fighting in war (what is traditionally called, *jus in bello*) and not on the morality of the initial decision to go to war (*jus ad bellum*). The book was begun in peacetime. It went to press in the midst of war. In the interim and concurrent with the run up to the war in Iraq, just war theory has been revisited both in the popular press and academy. One of the more interesting claims to arise in the debate is that we cannot decouple the resort to war from the prosecution of war. The consequence of this claim is that those combatants who fight for an unjust cause ought not be regarded as moral "equals" with those who fight with a just cause on their side.[3] The claim is intriguing, though I do not take a position on it in this book. My preoccupation remains with the moral and psychological character of combatants in general—with soldiers, sailors, marines, and aviators—who find themselves in war (or who train for war) and who need to conduct themselves with respect and dignity in their delimited role as potential or actual combatants.

The book is hybrid in content, taking seriously both military matters and Stoic theory. But it is also hybrid in methodology. It adopts the standard method of philosophers—namely, analysis of text and argument—but also the method of ethnographers who collect stories and anecdotes. Perhaps I have grown accustomed to the genre of "sea stories" from my time at the Naval Academy. But since so much of my understanding of the military has come from the storytelling of military men and women, it seemed only fitting to share those stories in the context of trying to understand stoic aspirations and themes.

My debts in writing this book are deep. I am particularly grateful to all those whom I have interviewed who have served in the armed forces in the United States or Great Britain and whose reflections inform these pages. My gratitude goes to Arthur Blank, Marvin Brenner, Ward Carroll, Hank Chiles, Michael Codner, Jonathan Coors, Bill Craft, James Ellery, Milton Friend, Betsy Holmes, Rick Jolly, Brad Johnson, Jerry Kerzinsky, Michael Nurton, Marissa Page, Tony Pfaff, Arnold Resnicoff, Seymour Sherman, Rob Stevens, James Stockdale, Hugh Thompson, Nick Wilkinson, Donald Vandergriff, and Ted Westhusing. My thanks go also to Mary King and Ilya Shabadash. For most helpful discussions about post-traumatic stress disorder, I am grateful to Matthew Friedman and Arthur Blank.

I remain deeply grateful to the United States Naval Academy for allowing me entry into that community. My special thanks go to Charles Larson, Superintendent of the Naval Academy during my years at the Academy, and William Brehm and Ernst Volgenau for their generous endowment of the Distinguished Chair in Ethics, which I held. I am also grateful to my military and civilian colleagues in the Leadership, Ethics, and Law division of the Academy for their support and insights in the teaching of the NE 203 military ethics course.

Numerous colleagues and friends have read various versions of chapters of this book. For their insightful comments on Chapter 4, I am grateful to Alisa Carse, Margaret Graver, Rebecca Kukla, Brad Inwood, J. P. Ivanhoe, Martha Nussbaum, Cass Sunstein, and Rebecca Walker. For comments on an ancestor of Chapter 3, I am grateful to Christopher Gill and Brad Inwood. I am deeply grateful to Tony Pfaff and Jonathan Shay for reading the entire manuscript in its penultimate stage and to Barry Strauss for encouragement at the earliest stages of the project. I am especially grateful to Peter Ohlin, my editor at Oxford. He has been enthusiastic about the book from its inception and has guided me with good judgment and editorial sense at each step of the way. I am also indebted to Helen Mules, Senior Production Editor at Oxford, for her peerless eyes, patience, and sound judgment.

My debt to my research assistants—Elisa Hurley, Carin Ewing, Joe Kakesh, and Julie Goldstein—is simply enormous. Each helped me at different stages of the project with uncommon professionalism and intellectual astuteness. Elisa Hurley and Carin Ewing read penultimate drafts of the manuscript with sharp philosophical and editorial skills. Elisa also helped with abstracts at an early stage of the work and Carin was tireless in locating art work at the end stages of the process. Joe Kakesh was invaluable in this transcription of interviews and preparation of abstracts early on in the project. Julie Goldstein helped me understand ancient practices of grieving. Each helped with the gathering of research. I cannot imagine having completed this manuscript without their superb assistance.

I have delivered early versions of chapters of this book in a number of seminars and lectures over the past few years. The final draft of the book benefited substantially from comments from the audiences at the Air Force Academy, the University of Denver, the Pontifical University of Santa Croce in Rome, the University of Maryland, the University of Chicago Law School, Dartmouth College, American University's 44th Annual Bishop Hurst Lecture, Edinburgh University, Santa Barbara City College, Santa Clara University, Oklahoma University, Emory University, Wake Forest University, the Royal United Services Institute at Whitehall in London, the Cornell University Peace Studies Program, the University of Exeter, and the University of British Columbia. I am also deeply grateful to my students at Georgetown University, who have heard me struggle with this material over the years. I am especially grateful to those in my violence seminar, co-taught with Alisa Carse in spring 2004.

Earlier versions of three chapters have appeared previously as independent articles. Versions of Chapter 1 have appeared as "Educating the Stoic Warrior," in *Bringing in a New Era in Character Education,* edited by William Damon (Stanford: Hoover Institution, 2002), and been reprinted in the Royal United Services Institute's September 2002 Whitehall Papers, *Morality in Asymmetric War and Military Intervention,* edited by Patrick Mileham. Another version of the chapter appeared as "Stoic Meditations and the Shaping of Character: The Case of Educating the Military," in *Spirituality, Philosophy, and Education,* edited by D. Carr and J. Haldane (London: Routledge Falmer, 2003). An earlier version of Chapter 3 appeared as "The Look and Feel of Virtue," in *Virtue, Norms, and Objectivity: Issues in Ancient and Modern Ethics,* edited by Christopher Gill (New York: Oxford University Press, 2005), and as "Virtue and Emotional Demeanor," in *Feelings and Emotions: The Amsterdam Symposium,* edited by Antony Manstead, Nico Frijda, and Agneta Fischer (Cambridge: Cambridge University Press, 2004).

Finally, I would like to thank those who have allowed me to devote my energies to this project for the past several years. A fellowship from the American Philosophical Society during 2002–2003, in addition to a sabbatical from Georgetown University, afforded me uninterrupted research and writing time. My chair, Wayne Davis, has made our department at Georgetown a wonderful home for productive research, teaching, and conversation; I am indebted to him for his support of my research over the years. My ultimate gratitude is to my family—Marshall, Kala, and Jonathan. Aristotle said the best kind of friends don't simply graze together but share in argument and thought. I have been blessed in having a husband and children who bring critical argument, inspiration, and wit to our home each day. To them, my gratitude is boundless.

STOIC WARRIORS

That person, then, whoever it may be, whose mind is quiet through consistency and self-control, who finds contentment in himself, and neither breaks down in adversity nor crumbles in fright, nor burns with any thirsty need nor dissolves into wild and futile excitement, that person is the wise one we are seeking, and that person is happy.

—Cicero, *Tusculan Disputations* 4.37
(Graver trans.)

Who is the happy Warrior? Who is he
That every man in arms should wish to be . . .
Who, with a natural instinct to discern
What knowledge can perform, is diligent to learn . . .
More skillful in self-knowledge, even more pure,
As tempted more: more able to endure,
As more exposed to suffering and distress.

—William Wordsworth,
"Character of the Happy Warrior"

Happy are men who yet before they are killed
Can let their veins run cold . . .
And some cease feeling
Even themselves or for themselves.
Dullness best solves
The tease and doubt of shelling . . .
Happy are those who lose imagination:
They have enough to carry ammunition.
Their spirit drags no pack.
Their old wounds, save with cold, can not more ache.
Having seen all things red,
Their eyes are rid
Of the hurt of the colour of blood for ever.

—Wilfred Owen,
"Insensibility"

1

A Brave New Stoicism

___

STOCKDALE'S EPICTETUS

In a remarkably prescient moment, James B. Stockdale, then a senior Navy pilot shot down over Vietnam, muttered to himself on September 9, 1965, as he parachuted into enemy hands, "Five years down there at least. I'm leaving behind the world of technology and entering the world of Epictetus."[1] Epictetus's famous *Enchiridion*, known in English as the *Handbook of Epictetus,* had been Stockdale's bedtime reading in the many carrier wardrooms he occupied as he cruised the waters off Vietnam in the mid-1960s; Stoic philosophy resonated with Stockdale's temperament and profession, and he committed many of Epictetus's pithy remarks to memory. And Stoic tonics would hold the key to his survival for seven and a half years of life as a prisoner of war. They would also form the backbone of his leadership style as the senior officer in the POW chain of command.

It doesn't take too great a stretch of the imagination to think of a POW survivor as a kind of Stoic sage, for the challenge the POW lives with is just the Stoics' challenge: to find dignity when stripped of nearly all nourishments of the body and soul. On a strict reading, Stoicism minimizes vulnerability by denying the intrinsic goodness of things that lie outside of one's control. For some, such as Stockdale, POW camp can offer an extreme experiment in Stoicism.

Most military men and women do not think of themselves in Epictetan terms. Yet they do think of themselves, or at least they have idealized notions of military character, as stoic in the vernacular sense of the term. The traits that go with that stoicism are familiar: control, discipline, endurance, a sense of "can-do" agency, and a stiff upper lip, as the Brits would say. In a less elegant American phrase, to be stoic is to be able to "suck it up." But while popular stoic ideals bear some fidelity to ancient teachings, the philosophical traditions of Greek and Roman Stoics are, not surprisingly, far richer and more interesting than our popularized notions, and more nuanced. Indeed, some Stoic writers themselves struggle with the very austerity of Stoic views and with the overall Stoic commitment to reduce human vulnerability.

In the pages ahead, I use the contemporary military as a lens through which to study and assess Stoic doctrines. Issues of military character bring into relief Stoic positions and encourage us to assess military practices as well as Stoic theory. In this way, the project of this book is dialectical—a back-and-forth movement from military character to Stoicism in an effort to shed light on both. While I suggest that we can better understand ideals of military character by turning to the Stoics, I urge that an appreciation of Stoic texts must always be critical and wary of the Stoic tendency to both overidealize human strength and minimize human vulnerability.

My own tour of duty with the military began on a drizzly February day in 1994. A Navy chaplain had invited me to brainstorm with the top brass about moral remediation for some 133 midshipmen implicated in an electrical engineering cheating scandal. The chaplain knew I was no Navy insider, but he wanted my input as an academic ethicist. That February meeting in 1994 led initially to a consultancy and visiting ethics lectureship whose audience was the implicated students. Later, in 1997, I was appointed by the then superintendent of the Naval Academy, Admiral Charles Larson, as the inaugural occupant of the Distinguished Chair in Ethics.[2] Larson, one of the Navy's most respected and highest-ranking brass (and a former superintendent of the Academy), had been brought back to help the Academy focus on the issues of character development and ethics. I was "brought aboard," in naval jargon, to teach what American and European universities had been teaching for the better part of the past century—essentially, Ethics 101. But at an engineering school such as the Naval Academy, introductory ethics had passed them by. Leadership courses were standard, with their mix of management and motivational psychology. Yet the far more ancient subject of ethics was viewed by some as newfangled, an academic course that would dare to teach what ought to be bred in the bone. I was to teach ethics for the military. That was contractual. What wasn't prearranged was what the military would teach me. It would allow me entrance into a world that for many of my generation had been cut off by Vietnam and had remained largely impregnable ever since. And it would offer living examples of the ideals of ancient Stoicism and its inherent tensions.

The allure of Stoicism became explicit at a certain point in the semester each term. The course I taught covered topical themes on honesty, liberty, virtue, and just war interwoven with the writings of historical figures, such as Aristotle and Aquinas, John Stuart Mill and Kant, and Epictetus as a representative Stoic. When we arrived at Epictetus, many officers and students alike felt they had come home. What resonated with them was what resonated with Jim Stockdale as he read Epictetus each night.

> Some things are up to us and some are not up to us. Our opinions are up to us, and our impulses, desires, aversions—in short, whatever is our own doing. Our bodies are not up to us, nor are our possessions, our reputations, or our public

offices, or that is, whatever is not our own doing. . . . So remember, if you think that things naturally enslaved are free or that things not your own are your own, you will be thwarted, miserable, and upset, and will blame both gods and men. . . . And if it is about one of the things that is not up to us, be ready to say, "You are nothing in relation to me."[3]

Epictetus's project is to show that our opinions, desires, and emotions are within our power in the sense that we can monitor our attitudes and reactions to the circumstances that befall us. They are "up to us" in a way that the external events themselves are not. A Marine may be killed in friendly fire that he had no way of avoiding; a sailor may be deserving of decoration and promotion, though she is overlooked because of gender prejudice that she alone can't change; an adoring parent or wife may receive a knock on a door from uniformed Marines, who begin, "We regret to inform you . . ." The circumstances may be beyond our control, but ultimately what affects us for good or ill are only our own judgments about them.[4] We undermine our own autonomy and dignity if we make material and external things responsible for our happiness.

It is tempting to read Epictetus as urging complacency in his listeners or at least a retreat to a narrow circle of safety. But this is not the message. We are to continue to meet challenges, take risks, and stretch the limits of our mastery. We are to continue to strive to the best of our efforts to achieve our ends. We are to push our agency to the limit. In this sense, the message is one of empowerment. But at the same time, we are to cultivate greater strength and equanimity in the face of what we truly can't change. We must learn where our mastery begins, but also where it ends. Epictetus puts the point here hyperbolically—what we can't control ought to be a matter of indifference: "Be prepared to say that it is nothing to you." But Stoic writing can be at once hyperbolic and highly nuanced. What we can't fully control, we still must care about and "select," in traditional lingo, as "preferred" indifferents or "disselect" as "dispreferred" indifferents. Thus we ought to select health as a natural advantage (as being "in accord with nature") and reject illness as a natural disadvantage.[5] We shall have much to say

Stockdale emerging from his plane one week before he was shot down.

about this: is the idea of a "preferred" indifferent a sleight of hand, as some ancient critics charged, or does it capture a distinct kind of value that is substantively different from what affects our happiness? But for the moment I put these questions to the side and return to Stockdale's Epictetan experiment.

How to define a sense of self in a way that preserved autonomy became Stockdale's preoccupation in his years as a POW, more than four of which were spent in solitary, and the first two of those in leg irons. Epictetus's *Handbook* had been a parting gift from a philosophy professor at Stanford, where Stockdale studied for his master's degree. Stockdale himself was a no-nonsense aviator, a graduate of Annapolis, where engineering and technical sciences were, then as now, the principal fare. After a first and second read-through of the *Handbook*, he was sure that Epictetus had little to offer him. The epigrammatic language of the text hardly spoke to the heart of this martini-drinking golfer, as his wife was later to put it to me.[6] But out of respect for his professor, he diligently returned to the book, eventually finding more and more of it congenial, and soon committing much of it to memory. Thirty-five years later, he still recites verses that were his salvation, his own words seamlessly blending into Epictetus's, and Epictetus's into his own. Indeed, in conversation with Stockdale, I found it hard to keep track of when he was quoting and when he was speaking in his own voice, in spite of my own familiarity with Epictetus. Physically, too, Stockdale and Epictetus both shared the fate of being crippled in the left leg (Stockdale as a result of being pummeled by a street gang as his parachute landed him in a village in North Vietnam). When I reminded Stockdale of the uncanny coincidence, he shot back Epictetus at me, in his own James Cagney voice: "Lameness is an impediment to the leg, not to the will; and say this to yourself with regard to everything that happens. For you will find such things to be an impediment to something else, but not truly to yourself." He admits, though, that the words gave him "only minor" relief once he was confined to his cell and realized that his broken leg would be with him for life. Indeed, his left leg is still unbendable at the knee joint, and he walks with a slight hobble. When he sits in a chair, the leg juts straight out from his hip at a sixty-degree angle (although this doesn't prevent him from swimming a mile most mornings).

As the senior officer in the POW chain of command, Stockdale needed to answer the "young Turks," as he affectionately referred to them, who demanded to know what sorts of behaviors they should be willing to engage in, knowing that the punishment for those behaviors would be torture. He vividly recalls their request:

> We are in a spot like we've never been in before. But we deserve to maintain our self-respect, to have the feeling we are fighting back. We can't refuse to do every degrading thing they demand of us, but it's up to you, boss, to pick out things we must all refuse to do, unless and until they put us through the ropes again.[7]

"Taking the ropes" became the euphemism for the sustained and methodical torture they were to endure. Forty years later, sitting at his dining room table in Coronado Beach, California, Stockdale described the ordeal calmly but vividly: "They would start by clanging a big heavy iron bar down [about eighty or ninety pounds in weight], and then tie your feet to it so that you couldn't lift it. Then they'd sit you up and jackknife you over and tighten the ropes around your arms. Next, they'd put you through [con]tortions to the point that they would be pulling the rope so hard that the blood circulation in your upper chest would shut off." At this point, he continued, the guard would dig his heels into the back of the prisoner's head and push his nose into the cement. With panic and claustrophobia setting in, the prisoners could be made to blurt out information, some of which would be false, but other bits of which would be true.

Stockdale as prisoner, 1966.

The confession was followed by a "cold soak"—six or eight weeks of total isolation "to contemplate one's crimes." This was standard treatment.

As commander of the prison resistance, Stockdale came to view himself as something like the sovereign head of an American expatriate colony. No one back home knew the details of their subsistence the way they did. They were on their own, an isolated colony, in need of its own governance and rules of engagement in fighting the enemy:

I put a lot of thought into what those first orders should be. They would be orders that could be obeyed, not a "cover your ass" move of reiterating some U.S. government policy like "name, rank, serial number and date of birth," which had no chance of standing up in the torture room. My mind-set was, "We here under the gun are the experts, we are the masters of our fate. Ignore guilt-inducing echoes of hollow edicts, throw out the book, and write your own." My orders came out as easy-to-remember acronyms. The principal one was BACK US. Don't Bow in public; stay off the Air; admit no Crimes; never Kiss them good-bye.

He went on to say that while the abbreviation *US* could be interpreted as referring to the United States, "really it meant 'unity over self.' It's always 'we,' not 'alone.'"[8]

In all this, Epictetus was Stockdale's implicit guide. Following the Stoics, harm came to mean not a broken back or leg but the guilt and shame of betrayal of the self and the group. Harm was underestimating the agent in the self who could still have authority. Harm was mistaking the taste of a cigarette or a night out of leg irons for real autonomy.

Even so, Stockdale's Epictetus was never overtly preached, except once, when he tapped out some of it in code to a prison mate whose spirits he was trying to raise. The response through the cell wall was a deadening silence: a boundary had been crossed. Camaraderie had passed into didactic philosophizing. After that, "I never tapped or mentioned Stoicism once. You soon learned that if the guy next door was doing okay, that meant that he had all his philosophical ducks lined up in his own way."

Still, Epictetus had become internalized into Stockdale's own command, however tacit the doctrine. It governed what he was to call the mind-set of a "slow-moving, cagey prisoner," adapting Ivan Denisovich's language from the Solzhenitsyn novel. It became Stockdale's way of staying aloof, of not being desperate for what those in power have to give, of not compromising himself, however dependent his existence. He recalls:

> I took those core thoughts into prison; I also remembered a lot of attitude-shaping remarks. Here's Epictetus on how to stay off the hook: "A man's master is he who is able to confer or remove whatever that man seeks or shuns. Whoever then would be free, let him wish nothing, let him decline nothing, which depends on others; else he must necessarily be a slave."[9]

For Stockdale, prison was unabashedly a laboratory in which to test Stoic postulates. It was there that even the most brute external forces—such as repeated, severe torture—still demanded something of the will and mind, something that could be parlayed into the Stoic category "what belongs to oneself" and "what is within one's power." On his telling, it was his Epictetan Stoicism that enabled him to regain his dignity, if and when he broke in torture.

Stockdale's POW experience is an extreme application of Stoicism. It is literally about empowerment in enslavement. But the appeal of Stoicism within the military goes well beyond the life of the POW. And Epictetus in particular, with his mix of Socratic examination of the lived life and exhortative, concrete maxims, has a special appeal. Consider Commander Ward Carroll (ret.),[10] a former colleague at the Naval Academy. Ward cuts a dashing image—he is tall and lean and looks good in naval whites. He is the son of a Marine Corps pilot and himself a graduate of Annapolis. He is a talented satirist and cartoonist, not your usual officer stuff. By training he is a flight officer who for several tours of duty served aboard Tomcats (F-14's) as a back-seater or RIO (radar intercept officer) in charge of locking radar contacts for weapons system deployment. In his twenty years of naval service he has seen little of the war front, though, like Stockdale, he frames much of military life in Stoic,

Jim and Sybil Stockdale.

Epictetan terms. His Stoicism emerges in his recent *Catch 22*–esque military novel, *Punk's War*, which features a brainy RIO, Einstein, who is twice paired with an incompetent, braggadocio pilot who nearly kills both of them in a daredevil mission meant to fix the pilot's tarnished reputation. Though Einstein's role as RIO prevents him from controlling the plane's throttle, he never gives up the idea, Ward later explains to me, that he is "allowed to have a vote." As his buddy Smoke tells him in the novel, "Rank has no place in the cockpit, Einstein." Ward elaborated as we chatted over coffee in Annapolis:

> You've got to be sure you don't relinquish control too far. That's Smoke's petition. But what's the irony of this chapter? Smoke seems to have said, "You've got a second throttle, you've got a second throttle." But guess what? The airplane's getting driven someplace he didn't want it to go. So has he suddenly become a non-Stoic? No. He may not be able to control where the plane goes. But he can control ejecting when the airplane gets hit by a missile. He can control how he acts when he's on the ground, and he does it the right way. That's why he gets picked up in the rescue operation.

Carroll's point is that those in subordinate roles nonetheless can control how they are to be subordinated. "Smoke is telling Einstein not to draw the circle too close to himself. Don't be passive, don't be apathetic," even when, by all external measures, the circle has become more and more constrictive.

Carroll goes on to cite an example from his own life—an unexpected extension of his deployment at sea. For those in uniform, getting such news is not uncommon. But reacting with equanimity is. It was about March 1987; the ship had been deployed for five and a half months in the Mediterranean and was scheduled to turn home soon. In Carroll's case, he was due home for his own wedding that summer. But suddenly the ship received new orders, and the return date now looked like mid-June. If things kept to the new schedule, though he wouldn't *miss* the wedding date, he would get there just in the nick of time. The reason for the extended tour was that Terry Waite (the special envoy to the archbishop of Canterbury) had just been taken hostage by factions in Lebanon and was missing. In the new deployment plans, the ship was to cruise near Israel and Lebanon in a strong show of American military presence. However, morale on the ship was at an all-time low, according to Ward, even after the visit of John Lehman, then secretary of the Navy, who personally implored the crew to take seriously their role in what would become this pre–Desert Storm Mideast crisis. Carroll, in a state of near apoplexy about his wedding, finally realized that the date of his return home was out of his control. What *was* a matter of his control, however, was his commission—that he had signed up, as he put it, "to do somebody's bidding" (within the limits of just orders), and that somebody else was going to tell him when he could go home. The "epiphany," he says, was in that moment of knowing that the return date was not his to choose. He had to give up the illusion that his vote mattered, that if he argued loudly enough to his skipper, the deployment plans would change. Unlike Einstein in *Punk's War*, Carroll didn't have a second throttle to control the deployment. But he did have one to control his own attitude, and to discover *that* was liberating.

But isn't it self-deluding to think one can have truly meaningful control, especially in moments of forcible coercion? How can even a sage's life be "well-flowing," to use a stock Stoic phrase, in moments of brutal torture? True, prisoners at the "Hanoi Hilton," like Stockdale, made decisions as to what they would take torture for. And that certainly is a form of empowerment. But at the moment of ultimate coercion, one seems to be a victim, in the most basic meaning of that term. In what sense can one be in charge then?

Epictetus will answer repeatedly that one's autonomy lies in "using impressions correctly."[11] By this he means we exercise our will or choice in accepting or rejecting (i.e., "assenting" or not to) certain appearances and evaluations about the world and, derivatively, in experiencing emotions that are based on those impressions. In the specific case at hand, the enlightened Stoic will neither assent to torture as a genuine evil nor fear it as a threat to his well-being or happiness. For he will hold that only one's own vice or failure of character is truly evil and, conversely, that only virtue is unqualifiedly good and the source of genuine happiness. These substantive claims are extreme, and they clash, at least intuitively, with our own conceptions of good and evil and happiness. We shall come to this. But what is crucial to acknowledge at the moment is that someone such as Stockdale, a non-sage, found inspiration and empowerment in Stoic teaching. And in that, he is not alone. Our task in the pages ahead is to explore the basis of such an attraction.

EMOTIONS, CONTROL, AND HAPPINESS

A central Stoic view that we have just encountered and to which we shall return repeatedly in this book is that emotions are, by and large, "things within our control." We go seriously wrong when we think that emotions just happen to us and that the attachments and losses they represent are beyond our control. Indeed, the Stoics hold that an ordinary emotion such as fear or distress is not primarily a sensation or feeling but rather an opinion or cognition that something bad is happening (or about to happen) and a second opinion that a certain course of action is to be taken or avoided. So to feel fear is not simply to be *struck* by the appearance or impression (*phantasia* is the Greek term) of something dangerous. Rather, it is to have opinions, which the Stoics analyze as assents (saying yes) to impressions. To assent is, in a sense, to endorse an appearance and its practical import for behavior. Put this way, an emotion becomes something of an act of judgment and will, and a matter of our own responsibility. This is to say not that we can control external stimuli but rather that we can learn to assent to or withhold assent from the presentation of those stimuli as something good or evil. Put concretely, we can control whether or not we say yea or nay to the suggestiveness of wealth and status or to the negative connotations of various forms of offense or hurt. Moreover, even if, say, hurt and offense continue to cause a spontaneous twinge, we can put a buffer between those negative impressions and our responses to them, on one hand, and how they go on to affect us upon consideration, on the other.

But the Stoics go further. They hold that emotions, as most of us experience them, typically involve assent to *false* opinions. That is, the impressions we assent to have a propositional structure (are capable of being true or false), and emotions typically involve *false* opinions of good and evil. Thus the Stoics claim that emotions are cognitive (i.e., constituted by reason in a thoroughgoing way), but they are nonetheless misguided applications of reason: they are irrational cognitions, false opinions. So, for example, the fear that comes with anticipating physical harm is based, they hold, on a false opinion that physical harm is a real evil in the way that vice is; conversely, the joy that comes with health, wealth, or fine reputation is based on mistaking those goods for the real good that virtue is. The point draws to some degree from Socratic teaching and its distinction between external goods (such as wealth) and internal goods of the mind or psyche (wisdom, for example). Wisdom is stably beneficial to its possessor; it cannot be misused in the way that money without wisdom can be.[12] We might say wisdom does not depend upon anything outside itself in order to be beneficial to its possessor. The Stoics strengthen the position, holding that only virtue (that is, wisdom) is a genuine good and only vice a genuine evil; everything else is an "indifferent." An emotion such as fear, through which one assents to an impending danger as a real evil, misevaluates what is really evil in the world. Impending danger is in fact only an indifferent that cannot affect one's real happiness in the way that vice or a loss of virtue can.

In holding that indifferents are not genuine goods or evils, the Stoics maintain that their presence or absence cannot add or detract from genuine happiness, as experienced by the perfectly rational Stoic sage. But there are few to no bona fide sages, whether in ancient or modern times, however earnest any given individual's aspirations. Losing all our worldly goods, being tortured repeatedly and mercilessly, or watching our loved ones wither from hunger, deprivation, or disease tends to eat away at the happiness of the best of us. It would be hard to watch up close the human horrors of Rwanda's civil war or the Sierra Leonean rebels' practice of punishing villagers by lopping off hands without a sense that the chances of happiness of the victims, should they survive, will be compromised.

As we shall see, some Stoics, notably Epictetus and Seneca, are at times more than eager to downplay the unworldly perfectionism of strict Stoicism. Stoicism must have appeal, they urge, even to those non-sages such as themselves who will never be more than moral aspirants. For such an aspirant, catastrophic loss may well upset happiness and throw substantial challenges in the path to regaining it. But even so, as Epictetus puts it, we do best if we fight the good fight and try to recover an attitude that puts us back in charge. Our job is to find and refind our agency, however vulnerable and constrained it is. In the passage below, the athletic metaphor for Stoic training is explicit:

> Consider which of the things that you initially proposed you have managed to achieve, and which you have not, and how it gives you pleasure to remember some of them, and pain to remember others, and if possible recover the things that have slipped away from your grasp. For those who are engaged in this greatest of contests must not shrink back, but must be prepared to endure the blows. For the contest that lies before us is not in wrestling or the pancration, in which, whether a man succeeds or fails, he may be a man of great worth or of little . . . no, it is a context for good fortune and happiness itself. What follows, then? In this, even if we falter for a time, no one prevents us from renewing the contest, nor need we wait another four years for the next Olympic games to come, but as soon as a man has got a hold on himself and recovered himself, and shows the

same zeal as before, he is allowed to take part in the contest; and even if you should falter again, you may begin again, and, if you once become the victor, you are as one who has never faltered.[13]

The passage is honest about the "faltering" nature of our progress in living the good life, and yet it is optimistic about opportunities for reversal and for recovery of agency. We are buffeted by unfavorable externals and hostile blows from others—some of us more severely than others. But still Epictetus insists that there is inestimable value in constantly pushing our agency against those obstacles and limits, to the degree we can. Conversely, neglect of our agency or failure to take seriously its potential for excellence and wisdom (that is, vice) damages us in a more profound way than external blows do. This, we might say, is the Socraticism that underlies the Stoic moral point of view—namely, that a person who lives a life of vice damages his soul (*and* chances for happiness) in a more profound way than one who suffers evil at the hands of others.

So when the young Turks demanded that Stockdale tell them what they could take the ropes for so as to best maintain their self-respect, we can reconstruct their request along Stoic lines as saying, "We do not fear these bodily harms as genuine bads, but regard them as indifferents, however dispreferred and contrary to what, by nature, we would select." Further, we can reconstruct them as saying that the kind of bad that constitutes physical harm is of a different order than the bad that comes from betrayal of one's prison mates or country. This is not to say that Stockdale or his fellow prisoners were anesthetized to physical pain or were indifferent to averting the next round of torture. The point, rather, is that they came to see that kind of bad as, in principle, categorically different from the bad, or evil, of compromising one's integrity or virtue.

When integrity was inevitably challenged under torture, self-shame became the residue of perceiving oneself as falling short, as having traded betrayal for relief from pain. So when a prisoner would return from the "cold soak," another prisoner in the same cellblock would often try to make contact through the adjoining wall as a sign of solidarity. The typical whisper back, as Stockdale recounted to me, was: "You don't want to talk to me, I'm a traitor." To that, the initiator replied in essence, "Listen, pal, there are no virgins here. You should have heard the kind of statement I made."

These brief remarks suggest both the appeal of Stoicism to military life and the subtlety, at times, of its doctrine. In the pages that follow I take up Stoic and military themes in a synergistic and dialectical way, beginning in some cases from clearly Stoic topics and in other cases from military themes. But whatever the starting points, the aim is to exploit the self-image of the military person as stoical in order to expose the tensions and richness in actual ancient Stoic theory as they relate to military life. In many cases we shall discover (perhaps not surprisingly) that tensions internal to the Stoic debate—about rigor and lassitude, agency and vulnerability, courage and fear, self-reliance and dependence, stolidness and emotional sensitivity, perfectionism and fallibilism—mirror tensions the military person faces in his or her own struggle with stoicism. But while military life, not civilian life, is my explicit focus, the implications for those of us who are not in uniform are never far from the surface.

This leads to a word of caution. Stoic consolations can soothe the soul and, as the Stoics say, lead to an "even-flowing life." But as we approach Stoic and military themes, we should not be so zealous as to demand of ourselves or others either *infallible* control or *perfect* virtue. Just as there has never been a certified Stoic sage, so too, I believe, we can vouchsafe that there has never been a military leader who has made no command mistakes. Any reasonable conception of morality requires that we hitch our wagon to high stars. But none ought to require that we be merciless in our punishment of ourselves or others when we fall short of the highest standards. A "zero-defect" policy (such as the one the military has promoted in recent years) is simply unreasonable.

In the course of examining Stoic and military themes, I argue for a brand of Stoicism that is moderate and mild. In the view of such a Stoicism, the task for the individual, whether civilian or military, youth or adult, is to temper control with forgiveness, soldierly strength with tolerance for human frailty. A healthy Stoicism of this sort, if we can successfully reconstruct such a thing, would push us to self-mastery, but never at the cost of self-renunciation or excessive self-punishment. It would exhort us to be sturdy in the face of disappointment, but not fully invulnerable. It would teach us to value self-reliance and a can-do spirit, but at the same time it would encourage us to know the place of fellowship and mutual support. In the face of our defects and vulnerabilities, empathy and compassion toward self and others would be recognized as crucial tonics.

This picture is eclectic and at times puts us at some distance from orthodox Stoic sources. In this sense, it is not a comprehensive guide to Stoic theory. Still, I argue that the conception has its roots in a number of key Stoic texts that we shall explore in depth. These, often in surprising ways, recommend important elements of the above picture.

THE CAST OF CHARACTERS

Just who are the Stoics and what are their textual traditions?[14] It is time to say a few brief words here to provide the broad philosophical and historical setting for our discussions. Roughly speaking, the ancient school of Stoicism spans the period from 300 BCE to 200 CE. The Stoics are part of the Hellenistic movement of philosophy that follows upon Aristotle and includes, in addition to Stoicism, ancient Skepticism and Epicureanism. The early Greek Stoics, known collectively as the old Stoa (taking their name from the *stoa*, or painted colonnade near the central Athenian plaza, where disciples paced back and forth), were interested in systematic philosophical thought that joined ethics with studies in physics and logic. The works of the founders of the school—Zeno of Citium (335–263 BCE), Cleanthes (331–232 BCE), and Chrysippus (280–207 BCE)—survive only in fragments, quoted by later writers. Indeed, much of what we know of them comes to us through second- and thirdhand sources, both Stoic and non-Stoic. Prominent among these are Roman writers, including Cicero, Seneca, Epictetus, and Marcus Aurelius, all of whom except Cicero explicitly identify themselves as Stoics. These Roman interpreters, some writing in Greek, as did Epictetus and Marcus Aurelius, others writing in Latin, such as Seneca and Cicero (and actively retooling Latin for philosophical usage), viewed themselves as public philosophers at the center of public life. In this work, the Stoic texts I most frequently draw upon are those of the Romans, in part because their texts survive whole, and in part because of their own self-defined mission to offer a publicly accessible philosophy with clear practical application.

Despite his humble origins, Cicero (106–43 BCE) rose meteorically through the ranks of the Senate to become consul at the young age of forty-three. A well-known Roman political orator, military leader, and ally to Pompey, he devoted his energies to philosophical writing at the end of his political career, after Caesar's assassination and while in hiding from his own future assassins, Antony and the other triumvirs. Philosophical writing also became a consolatory tool to help assuage his grief after the death of his beloved daughter Tullia. Although himself not a Stoic (he identified as a member of the New Academy or school of Skepticism), he wrote extensively on Stoic views, and his works, especially *On Moral Ends* and *On Duties,* remained highly influential throughout the Renaissance and Enlightenment as statements of Stoic positions.

While Cicero was no self-styled popularizer, through his Latin translations of Greek philosophical vocabulary he was committed to making philosophy widely accessible to an intelligent but non-Greek-reading audience. Moreover, his philosophical writings tend to have an implicit political dimension, promoting the view that a decline in contemporary ethical standards was a principal cause of the fall of the Roman Republic and that ethical instruction is necessary to reinstate a climate hospitable to political liberty.

Seneca (4 BCE–65 CE), the son of an eminent family, was groomed early on for a political career. However, after repeated bouts of tuberculosis, resulting in a suicide attempt in adolescence, he turned to philosophy for consolation. Chronic ill health and a passion for philosophical studies delayed his entry into public service until his mid-thirties. With several philosophical treatises already penned and a rising reputation as an orator, he entered the Senate and in due course was appointed the tutor and political advisor of the young emperor Nero. Though he formally taught rhetoric and not philosophy to the emperor, his commitment to Stoicism influenced his role as Nero's minister and moral adviser. His tract *On Mercy*, addressed to Nero, urges that Stoicism need not be construed as an overly harsh doctrine. "I know," he says, "that the Stoic school has a bad reputation ... for being too hard and most unlikely to give good advice to princes and kings. The objection is that it will not allow the wise man to pity or pardon. . . . In fact no school of philosophers is kinder or more lenient, more philanthropic or attentive to the common good."[15] "Mercy" or "leniency," he repeats routinely, "enhances not only a ruler's honor but his safety."[16] In our own study of Seneca, we shall pay special attention to his discussions of emotions, such as anger and fear, and to his remarks on emotional comportment and demeanor. I shall argue that Seneca remains compelling, in part, because of his own resistance to orthodox Stoic positions.

Epictetus (55–135 CE) was a slave (most likely by birth rather than seizure) from Phrygia, a Greek-speaking province of the Roman Empire. He was acquired (and later emancipated) by Epaphroditus, a wealthy freedman and secretary of Nero. While still a slave, Epictetus studied philosophy with the Stoic Musonius Rufus, and eventually he began teaching Stoic thought himself. Like Socrates, whose style Epictetus may have modeled, Epictetus is exclusively an oral philosopher whose audience is primarily boys in their late teens and early twenties. His work comes to us through one of his students, Arrian, who compiled his detailed teachings (in Greek) in four volumes, known to us as the *Discourses*, and in a more popularized short manual, the *Handbook*.

The suffering of a slave permeates Epictetus's writing. He was a cripple— according to some accounts as a result of disease, according to others as a result of beatings from masters. Even as a freedman, he chose a life of little luxury and material comfort, furnishing his home, it is said, with only a pallet and a rush mat. Though his writing in the *Handbook* is sometimes condemned by academics as overly aphoristic, potted "wisdom" philosophy, his style in the *Discourses* is fairly systematic and argumentative. Most recently, A. A. Long makes a compelling case for reading Epictetus as a self-styled Roman Socrates.[17] In this view, his writing is at once elenctic (that is, in the Socratic mode of question-and-answer cross-examination, or *elenchus*, that shows people the inconsistencies in which they are caught up in living their lives) and protreptic (exhortative and reproving about how we ought to live). To these two Socratic elements, according to Long, Epictetus adds the methodology of traditional Stoic didactic or doctrinal teaching. Finally, he adapts his style to his special audience—boys on the cusp of manhood, whom he can best reach with irony and hyperbole. The overall result is an unusual mix of rhetorical and philosophical dialectic that takes seriously, as Socrates famously did, the self-examined life and the commitment to purge oneself of inconsistency and ignorance in living one's life.

Marcus Aurelius (121–180 CE) was deeply influenced by Epictetus, despite their diametrically opposed positions in life. Marcus was born into a noble family with a long tradition of military and public service, and he himself served as emperor for the last two decades of his life. Like Seneca, Marcus was a sickly youth who became passionate about Stoic philosophy as a young boy. He wore the dress of the Stoic sect and practiced its abstemious ways to the point of imperiling his already fragile health. But unlike Seneca, whose writings are often addressed to others, Marcus's meditations are exhortations to himself. Despite an adult life of pomp and circumstance, he never abandoned his philosophy of the simpler life, and as Roman emperor and warrior, he wrote his famous *Meditations* in 172 CE in the fleeting moments of quiet during the Germanic campaigns. The Stoic idealism and search for a simpler life were still with him at the end: "I preserved the flower of my youth and did not play the man before my time, but even delayed a little longer."[18] He wrote this knowing that he had become larger than life to many: a colossal gold statue of the emperor was wheeled onto the battleground each day and to the campsite each night for a kind of hero worship.

A repeated theme in Marcus's writings is that we live in a world of flux, like the one the pre-Socratic philosopher Heraclitus once described. To find happiness, we cannot hold on too tightly to what is transient and beyond our control. Drawing on an ancient Cynic teaching repeated in Epictetus, Marcus also reminds himself that his ultimate political status is as a "citizen of the world" and that he serves in a community of humanity and God that partakes of the same reason: "enter into the governing self of every man and permit every other man to enter into your own."[19]

A PREVIEW OF THEMES

In the next chapter, I take up the issue of discipline as it affects the development of both mind and body. Americans have become a culture obsessed with excessive eating but also, paradoxically, with physical fitness and the demands of fashioning a hard, strong body. Here I suggest that the stripped-down life of military endurance offers something of a model of discipline and control. The view seems Stoic, but ancient Stoics view bodily health and vigor as indifferents, not valuable in their own right or fully within our control. Stoic doctrines force the questions of how we are to live with the fragility of our bodies, what efforts we are to put into their adornment and sculpture, and what attitudes we are to take when our bodies fail us.

In Chapter 3 I consider the important role that manners and demeanor play in the cultivation of virtue. The issue is central to the military and its core belief that training in decorum is an integral part of training character. Seneca, in particular, offers instruction here, giving support to the notion that a virtue, such as doing kindnesses, can be expressed in acts of decorum and facial and bodily comportment. Included here are facial expressions of emotion. But which emotions, on a Stoic prescriptive view, may we indulge in and which ought we try to eliminate or transform? These questions take us to the theme of the next four chapters and to Stoic views on emotions.

The Stoics push the Aristotelian study of the emotions to new frontiers, paralleled only by advances in contemporary psychology. Indeed, the Stoic view that emotions are robustly cognitive has been embraced by contemporary psychology, despite its virtual neglect during the Renaissance, Enlightenment, and early modern period. The Stoics also advance important discussions about the possibility of emotional regulation and transformation. Some authors, such as Seneca, actively struggle with the conflict of wanting both to minimize the vulnerability to which an emotional life exposes us and to preserve emotions as the lifeblood of human exchange and fellowship. In the military, unforgiving views toward the expression of emotions have led in the past to disastrous treatment of shell-shock victims and to demands for military men and women to compartmentalize their emotional lives in ways that both tear military bonds and strain service members' reintegration into their families and the civilian community. Appraising Stoic views and appreciating that the Stoics themselves embrace options other than a stolid repudiation of emotional life provides a bold lesson for the military.

The specific theme of Chapter 4 is the Stoic conception of anger and its control. The recurrent question in ancient texts from Homer to Seneca is whether a warrior needs anger to go to battle. Seneca, like many moderns, says no, but he then proceeds to eliminate other, more constructive forms of anger that we might think essential to good moral character in general. In Chapter 5 I raise questions about fear and resilience: Can we eliminate the terror of killing and being killed, and what is the cost of a warrior learning to do so? What is resilience? What are our own contemporary notions of resilience, and how, if at all, do they resonate with earlier, Stoic models of psychic strength and endurance? Chapter 6 turns to the issue of grief and to Stoic notions of mourning and appropriate decorum in grieving. Cicero's candid reflections about the loss of his beloved daughter Tullia in letters, and his developed ideas about a therapy of grief in the *Tusculan Disputations*, provide some of the most insightful writings we have on the subject.

I conclude, in Chapter 7, with issues of camaraderie, empathy, and respect. In particular, I address the fact that warriors are motivated to fight by their love for their buddies and that they often survive their ordeals by returning to the bosom of those buddies. I shall argue that while the Stoics may fail to adequately appreciate feelings associated with intimate friendships, they offer profound insight about a more far-flung sense of affiliation, built on shared humanity and common reason. With Diogenes the Cynic, they hold that each of us is a "citizen of the world" (*kosmopolitēs*), a member of a global community. Universal reason is the collective tissue of that community, whose boundaries stretch beyond those of country, city, and family. The implications of this groundbreaking idea are vast. The notion would come to have a profound influence on the Church fathers and subsequent notions of reason and the laws of nature. Stoic cosmopolitanism also greatly influences the rational Enlightenment and, in particular, Kant's eighteenth-century project of grounding moral law in universal reason accessible to all humans.

As I finish the writing of this book, U.S. troops are still deployed in Iraq and views of the United States' membership in a globalized world are routinely tested. One such test has been in the American prisons in Baghdad, including Abu Ghraib. I end the book with a consideration of how a stern lesson in Stoic cosmopolitanism, with its inherent notions of respect and empathy, might have led to a substantively different treatment of prisoners in Abu Ghraib.

Aren't these . . . [guardians] athletes in the greatest contest?

Then our warrior athletes need a more sophisticated kind of training. They must be like sleepless hounds, able to see and hear as keenly as possible and to endure frequent changes of water and food, as well as summer and winter weather on their campaigns, without faltering in health.

—Plato, *Republic*

"You want to look like *that*?" Sweepea asked, incredulous.

Again, the pregnant pause. This time Mousie said it: "Then you best be prepared to make the necessary adjustments." . . .

First off, I would have to start eating five meals a day, plus special protein milk shakes. Then, I would have to adopt the double-split, three on, one off exercise program. It meant twelve workouts per week instead of three. . . .But above all, they said, it meant "The Three D's." . . .

Mousie nodded sternly. "Dedication, Determination, Discipline. *That's* bodybuilding."

—Samuel Wilson Fussell, *Muscle*

2

Sound Bodies and Sound Minds

———

A NEW BREED OF WARRIOR ATHLETE

On a sticky June morning in the D.C. area, I drove my daughter to a triathlon at a Navy base some two hours south of our home. The event (three-quarter-mile swim, six-mile bike ride, and three-mile run) drew a lot of military athletes, but there were also civilians interested in the same exhilaration of hard physical activity. As I helped my daughter unload her bike, I found myself gawking at the sculpted bodies that surrounded me, especially those of the men: V-shaped torsos and six-pack fronts, well-developed biceps, broad, muscular shoulders, thickened necks, well-defined pectorals, thighs pumped and strong like stallions' legs. For the most part, I found them beautiful. I had become used to the sight during my time at the Naval Academy, and as one sitting squarely in middle age, I found the well-kneaded, non-saggy bodies even more attractive. Still, I knew most of these fit bodies were the product not just of youth or nature but of vigilant labor—hours of biking, swimming, or running logged each week. For some, additional hours had been spent at the gym in weight training.

Many participants had woken up at 3 a.m. or earlier to arrive for the 7 a.m. start time—some did it regularly as part of the weekend triathlon circuit. But despite the hour, people were cheery and chatty, even the most serious-looking athletes. Among them were two USNA triathlon team members, who meticulously greased their bodies with a product called Glide so that they could slide into their full-length wet suits easily and slither out of them the moment they hit the shore and dashed for their bikes.

Side by side with this spirit of camaraderie was a subtle but unmistakable combat element. It came not just from the military types who flocked to this navy base and whose bodies have long been thought of as "war machines"—equipment that is part of the armor and weaponry of the military mission, bodies that are a public investment. It also emerged in the logos on equipment that civilians brought with them: racing bike tires emblazoned with the words

"Speed Weaponry," a T-shirt that featured a bodybuilder in combat fatigues and the caption "Take No Prisoners," another T-shirt with a lighthearted revision of an Army recruiting slogan: "Be All You Never Were." The scene confirmed something quite noticeable these days—that the fitness of the classic warrior has become a model for many Americans who have no military experience and little appetite for it.

The phenomenon has become conspicuous in the tony gyms and fitness programs that have mushroomed throughout the American landscape. In my neighborhood alone one finds the Fitness Corps, the Sergeant's Program, Basic Training, and the Fitness Force. They are our local boot camps. In these programs, well-heeled men and women pay good money to subject themselves to self-fashioned drill sergeants who specialize in just the sort of abuse that real military drill sergeants are now under pressure to abandon. Indeed, at 5 a.m. in my neighborhood, fitness sergeants are kicking the saggy butts of middle-aged folks who willingly accept the abuse. One winter my husband became a self-appointed victim. He would wake up before sunrise to endure the boot camp he'd managed to escape during the Vietnam years. One morning he lagged in his warm-up run around the park. The drill sergeant didn't fail to notice and instantly ordered him to pay for his sloth by doing twenty push-ups on the frosty ground. As if this weren't enough of an indignity, the sergeant then barked out: "Presser, you little piece of shit, do them like you mean them, or else you'll do twenty more." It is not just men who subscribe to civilian boot camp. Women too flock to fitness corps, to be all they can be and everything they weren't. One women's workout group in our neighborhood has a four-D slogan: "Drill, discipline, dedication, dignity." At a local 8K charity race I ran (my only competitive race in some twenty-five years of running), it was just those fitness drill sergeants—many of whom, I am sure, are former military men and women—who goaded the runners on from the sidelines to run harder and faster than we thought possible: "Push it out, push it out," they yelled, and "Make it happen!" "Hey, ho, hey, ho!" they chanted in military cadence. If Jane Fonda's best-selling 1983 workout video first launched the fitness craze, military-minded trainers are keeping it alive and well.

Still, the American fascination with the military image, even if primarily the body image portion of it, is something not to be taken for granted. Before the events of 9/11 and the widespread mobilization of permanent and reserve troops in Afghanistan and Iraq, many argued that there was a growing gap between the military and civilian worlds.[1] Indeed, in 1997 Tom Ricks, a Pentagon correspondent, argued in his book *Making the Corps* that this gap is widening as the result of a number of factors: the end of the draft in the early 1970s and the institution of an all-volunteer army with lengthened periods of enlistment, a swelling in non-middle-class recruits at the bottom end of the chain of command matched with a growing professionalization within the officer class at the top, and a new partisan conservatism among officers that no longer reflects the partisan divisions in the general public. Add to this the diminishing number of ROTC units on campuses, the dwindling number of congressmen who have served in the military, and the military's own prolonged "Vietnam hangover" (its sense of civilian betrayal during that war), and one gets a fairly vivid picture of weakened links between those who wear uniforms and those who don't.[2] Ricks's own experience comes from covering Marine boot camp at Parris Island. After eleven weeks of deprivation and drill, recruits were not simply alienated as they returned to their largely working-class communities but disgusted at the corpulence and unkempt lives they had left behind.

It is not just Marine recruits who harbor these views. Increasingly, many civilians do, and some of it is self-directed. Indeed, for those tired of pleats of adipose tissue, modified boot camp seems to offer an attractive tonic. In a country of extremes, it is the antidote to Homer Simpson's gluttony and lassitude.

This renewed interest in hard control of the body may sound Stoic in spirit, especially in terms of its emphasis on self-toughening through severe training and drill. Epictetus, in particular, routinely employs athletic metaphors to capture the dedication and discipline needed for Stoic training: We are to be like the "invincible athlete" who continues to prove himself even after "he has been victorious in the first encounter," even if it is "burning hot," even if there are naysayers who try to bring him down.[3] No one can be "an Olympic victor . . . without sweat." "Remember that god, like a wrestling master, has matched you with a rough young man."[4] But training and discipline, whether physical or mental, are one thing; attachment to the body is another. And Epictetus himself will argue, in Stoic fashion, that while we have a duty to care for the body, ultimately our bodies should be regarded as indifferents, not as intrinsic elements of our good.

This can be difficult advice to swallow. We non-Stoics tend to view ourselves as embodied and our identity as a function of our bodily existence. We may overexaggerate that identity and become obsessive in our care and cultivation of the body, but a healthy sense of self does not leave the body behind. Soldiers who return from war with bodies maimed and disfigured lose more than just a physical part of themselves. They sacrifice a fundamental part of what shapes their sense of self and good living—easy mobility, full and independent use of arms and hands, sightedness and hearing, and in many cases a fitness for competitive physical adventure and risk that made the military attractive to them in the first place. They may also have to live with the fact that they inflicted comparable losses on others. The bitter irony of war is that the fittest risk becoming the most disabled. As we shall see, cutting-edge technology has transformed the lot of veterans, with many more surviving the sort of severe injuries that would have killed them in past wars. Even so, they still must adjust to a new kind of life, lived with a new kind of vulnerability and set of compensatory skills.

In a sense, the Stoics address fragility of just this sort. We are vulnerable to disease and disability, whether through war, sickness, or old age. We need lessons for preparing for this—indeed, hard training and drill—if we are not to be totally undone by life's tragedies. What I shall be exploring in this chapter is whether Stoic teachings about our relationship to our bodies offer sage counsel.

I come to this by first considering in greater detail the current American fascination with images of the warrior body and attendant dangers of overly ambitious bodily control and idealization. This takes us to Stoic images of the body and its discipline, and to a consideration of Stoic views of our relationship to our bodies. How might Stoic consolations help a soldier face the gruesome casualties of war? Underlying my remarks is a striking paradox about which there has been a stunning silence: a warrior's body is in many ways a public investment, and yet the sacrifices he or she makes are harrowingly private. Can Stoic doctrines help in facing those losses?

THE HARDENED BODY
(AND FUSSELL'S MUSCLES)

Americans are extreme about their bodies. On one hand, there is an epidemic of adult and juvenile obesity, with nearly two-thirds of adults overweight and nearly one-third obese.[5] Jumbo clothes, seats, beds, roller coaster lap straps, coffins, and so on are all available to accommodate the epidemic. Jumbo portions of food continue to feed it. On the other hand, there is a conspicuous rise in interest in muscularity and reduced body fat. There is a desire to take control of the body, to make it hard, angular, and warriorlike, through both exercise and an obsessive interest in the latest diets and diet supplements. Both trends are out there, and no doubt there are complex sociological, psychological, and hereditary factors that help explain who is in which camp.

It should not surprise us that one's own body is, in principle, a primary locus of self-control. If all goes well, at an early age we learn bladder and sphincter control, and these are no small personal and social achievements. In due time we become responsible for the care and feeding of our own bodies and for our fitness. And when at different points in our cultural and social trajectories our bodies become our own, we may be given autonomy about how to dress them up or down—not just in terms of the muscles we sport and the clothes we wear, but also, in some cases, in the realms of body art, piercing, and cutting.

The athlete's or warrior's body has long been idealized for its hardness. Painted Attic amphorae, awarded to victors in the Pantheneic Olympics, show well-muscled runners with cleanly articulated pectorals and the ripples of a taut chest. The bulge of muscles is unmistakable despite the flat perspective of

Michelangelo's *David*.

Attic style. The ancient Olympics are celebrations of the union of military and athletic events—and the union of military and athletic bodies. For post-Renaissance moderns, Michelangelo's *David* is probably the best-known example of the athletic or warrior body. The statue's forearms, biceps, and pectorals are clearly defined; the torso bears the lines of washboard abdominal muscles. Yet in this great statue physical control is at the same time mental control. With his left hand curled upward toward the leather catapult on his shoulder and his right hand by his side gripping a stone, David is poised for action and for military strategy. His piercing gaze emits determination and focus against an assumed Goliath.

David's body is not Goliath-like. Yet in our own culture, Goliath bodies of oversized muscle and heft seem to compete for the image of hardened strength and discipline. Indeed, some researchers claim that among boys and young men there is an underrecognized body obsession analogous to anorexia in women. They dub it "bigorexia," a species of body dysmorphic disorder that focuses on fear of not being big enough in muscle size.

"People with anorexia nervosa see themselves as fat when they're actually too thin; people with muscle dysmorphia feel ashamed of looking too small when they're actually big."[6] So argue the authors of *The Adonis Complex*. In their book we meet men like Scott, who is lifting weights at a Boston gym and fixated on turning his body into a perfect physical specimen:

> To a casual observer, Scott seems like a perfect picture of fitness and health. Five feet nine inches tall, with shortly cropped dark brown hair and handsome facial features, Scott weights 180 pounds and has only 7 percent body fat, making him leaner than at least 98 percent of American men his age. Beneath his worn gray sweatpants and sweatshirt, he has the proportions of a Greek statue. He has a 31-inch waist, a "six-pack" of sculptured abdominal muscles, a 46-inch chest, and shoulders as big as grapefruits.[7]

Though massively built, Scott sees himself as puny. "I know it sounds silly," he explains, "but there are times that even on hot summer days, after getting a bad shot of myself in the mirror, I'll put on heavy sweatshirts to cover up my body because I think I don't look big enough."[8] On days when Scott can't work out, he feels trapped and starts bench-pressing furniture in his home. His preoccupation with muscle building has led to a breakup with his girlfriend: she was tired of playing third fiddle to his diet and workout schedule, though in his mind, the only reason she would leave him was to find a bigger guy.

Consider another vignette from a friend who is a psychotherapist. When I asked her about male body obsessions, she told me about a patient named Bill, a gay thirty-five-year-old who routinely used to come to sessions wearing heavy sweaters to cover what he viewed as a flabby body. To her eyes, she said, he was a trim man, in relatively good shape. But he was obsessed about his body fat percentage and during the clinical hour would often grab his waist area to measure for any rolls. At home, he reported, he would do it more scientifically, with calipers. Another psychotherapist friend told me of a patient who was obsessed with developing a muscle builder's body, to which end he often worked out three times a day and took muscle-enhancing anabolic steroids over a period of years. Workouts and therapy, however, could not relieve his low self-esteem and severe depression, and ultimately he committed suicide.

Perhaps the most gripping story of bodybuilding, and what may seem at first glance to be the most Stoic, comes from Samuel Fussell in his memoir *Muscle*. Fussell is an unlikely bodybuilder, for he is the son of two university professors of English and himself a student of American literature. (His father, Paul Fussell, is the noted author of books with World War I literary themes, including *The Great War* and *Siegfried Sassoon's Long Journey*, the latter of which we take up in Chapter 7.) As Sam Fussell tells the story, he came to bodybuilding, at age twenty-six, as a way of making himself invulnerable. He had just moved back to New York City after spending a year studying at Oxford and before beginning graduate school. And then suddenly—"spectacularly," as he puts it—his health began to deteriorate. He recognized that living in the city created absolute terror in him and that it had manifested in a kind of somatic breakdown. In his mind, he needed to find an armament. Bodybuilding was the answer. The specific inspiration came in the autobiography section of a bookstore: "It was in this aisle, in this store, in September of 1984, that I finally caught 'the disease.' Here it was I came across *Arnold: The Education of a Bodybuilder,* by Arnold Schwarzenegger." In moving prose, Fussell describes his reaction to the cover of the book:

> As for his body, why, here was protection, and loads of it. What were these great chunks of tanned, taut muscle but modern-day armor? Here were breastplates, greaves, and pauldrons aplenty, and all made from human flesh. He had taken

A promotional image from a bodybuilding Web site.

stock of his own situation and used the weight room as his smithy. A human fortress—a perfect defense to keep the enemy host at bay. What fool would dare storm those foundations?[9]

With Arnold as his model, Fussell set out on a bodybuilding mission to make himself "larger than life," "less assailable," and "a little less human."[10] His six-foot-four body, once 170 pounds, eventually turned into a machine (he doesn't actually give us his final weight) that could bench-press 405 pounds, squat 545 pounds, and pump out ten reps with 315 pounds on the incline bench. His weightlifting and food regimens were merciless. But for the kind of "thickness" and "muscle maturity" he aimed for, daily anabolic steroidal injections were essential.[11] Pumped up with iron, he became a competitor in the California bodybuilding championships, with poses (the book has an insert of photographs) that make him look like Goliath to Michelangelo's *David*. But what is most stunning about Fussell's story is that bodybuilding was for him a way to leave behind his humanity. With maniacal control, he used it to create a rite of passage that just might lift him out of human frailty: "I hated the flawed, weak, vulnerable nature of being human as much as I hated the Adam's apple which bobbed beneath my chin. The attempt at physical perfection grew from the seeds of self-disgust."[12]

Now, not all bodybuilders are as articulate or literary as Fussell or as self-reflective. But for most, at some level, the idea that muscles are an armament that can make one invincible may resonate. We need to be careful here. We are not talking about the muscles one builds to ward off osteoporosis, or to develop a strong pitching arm, or to stay lean and strong and fit through moderate exercise. Nor are we talking about muscles built for the line of service—for

becoming a Ranger or SEAL or Royal Marine Commando. Rather, we are talking about muscles as a complete end in themselves. Fussell says in the first line
of his memoir, "Bodybuilders call it 'the disease'" because it involves "a *complete* commitment to all matters pertaining to iron."[13] It is an exclusive commitment that crowds out all others in one's life. In *The Adonis Complex,* many
of the young men interviewed were like Scott, discussed above—they could
not be committed to their Adonis bodies *and* maintain an ordinary family life,
romantic relationships, or a job. Fussell is insightful on the point. Bodybuilding, unlike his past bookish pursuits, taught him that he *could* finally become
the person he dreamed of being. Perfection was possible; it just depended on
what "you're willing to give." "If it meant feeling safe and protected, I was willing to give up *everything.*" And so he gave up his job, his Upper East Side apart-
ment, his non-bodybuilding friends. Arnold directed his new bunker mentality:
"As they say, if you stick around cripples—mental or physical—long enough,
pretty soon you'll learn how to limp."[14]

I dwell on muscle building and in particular Fussell's remarkable self-
portrait because it seems to carry with it a whiff of Stoicism. Muscle massing
is done in the service of limiting vulnerability, of "keeping an enemy at bay." It
involves a metamorphosis of the body into something staggeringly (albeit gro-
tesquely) idealized. It involves control, austerity, and denial. It invokes the will
in an extreme and straightforward way. It is the will defying human limits.
Stoicism, too, is a philosophy about disciplined control and perfectionism,
and its practical focus is in limiting our vulnerability to goods and circumstances that lie outside our dominion. More specifically, our happiness, the
Stoics argue, cannot be vulnerable to what lies outside our vigilant control. To
this end, Stoic practice aims to help us cultivate the kind of mind-set whereby
we might be able to endure the cruelest torture and survive the most devastating psychological deprivations.

But the program Sam Fussell undergoes, to transform the body into an
invincible fortress, is not, strictly speaking, in line with ancient Stoicism. The
body, on the Stoic view, can never be a proper object of full control (the muscle
builder's dependence on anabolic steroids is a telling concession to this) nor,
for that matter, an object of worship. We may invest in it, but like our material
possessions or, indeed, bodily adornments—muscular or otherwise—it can
become damaged and break, cease functioning, or at least cease functioning
smoothly or with grace. And it can be used for good or ill, as an instrument of
benefit to self and others or as a tool of destruction (dramatically so in the
case of suicide bombers, where the expendable body is itself is a part of the
operation of the weapon).[15] In these ways the body is neither a permanent
good nor an unequivocal one in the way that Stoics allege virtue alone is.

With this as preface, I am almost ready to turn to Stoic images of the body
and assess the plausibility of their views. But first I prepare the way with some
background to help locate the Stoic conception.

STOIC IMAGES OF THE BODY
AND ITS DISCIPLINE

The Stoics argue that human flourishing—that is, our happiness or well-being (what the Greeks call *eudaimonia*)—is not a matter of the state of one's body, even its global condition of being healthy or diseased. Rather, as I have noted before, the body and its states constitute what the Stoics call "indifferents," that is, external goods, outside our full control, to which happiness is indifferent, so to speak. In making this claim, the Stoics will agree with Aristotle, and most of the ancient tradition, that human flourishing is marked above all else by a sense of completeness and self-sufficiency. But they part company with Aristotle in giving a narrow reading to the meaning of those terms. Happiness is complete and self-sufficient in the sense that it must be strictly within our control. If it is to be the highest and most final or complete kind of good, and if it is to have the permanence and stability befitting such a good, then it must be protected against the vicissitudes of life that come from loving and losing, from being healthy and infirm, from being subject to nature's plenitude and famines and to the whims of tyrants, thugs, and captors. It cannot, as Aristotle holds, be a mix of virtue *and* external goods. Rather, happiness must be a matter of virtue alone.

The Stoic view, with its retreat inward to the virtuous state of the psyche, is itself rooted in a Platonic reaction to Homeric or archaic values. In the world of the *Iliad* and the *Odyssey*, the good and happiness are in no small degree a matter of fortune and status, of tangible honor, measured in war booty, strength, and wealth. These are largely external goods, tied up with the gods' will and with the caprices of war's victories and losses. Socrates's radical move, transmitted to us through Plato, is to shift virtue and happiness inward to the soul or psyche—to make honor a matter of virtue, and virtue largely achievable by a training of the soul. Virtue alone becomes sufficient for happiness, without dependence on external goods or luck. This position, in essence, is what the Stoics return to and embrace.

It is against this backdrop that we should read Epictetus, a fairly orthodox Stoic, when he claims: "In our power are moral character and all its functions; not in our power are the body, the parts of the body, possessions, parents, brothers, children, country and associates in general." And again:

> When you wish your body to be sound, is it in your own power, or is it not? — "It is not." When you wish it to be healthy? — "Nor this." When you wish it to be handsome? — "Nor this." And to live, or die? — "Nor this." Our body, then, is not our own, but subject to everything stronger than itself.[16]

The "paltry body," Epictetus continues, is an external, to be compared to a petty estate or reputation.[17] It is something you may think you possess, but it can be easily taken from you by disease or death. It is a mere matter or clay, "a corpse" that must be animated and directed by a separate, lifegiving substance in order to function properly.

On this view, the body is itself an external, which in virtue of its needs and desires, is encumbered by a further layer of externals. So hunger, thirst, and sexual urges direct us outward and make us dependent on what we find and lose: "For seeing that we are on earth, and confined to an earthly body, and amongst earthly companions, how was it possible that in these respects we should not be hindered by external things?"[18]

> Is your poor body, then, enslaved or free? . . . Do you not know that it is a slave to fever, gout, eye-disease, dysentery; to a tyrant; of fire, and steel; to everything that is stronger than itself? — Yes, it is a slave. How then can anything belonging to the body be unhindered?[19]

> You ought to treat your entire body like a poor, overburdened ass, as long as it is possible, as long as it is allowed you; but if it is pressed into public service and a solider should lay hold of it, let it go. Do not resist or mutter, otherwise you will get a beating, and lose your poor ass just the same. When this is the way in which you should conduct yourself with regard to the body, consider what is left for you to do about the things that are procured for the sake of the body. If the body be a little ass, those other things become bridles, pack-saddles, shoes, barley, fodder for the ass. Let these go too; dismiss them more quickly and more cheerfully than the little ass itself.[20]

We, as bodies, are little donkeys, weighted down by our worldly loads. We hold tightly to those material loads, though they enslave as much as nurture. So, too, we long for our old body's shape, beauty, and fitness after indignities such as those that combat serves up. But that is a kind of enslavement. It is for reasons such as these that the body is to be regarded as an indifferent that does not contribute to our happiness. And, as already noted, it is excluded from happiness because it is not an unequivocal good. Reissuing a Platonic argument, the Stoics argue that goods such as physical health and strength can be used for good or ill in a way that genuine virtues cannot.[21] We can use our healthy bodies or strength either to rescue innocents who are trapped or to impede their safety. But true courage or kindness are unconditionally good— they can be used only for fine ends. Epictetus asks, "Is health a good, and sickness an evil? No, man. What, then? Health is good when used well, and bad when used ill."[22]

This general view of the body seems unduly harsh. Cicero registers a blunt complaint in his interpretation of this argument, commenting that the Stoics "show concern for nothing but the mind, as if human beings had no body."[23] "When it comes to a happy life," the Stoics simply argue that "the amount of bodily advantages has no relevance at all."[24] We can add to this criticism that even if it is plausible to think of goods such as physical strength and fitness as only conditionally good, they are nonetheless not typically fully outside our ministry. Muscle building, in Fussell style, illustrates in an extreme way the body as an object not just of self-discipline but of obsessional control. And this control can produce highly tangible results. Of course, the most diligent effort never *guarantees* intended results. But this does not make us thoroughly helpless in terms of our bodies. Our habits of diet, hygiene, and fitness all contribute to physical well-being, even if they are not sufficient for it.

Epictetus is concessive about these commonsense points. The Stoic notion of what is "appropriate" and in accord with nature (*ta kathēkonta,* which becomes *officia* or "duties" in the works of Latin writers) requires that we care for our bodies.[25] But the accent always falls on acknowledging the limitations of our efforts and recognizing that the effort, not the result, is what matters. Death and disease, disfigurement and disability are conditions we must learn to face with equanimity. The more frequently and matter-of-factly we remind ourselves of our fragility, the more prepared we will be to face adversity. So someone might ask: "But what if my friends should die?"

> What else could that signify except that men who are mortal have died? Do you at once wish to live to be old, and yet not to see the death of any one you love? Do you not know that, in a long course of time, many and various events must necessarily happen? That a fever must get the better of one person, a highwayman of another, a tyrant of a third? For such is the world we live in; such are those who live in it with us. Heat and cold, improper diet, journeys by land, voyages by sea, winds, and all kinds of accidents destroy some, banish others, and send one on an embassy, another on campaign.[26]

Such are the facts of luck and circumstance. We are ultimately all vulnerable.

But it is crucial to note that dispassionate care of the body need not entail indifference. And it does not, in Epictetus's considered view. With regard to "appropriate action," he insists, "I should not be unfeeling like a statue."[27] And so he says, following Stoic tradition here, that it would be foolish to fail to supply the body with the nourishment and care that is suitable to it, or to avoid the advice of a good doctor when it is warranted.[28] This is to say we should care for our bodies in ways that are overall advantageous, or "in accord with nature," selecting and disselecting accordingly. What we should not do, however, is what most of us do—invest in our bodies in a way that amounts to emotional attachment.

Epictetus's most colorful reflections on the body form part of a criticism of Cynics and their unconventional views about cleanliness. It is worth pausing over these texts for a moment, both because of their didacticism about bodily hygiene and because of the touch of comic irony they provide in a work that can, at times, be unduly severe. Here we imagine Epictetus clearly in high performance mode before his teenage male audience. A lecture such as this one might wake up even the most bored listener.

We begin with his harangue against the Cynics for their public displays of nudity and for their failure to appreciate the social and moral utility of a good bath. The practitioners, he laments, have evidently gone astray, for their leader and the founder of the movement, Diogenes, was himself a man who "walked about radiant with health, and would draw the attention of the crowd by the very nature of his body."[29] And even though Socrates, the model for the Cynic sage and notorious in historical depictions for his neglect of worldly matters of the body, "rarely bathed,"

> yet his body looked radiant, and was so agreeable and pleasing, that the most handsome and noble were in love with him, and desired to sit by him rather than by those who had the finest features. He might have never washed or bathed if he had pleased, yet even the few baths he did take had their effect.[30]

This is high polemic. If Socrates, a near god for Cynics and Stoics alike, deigned to take baths (however few), then we lesser mortals ought to as well. Moreover, in Socrates's case, the occasional bath seems to have enhanced his success at courting his beloveds. As a Greco-Roman, Epictetus is unlikely to teach through pederasty. But he seems to think he can attract his young listeners by reminding them of Socrates's practice!

In other passages, Epictetus weaves together, with a similar sense of comic irony, related claims about the body. The following claims are implicit in the texts and worth untangling: (1) discipline of the body prepares one for discipline in general, (2) duties of bodily care are social duties as well as duties of respect to self, and (3) appreciating bodily beauty can be an indirect path to appreciating inner, psychic beauty.

With regard to the first point, Epictetus states, "Whatever means are applied to the body by those who are exercising it, may also be valuable for [character] training."[31] The point underlies his repeated metaphors, discussed earlier, for framing character training in terms of athletics. But here the point is not just metaphorical: the very same qualities cultivated in athletics—for example, stick-to-itiveness, drive, concentration, dogged commitment—stand one in good stead in other arenas.[32] They are the same habits of mind.

Epictetus goes on to sketch his version of the teleological function of a hygienic body. In a roundabout way, he takes us to the second claim of care for bodies as grounded in social duties to others. For instance, nostrils are among the channels that dispel the humors, and if we sniff up their mucous discharges, we are violating the course of nature. Too, we violate our nature when we leave food between our teeth, allow dirt to cake on our bodies "as the result of perspiration and the pressure of our clothes," or fail to make use of "water, oil, our hands," and soap and towel to remedy the problem. In response to an imaginary interlocutor's protest of "Why should I?" Epictetus appeals first to a not very informative nature argument: "I will tell you again. In the first place [be-cause one is] to act like a human being." But then he adds a social dimension: "And, in the second, so as not to cause distress to those you meet."[33] In short, we may fail in our social duties to others when we neglect our hygiene:

> You think you deserve to have your own smell? So be it. But do you think those who sit by you deserve it too, and those who recline by you, and those who kiss you? Go away, then, to some wilderness or other, where you deserve to be, and spend your life alone, smelling yourself; for it is right that you should enjoy your uncleanness alone. But since you are in a city, what sort of person do you suppose you are showing yourself to be, to behave in such a thoughtless and inconsiderate manner?[34]

Not bathing is a social offense. This may explain why the Cynics' popularity started to decline—it may have been the stench. While philosophers shouldn't have to issue invitations—"What physician invites anyone to be cured by him?"[35]—if you really want your philosophy to attract listeners, you may need to engage in a little bit of image control. The Cynics should have known better than to sport a "consumptive" and "thin and pale" body or bear the "figure and visage of a condemned man." Who would want to take up that kind of lifestyle?[36] A groomed and nonodiferous body is a social must for anyone who wants friends and admirers.

> But who does not avoid a man who is dirty, and smells and looks unwholesome, even more than a man who is befouled with dung? The stench of the latter is external and adventitious, but that which arises from want of care comes from within, as though from a kind of inward putrefaction.[37]

Epictetus's final concession to spending time on bodily hygiene hinges on the idea that the activity, even if ultimately misplaced, can indirectly lead one to the more worthy end of cultivating a beautiful soul. The young disciple who is preoccupied with the body at least has *some* vision of beauty. "With that as a starting point," Epictetus optimistically suggests, "all that is necessary to do is to show him the way" toward more appropriate objects for his devo-tion. Transference and growth are possible here in a way that is simply more problematic for one who lacks any aspiration to beauty, whatever its form:

> But if he should come to me befouled, dirty, with whiskers down to his knees, what can I say to him, what sort of comparison can I use to draw him on? For what has he ever concerned himself with that bears any resemblance to beauty, such that I can redirect his attention, and say, "Beauty is not there, but here"? Would you have me say to him, "Beauty lies not in being befouled, but in rea-son"? For does he in fact aspire to beauty? Does he show any sign of it? Go and argue with a pig, that he should not roll in the mud.[38]

Epictetus's point, reminiscent of that of Diotema in Plato's *Symposium*, is that even if beauty's proper home is not a body, to care about beauty in bodily form can jump-start dialectical progress upward.[39] Still, Epictetus, like Diotema, warns that bodily beauty is no more than a starting point for a nobler kind of beauty. Moreover, to remain obsessively fixated on one's physical beauty, however produced—by nature, grooming, physical workouts, or muscle enhancers—is narcissistic folly:

> In conclusion, whatever means are applied to the body by those who are exercising it, may also be valuable for training [in general] . . . ; but if their aim is mere display, these are the traits of a man who has turned to externals, and is hunting after something other, and is seeking for spectators to exclaim, "What a great man!"[40]

Taken to an extreme, it becomes an Adonis complex.

The texts are full of sarcasm but nevertheless are didactic: regarding the body as an indifferent is not to be "unmoved as a statue." It still involves, practically speaking, its own form of commitment. Seneca puts the matter aptly: "I do not maintain that the body is not to be indulged at all; but I maintain that we must not be slaves to it."[41] Becoming a slave to the body, even if, paradoxically, through relentless exercise of the will, is not a Stoic posture.

More positively, the Stoic position that we have been drawing from Epictetus can be summed up this way: the body and its care and fitness are conditional goods that have significance in the good person's life. More specifically, a physically fit and well-groomed body can tell us something about its owner's level of self-respect and about her regard for others around her. And it can reveal habits of discipline and care that may well generalize to other arenas of life. Finally, devotion to physical beauty may be an important step in cultivating aesthetic beauty in other places where beauty is less ephemeral. These, taken as a package, are not unreasonable arguments to consider in assessing the place of a fit body in our lives.

Still, how satisfying are these claims if Stoics ultimately deny fitness and physical well-being a proper place in their conception of flourishing? One way to press this question is to explore further the relation of "indifferents" to virtue. This will help us ask, ultimately, how Stoic consolations might address the concerns of combat soldiers who risk life and limb, putting themselves in harm's way.

THE INDIFFERENTS AND HAPPINESS

We can frame our present question in this way: in what sense is the strong and healthy body an object of our rational concern if it is not a part of our happiness? That goods such as health and a fit and strong body are "preferred" goods is a Stoic concession to the fact that they are not unimportant, even if they don't make or break one's happiness. The crucial qualification is that they do not *add* to the overall goodness of virtue. That is, virtue and health are not worth more than virtue on its own, and the absence of health does not mar happiness.[42] Cicero argues by analogy: a drop of honey does not make the Aegean Sea any sweeter; a penny does not add to the riches of Croesus; taking only one step on the road from here to India does not get one substantially closer to one's goal; turning on an artificial light when one is already in full sunshine adds little to the overall illumination. In a similar way, external goods don't contribute to the goodness of virtue.[43]

And yet the fact that these externals have preferred or selective value bears some weight in our rational deliberation. But in what way? Why should we choose virtue plus health or virtue plus bodily fitness if it makes us no happier than virtue alone? What is the selective advantage of externals if they don't contribute to happiness? The Stoic defense is complex, and a full examination of texts would take us too far afield. Still, a few remarks are important for clarification.

One way of conceiving of the Stoic defense is to claim that not all of the objects of our rational deliberation and concern have the same kind of value.[44] To be concerned with happiness as an end, the Stoics argue, is to be concerned with virtue in the sense of what a person can bring about through his own powers and rational agency. Accordingly, they will argue, happiness is not virtuous action—an external act that Aristotle describes as an actualized choice requiring favorable circumstances and success (more or less) in hitting one's target. Rather, happiness is virtuous activity in the leaner sense of skill and effort, of doing all one can to act from the right motives with external objectives in mind (a successful performance, in their view), whether or not one successfully achieves the objectives. Cicero gives the example of an archer: "One's ultimate aim is to do all in one's power to shoot straight." Living the life of virtue is a skill like this. Achieving that aim, like being a good archer, is compatible with missing the immediate target or external objective. "To actually hit the target," he adds, is "to be selected but not sought."[45]

"To select," in Stoic idiom, is shorthand for treating goods as preferred indifferents, that is, as something we value as having natural advantage, though we do not seek or choose it as part of happiness. The wise person will make such selections, preferring health to disease, fit sensory and mental faculties to deficient ones, wealth and freedom to penury and slavery.[46] He will view them as important and of rational concern but nonetheless as distinct from the value of happiness, and their absence does not detract from happiness.

But to this we might make an objection: can't we conceive of a kind of happiness that *combines* goods of different scalar values, and perhaps even ranks those goods *within* happiness, with external goods conditioned by (or hierarchically ordered by) virtue or wisdom? In this sense, for the sage at least, the possession and use of external goods will always be constrained by conditions implicit in virtue.[47]

In many ways this is Aristotle's view.[48] As I noted earlier, happiness is a composite, in his view, of virtues plus the external goods and luck that are both necessary for the full exercise of virtue *and* valuable simply in their own right (as in the case of friendship) for human forms of good living. To be virtuous but to have catastrophic bad luck or deprivation—think of the fate of Priam, who loses his country and tens of sons in battle—is to suffer ills that "crush and maim" happiness.[49] Still, Aristotle equivocates on the point. If virtuous activities characterize the goodness of life, then the person who lives virtuously, doing nothing hateful and mean, may not reach the height of happiness, but at least he will not be miserable, in the sense of being morally wretched. "For the person who is truly good and wise, we think, bears all the chances of life becomingly and always makes the best of circumstances, as a good general makes the best military use of the army at his command."[50]

It is this latter, Socratic point that the Stoics isolate and ultimately stress. Isn't the part of happiness that we prize most not prosperity or luck, but how we bear up and make the best of ourselves, whatever the circumstances? Isn't real happiness, then, the strength and dignity we show in facing whatever hand we are dealt, and the stability and equanimity with which we pursue our desires in those circumstances? Aristotle himself lays stress on the point when he says, "The good . . . is something of one's own and not easily taken from one."[51] Most of us can agree with this. Still, we are probably unwilling to go all the way with the Stoics and argue that virtue exhausts our happiness.

Even so, we might hold that if we are truly to work at finding happiness, then it is better to err on the Stoic side—it is better to design a life in which we are empowered rather than helpless. And if and when we are victims of misfortune or oppression, we must still try to find some measure, however slight, of dominion and resilience. These are Stoic sentiments, and Epictetus expresses them powerfully, again through an athletic metaphor I have quoted before:[52]

> Consider which of the things you proposed initially you have mastered, and which you have not, and how it gives you pleasure to remember some of them, and pain to remember others, and, if possible recover the things that you have let slip. Those competing in the greatest contest should not fade out, but take the blows too. For our competition is not to do with wrestling or the pancration—where success or failure can make all the difference to a man's standing—and indeed make him [in his and the world's eyes] supremely fortunate or unfortunate—but over *real* good fortune and happiness.
>
> *What then?*
>
> Even if we fail here and now, no one stops us from competing again; we don't have to wait another four years for the next Olympics, but as soon as a man has

picked himself up and renewed his grip on himself and shown the same enthusiasm he is allowed to compete. And if you give in again, you can compete again, and if once you win, you are like someone who never gave in. Only, don't let sheer habit make you give in readily and end up like a bad athlete going around beaten in the whole circuit like quails that run away.[53]

As Tony Long has argued in his masterly commentary on Epictetus's *Discourses*, the above passage is crucial in understanding Epictetus's conception of happiness. The contest of life has as its prize our own individual happiness. We compete against ourselves, not others. And we compete over and over, through repeated opportunities for achievement. To be defeated need not mean that we are out of the race. Life gives us new contests and new opportunities in which happiness can prevail.

Epictetus's tone is optimistic. And yet, following traditional Stoic doctrine, he leaves the door open for a "well-reasoned exit" (*eulogos exagōgē*) through suicide in extreme circumstances when one can no longer have the happiness that consists in practicing virtue.[54] Still, Epictetus is far less intrigued by suicide than, for example, Seneca, who famously committed suicide at the order of Nero.[55] Epictetus follows his master, Socrates, in holding that no one should leave the prison house of the soul unless God has given the signal.[56]

I cannot take up the complex issue of the Stoic view of suicide here. What I wish to stress, however, is Epictetus's general view that our happiness rests on our achievement of (virtuous) agency and not, as we moderns tend to think, on a feeling of prosperity or satisfaction.[57] The point, as I have said, appeals to many of us. But it must not blind us to the real fragility of human agency and to the brute fact that even at our strongest moments we are only finitely strong. *Human* agency is always vulnerable, and the frailty of our bodies is a constant reminder of that.

With this as background, I turn to the issue of physical injury and disfigurement. What of the men and women returning now, as I write, from war in Afghanistan and Iraq maimed in some way—who are amputees at the elbow or knee, or who are blinded, or who have a hollow socket in place of an eye or nose? What is the contest for happiness like for those who are no longer able to touch their children with hands and fingers, or see a loved one's face, or walk when they used to be the most physically elite among soldiers? The moral and psychological questions of how to cope with injury, and in these cases a radically new embodied identity, can shift quickly, in Stoic teaching, to more abstract metaphysical themes of the value of external goods in relation to an unconditional good such as virtue. But the moral and psychological questions remain. It is time to explore these questions by taking up a number of concrete cases. Can modified versions of Stoicism provide consolation for those who face severe physical loss?

"THE BICEPS I LEFT IN IRAQ"

In the current wars in Afghanistan and Iraq, soldiers often survive wounds that would have been fatal in previous wars. But that survival, due to high-tech body armor and helmets, may still involve a new body identity—as an amputee, as a person without vision or hearing, as a burn victim. And while there may be prosthetics for amputees and plastic surgery for burn victims, there are no prosthetic eyes for the blinded.[58] (Nor are there prosthetic repairs of sexual identity for the millions of noncombatant women who become victims of wars' genocidal rape.)[59] These losses are brute reminders that technology goes only so far and that missing limbs or disabled and violated body parts are still catastrophic losses. A soldier may joke that he has left his biceps behind in Iraq, but if it means that not just that his hope of being Mr. America has been dashed, but along with it his hope of still being able to hug, or drive, or open the refrigerator door in the usual way, then more than just biceps has been lost.[60]

Much can be said intuitively about the injury to bodily identity caused by different kinds of physical losses. In an obvious way, there are aesthetic injuries that come with disfigurement and deformity. But just as fundamental are identity shifts having to do with restrictions of capabilities and functions that define a good life in general and a given individual's good life in particular.

In what follows, I want to consider briefly two anecdotal cases in which soldiers seem to appeal to Stoic-like sensibilities in facing risk and bodily injury. In each case, however, more than just resoluteness is at work. Each expresses an empathic connection toward others (and the self) in facing loss. I am reminded here of Shakespeare's mythic Stoic warrior, Coriolanus, who learns he can be tough and still show compassion: "Sir, it is no little thing to make mine eyes to sweat compassion."[61] We shall see in a later chapter that an attenuated form of empathy finds a place within some of the Stoic texts. But for now it is important simply to note that connectedness to others, in addition to a steely will, can be a factor that contributes to resilience.

"Baptized in Fire and Blood"

An Army captain named David Rozelle went into battle in Iraq wearing a belt buckle with the inscription "Brave rifles! Veterans! You have been baptized in fire and blood and have come out steel."[62] The words are from General Winfield Scott's 1847 address to cavalrymen during the Mexican-American War. Two months after Rozelle was deployed in Iraq, a mine blew off his right foot. With the help of technology and a relentless will, Rozelle returned to combat service as commander of an armored cavalry unit, just days away from the first anniversary of losing his foot. Rozelle was and still is an athlete and warrior. His recovery was a matter of grueling workouts—four hours a day of physical therapy, swimming, weight lifting, mountain biking, skiing. Some six months after his injury, he went skiing in the Rockies, using a prosthetic ski boot. Even without a foot, he passes other swimmers in a pool. Rozelle is tough, but he is also honest about his loss: "There are times I definitely feel disabled." "At least once a day," he says, "I miss my foot." He is in regular contact by e-mail with other amputees and has visited hospital units to encourage amputees to pull through: "I sat in rooms with guys and cried with them," he says. "I think I've made a difference with a few." He is committed to "plain talk" about life as an amputee, something he himself never got when he first lost his limb.

In some sense we can view Rozelle as coming to regard his body as an indifferent. In that he is not overly invested in having his foot and can carry on in its absence, in a way he exhibits Stoic sensibilities. He is flexible about his body image and ready to adapt to changes to it. And yet we should not idealize this

Photographer August Sander's "disabled ex-serviceman" (1928).

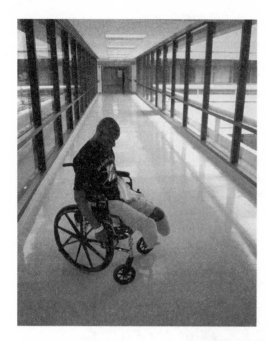

Coping with lost limbs.

The new prosthetics.

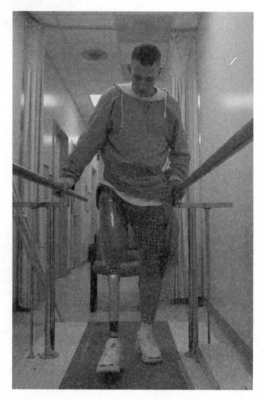

dispassionate stance. He is no sage—he acknowledges his loss, he misses his foot, and he spends a fair portion of his time helping others to acknowledge their loss. In this sense, he may believe that having a functioning flesh-and-blood foot is not at the core of his happiness, but it still *affects* his happiness, and had he no prosthetic, his adjustment might have been far different.

What is also striking about Rozelle as a kind of Stoic warrior is his combination of steely will and empathetic compassion. He is all about brawn and will, but he's also about humanity and the anguish of suffering war's indignities: "These guys with no arms who have to go home and learn to live again? Shoot, I've got it easy." In Rozelle, there is an optimism and can-do spirit we associate with Stoicism in its various stripes, but there is also a willingness to accept vulnerability that is all too often obscured by the austere lines of orthodox Stoicism. Too, there is a profound sense of solidarity with other warriors, both with those still deployed and with those who have returned home bearing the scars of war's hell. We return to this reparative role of affiliation in Chapter 7.

"Unscathed"

Major Phil Ashby offers another subtle mix of tough and gentle Stoicism. His story is the subject of his gripping memoir, *Unscathed*. Ashby served as a rugged Commando of the British Royal Marines, and later as a Marines Mountain Leader, undergoing what is arguably the longest and toughest special force training in the British military. Though Ashby was trained in the Arctic, Scotland, and Norway to lead warfare efforts in extreme cold-weather conditions (and out of uniform was a rugged Scottish mountaineering/Outward Bound type), his most perilous trial came in tropical terrain, in Sierra Leone. There, on May 6, 2000, while serving as an unarmed United Nations observer helping to implement disarmament, he and three others were taken hostage as civil war erupted. Three days into the siege, amid increasing worries that they would be beheaded, Ashby, who was in command, made the decision for the four to attempt an escape. With limited battery power in his satellite phone, he had to decide whom to inform of the escape plan and the likelihood of his not making it (he estimated his survival chances at 20 percent). He called a team leader, who was himself imperiled and unable to offer command advice. He then made three calls to the United Kingdom—to his father, who told him he loved him; to a training mate, to whom he gave funeral details; and to his wife, Anna, to whom he said it might be goodbye. "I couldn't think of enough ways to tell her how much I loved her and was missing her and it was hard to hang up. Our final message to each other was the same: 'Take care of yourself. I love you.'"[63] The conversations "relieve[d] a burden and emotionally fortif[ied]" him for his escape.[64]

Ashby's Stoic image is a complex one. In Stoic mold, he finds room to exercise strength and a robust will in the most constricted and adverse circumstances.

His escape in Sierra Leone is, as he puts it, a way of trying to survive rather than "simply do[ing] nothing and waiting for the worst to happen."[65] His resilience rests not only on his own strength and resourcefulness but also in the lifeline he finds in others—his father, his best friend, his beloved Anna. But there is a further point to make that is critical given the focus of this chapter— a point that emerges only in the final pages of his memoir. Ashby, the invincible mountaineer and superb military athlete, did not, in the end, escape from Sierra Leone physically unscathed. He returned to the United Kingdom with "a tiny part of Sierra Leone" having broken through his "defenses."[66] More precisely, a tropical virus attacked his spine, leaving him with significant neurological damage and physical and mental impairment. Ashby is under no illusions about how this is likely to affect his future:

> In some ways, I would rather have had a concrete, visible injury that I could point to and come to terms with—even a missing limb. Not knowing exactly what is wrong with you, or how bad or good it is going to get, is mentally as well as physically debilitating. It sounds big-headed, but I was used to being one of the best at whatever I set out to do and the thought of not being able to work hard and play hard is a pretty desperate prospect.[67]

To return to our earlier discussion, Ashby's worry is that the "contest" of life that he knows best and that has, in a sense, defined good living for him— namely, a life of extreme physical challenge and risk—is no longer one in which he can ably compete. No doubt there are other challenges, other competitions in life, Epictetus would say, against which to test one's excellences and agency. And some of these will be physical challenges, as Rozelle's story of recovery attests. Still, Ashby's voice ought not to be silenced. For him, like so many military men and women, "being able to work hard and play hard" is precisely a matter of having an exemplary body that can be routinely tested in grueling ways. To be deprived of that contest is no small change in the terms of one's happiness and conception of self.

We have seen in this chapter that physical and mental resilience in the face of vicissitudes, such as those Ashby and Rozelle face, tend to give Stoicism its appeal. But we have also seen that Stoicism can quickly become harsh. As Epictetus puts it, our bodies are paltry things that enslave us with disease and disability. We must be able to find a kind of happiness that is neither enhanced by clingy possession of positive bodily states (health and strength, bodily integrity and fitness) nor marred by their opposites (disease, disfigurement, physical fragility). It is this last claim, perhaps, that is the most difficult to accept. For even if we embrace the Epictetan point that much of our happiness has to do with our own attitudes and efforts in facing the contest of life, we are still likely to hold that severe bodily injuries—loss of limbs, sight, facial features, and more, all of which are losses that combatants, and noncombatants in war zones, routinely endure as the price of war—alter our sense of identity and our very chances for happiness. This is not to deny that some manage well under such circumstances. Indeed, we admire and are inspired by those who seem to find happiness despite severe bodily harm. But not all find that happiness, and toward them (whether they be others or ourselves) compassion is appropriate, not Stoic reproof.

"You! What d'you mean by this?" I rapped.
"You dare come on parade like this?" . . .

Some days "confined to camp" he got,
For being "dirty on parade."
He told me, afterwards, the damned spot,
Was blood, his own. "Well, blood is dirt," I said.

"Blood's dirt," he laughed, looking away,
Far off to where his wound had bled
And almost merged for ever into clay.
"The world is washing out its stains," he said.
"It doesn't like our cheeks so red:
Young blood's its great objection.
But when we're duly white-washed, being dead,
The race will bear Field-Marshal God's inspection."

—Wilfred Owen, "Inspection"

We should consider also in how much of our behaviour the benefit or injury resides mainly or entirely in the manifestation of
attitude itself. So it is with good manners, and much of what we
call kindness, on the one hand; with deliberate rudeness, studied
indifference, or insult on the other.

—Peter Strawson, "Freedom and Resentment"

3

Manners and Morals

———

MILITARY BEARING

Strong characters and strong bodies are part of the military appeal. But so too are manners. For those who believe manners build morals, the military offers the lesson in spades. At the mealtime formation at the Naval Academy, visitors line up daily to see a brigade of crisply pressed uniforms and taut, straight bodies. Officers and midshipmen generally greet civilians with a "sir" or "ma'am," locked eye gaze, and firm handshake. Hair is in place and uniforms are impeccable; shirts have creases like no civilian dress shirt has ever seen. It is not just a trim and neat uniform that an outsider notices, however, but a midshipman's overall demeanor and bearing—an attitude of politeness and respect, an air of somberness and civility. "Honor, courage, and commitment" may be written on Academy walls, replacing Harvard's "*Lux*" and Yale's "*Lux et Veritas.*" But inscribed on the faces and bodies of the midshipmen is a commitment not just to character but also to an "*aesthetic* of character."[1] The world of the military takes seriously both the inner stuff of character and its appearance. Military rules and regulations, and what can fall under the category of "conduct unbecoming," pertain to actions, but they also cover a more general sense of comportment, manners, and emotional bearing. Whether or not it is a throwback to Roman and medieval times, or the replacement of Homeric anger and lust with a chivalrous warrior's code of downcast eyes and stolid demeanor, an emphasis on the face and look of a warrior remains with us.[2]

As a moral philosopher, I found that the questions that nagged me during my time at the Naval Academy were these: How deep does surface conduct go? Do manners lead to morals, etiquette to ethics? Should the civilian world, baffled by the degeneration of civility in public life, take better notice of the role of decorum in military culture? Is good conduct a part of good character?

It is easy to be a skeptic here. Codes of conduct are highly local. What one group finds pleasing and a sign of respect, another may find overly formal or off-putting. Given the variability of conduct codes across cultures, how can

U.S. Naval Academy dress parade.

Finally letting loose at graduation, U.S. Naval Academy.

behavior that is so culture-specific get to the heart of what matters morally? Moreover, much military conduct is mindless drill and compliance motivated by fear of those higher up in the chain of command. Can motivation so tightly pegged to reward and punishment still help an individual secure inner virtue? If Stoic doctrine is right—that inner virtue is what matters—then shouldn't the focus be primarily on the inside, on motives of virtue, and not on the external trappings of deference and decorum?

These are legitimate concerns, not easily dismissed. They are criticisms most civilians, myself included, would bring to a military environment. And yet I have become persuaded that the military gets something right in thinking that manners matter. Side by side with moral acts such as helping or rescuing, or showing courage or generosity, comportment and demeanor are vehicles through which we routinely express our concern or respect for others. To display the proper eye gaze toward another, to bear oneself physically in a certain way, and to be mindful of what would offend, insult, or shame are in many cultures simply the ways we acknowledge others as worthy of respect. True, certain aspects of decorum and manner may have more local value than others. But the fact that codes of etiquette vary culturally and some codes are morally problematic does not impugn the connection of a good code of etiquette, in general, with morality.[3]

Stoic teachings are again instructive here. Cicero, in *On Duties,* a work that was mandatory reading for the well-educated classes right up through the nineteenth century, reports a Stoic view that decorum is inextricably woven into the fabric of virtuous character. And Seneca, in a less well known but remarkable text, *On Favors,* argues for the crucial role of emotional demeanor in acts of kindness and gratitude. Ever faithful to Roman decorum, Seneca seeks to revise and enlighten practice without dispensing with its crucial role in society.

But as we have seen before, Stoic texts are not without internal tensions. In the texts we will study, the authors are mindful of the powerful criticism that social conventions can be just facade and can corrupt purer, moral purpose. This, in essence, is the stance of the Cynics, who indeed are radically unconventional, shamelessly so—as shameless as a dog (*kunos,* from which our term "cynic" derives). The Stoics are inheritors of much Cynic doctrine, but the Roman Stoics, sensitive to Roman decorum, are particularly allergic to this unconventional stance. Yet the break is not completely clean; there are many moments in reading Seneca when one senses a palpable tension between laying stress on inner virtue and caring about its outer trappings.

There is a further tension in the Stoic texts that I will address: an ambivalence about the role of emotion in the expression of virtue (itself an issue of decorum). The Stoics, as I have stressed, aim to reduce emotional vulnerability in the good life, yet the texts we will take up encourage us to be respectful both of our propensity to express emotions and of our capacity to read them off the faces and bodies of others. In these texts emotional exchange becomes, surprisingly, a critical element of moral interaction. The fact that the Stoics, whose emphasis is typically on the internal aspect of virtue, nonetheless give an important role to the outer face is a good indication that this is a significant consideration for moral theory in general, and for its applications.[4]

We shall come to Stoic teachings in due course. But for now it is important to take seriously the objections to decorum and manners and to see how they can be met, especially from a military perspective.

CYNICISM ABOUT DECORUM, AND SOME REPLIES

The world of the military emphasizes matters of appearance and decorum—a spit shine on shoes, the right uniform with the right creases, a "cover" donned the moment one steps outdoors, and regulation socks, shoes, and underwear.[5] These are the ritualized aesthetics of garments, but then there is the aesthetic of the body and face—a ramrod-straight posture, a crisp salute to those of superior rank, a stolid but attentive gaze. At the Naval Academy at least, regulations about what is "seemly" and "proper" for a midshipman can at times extend to minutiae—to prohibitions on keeping Tupperware in one's locker or using an umbrella to take cover in the rain. It is not just an eighteen-year-old offender who might object, "But what does this have to do with honor or character?" A more neutral observer might wonder, too.

At one level, the cynicism is about symbols of deference and propriety. Why do these particular symbols matter? With respect to this question, explanations may not go much beyond the accidents of history, artifice, and stipulation. The Cynics themselves come to mind here, as they were keen to get rid of many of these artificialities. "Deface the coinage" was their slogan, and by that they meant abolish money—a global symbol of conventionalism and materialism. They also urged that buildings, courts, and gymnasia are no more than facades for the real virtue that rests within inner souls. In a pure world free from material clutter, we would have no need for those institutions or for the money required to fund and maintain them. They went further in their defiance of custom: incest is all right, public masturbation and copulation are fine, and eating people—"not only the dead, but our own flesh, if ever a part of the body should happen to be cut off"—can at times be appropriate.[6] Perhaps less radical was their advocacy of unisex clothing, though their recommendation of naked mixed-sex workouts raised many eyebrows even then.

The Cynics show the extreme side of irreverence for matters of decorum. What their fellow ancients (and we) often take for granted in our social customs and interactions, the Cynics throw to the winds. Moreover, the Cynics' list of examples shows that rituals of decorum govern not just peripheral matters of conduct but many of our core moral duties. Those rituals can give concrete form to how we respect the dead, honor the dignity of bodies, or take care not to offend our neighbors by how we draw the line between public and private space. Thus many of the specifics in how we fulfill duties are conventional, and the Cynics rightly call our attention to that conventionalism. In this sense they provide an important lesson, however hyperbolized, that even core moral practices can sometimes reasonably be the subject of reflection and criticism, both from within and from without. In civilian and military life, criticizing demeaning or degrading moral practices is often precisely the form that acting from moral conscience takes. Such criticisms contribute to a healthy moral atmosphere and are quite different from complaints grounded in expediency or self-interest.

In this vein, I recall a midshipman who, having just learned in ethics class about grounds for disobeying orders, came to my office to tell me that he planned to openly flout the fraternization rule prohibiting upperclass students from dating plebes, or first-year students. He was convinced that this rule was a violation of his rights as an officer and that issues of unit cohesion and impartiality within units did not trump his being able to date a plebe. In his case, his girlfriend from home had come to the Academy precisely so they could be together, and the fraternization rule was no small obstacle to their romance. As inconvenient as the rule was for them, I tried to show this young man that, overall, it was a reasonable rule for troop conduct, though neither I nor a four-star admiral could easily convince him of that. He was bent on flouting the rule, I think ultimately more out of self-interest than principle (though I'm sure he would disagree).

I have focused on the issue of conventionalism and particular rules and practices of decorum. But there is another set of factors that breeds cynicism, and that is decorum's alleged inauthenticity and superficiality. When we follow codes of conduct or rituals of decorum, we are often just playacting—acting appropriately in terms of outward conduct, irrespective of what is in our hearts. Politeness in a show of gratitude, for example, is often a mask that hides the feeling that we really dislike a gift and wish someone had not gone to the bother of giving it to us; we teach our children not to be too candid about disappointments when they unwrap their birthday gifts because we think avoiding offense to the benefactors in this case trumps honesty of expression. In a slightly different vein, junior officers salute more senior ones in a show of respect for the uniform, and the gesture has little to do with whether they think those officers actually deserve the honor. They adhere to the minutiae of rules that they may privately think not worth the bother. But at some point, isn't insincerity itself a kind of offense? Why reward the person who is good at "faking it"?[7]

The issue is complicated. But one place to begin is to note that even actions that are not part of codes of etiquette and instead seem more at the heart of morality, such as acts of generosity or bravery on the battlefield, can be done dutifully even though from less than wholehearted moral motives. Thus someone may act out of mixed motives at times—altruism as well as a bit of self-interest, or bravery but also a tinge of glory seeking. Purity of (moral) heart is something hard to achieve and hard to be fully honest with ourselves about. The eighteenth-century German Enlightenment philosopher Immanuel Kant is forever reminding us of this fact. Also, we might act to please others, as we do in the case of many etiquette-bound acts, knowing that we don't really feel in our heart what we show in our face, or fully endorse the practices to which the social conventions bind us. The commitment is to outward conduct, to what we show and display to others. In etiquette, we allow for a gap between candor and performance.

Put differently, in cases of etiquette or decorum, appearances sometimes matter for their own sake. The outer aesthetic is the thing, and it is recognized as essential to the mutual ritual. The legendary sociologist Erving Goffman brilliantly captures this insight in his research on deference behavior:

> It appears that deference behavior on the whole tends to be honorific and po-litely toned, conveying appreciation of the recipient that is in many ways more complimentary to the recipient than the actor's true sentiments might warrant. The actor typically gives the recipient the benefit of the doubt, and may even conceal low regard by extra punctiliousness. Thus acts of deference often attest to ideal guidelines to which the actual activity between actor and recipient can now and then be referred.[8]

Goffman continues, "Regard is something the individual constantly has for others, and knows enough about to feign on occasion."[9] Too, a recipient knows enough not to probe beyond facades: to "steal information," as Goffman puts it, that was intended to be hidden may show disrespect for others and be an invasion of their privacy.

In a striking way, the junior officer's salute or stolid gaze and the senior officer's acknowledgment of each are elements of such a pact. The point of the mutual ritual is to offer and accept just so much information, and no more. To look for more or to offer more is to break the pact. Indeed, interactions within the military are, in part, so ritualized precisely in order to draw sharp borders between public and private personae. That boundary is emphasized by war, when an individual, in her public, military persona, is trained in body and mind to carry out military functions and missions that she would not be asked to carry out as a civilian.

Goffman's pivotal point, relevant to matters of military role and decorum, is that a certain degree of pretense is a pervasive part of much social interac-tion, and especially so when it comes to etiquette rituals. Kant himself, fa-mously dogmatic about truth-telling, surprisingly anticipates (indeed embraces) Goffman's point on the role of pretense in social interaction:

> Men are, one and all, actors—the more so the more civilized they are. They put on a show of affection, respect for others, modesty and disinterest without deceiving anyone, since it is generally understood that they are not sincere about it. And it is

a very good thing that this happens in the world. For if men keep on playing these roles, the real virtues whose semblance they have merely been affecting for a long time are gradually aroused and pass into their attitude of will.[10]

Here Kant is not terribly worried about this sort of semblance counting as a case of deceit. The game is transparent: it is wink, wink, nod, nod. No one is manipulated. The feigned smile keeps under wraps less generous feelings, which a duty of beneficence demands be kept there. A cold-hearted misanthropist, even if he is acting from duty, should not wear his misanthropy on his sleeve.[11] Decorum is important for its own sake, whether or not it conceals inner feelings.

However, Kant concludes by suggesting that decorum can, in some cases, change inner states. That is, semblance can catalyze a change of heart. As he puts it elsewhere, with a sexism that runs through his work, when a woman practices smiling, the facial gesture helps to promote an inner spirit of benevolence. Put more benignly, "posed" facial expressions may please and show respect.[12] But in addition, they can be self-exhortative, a way of coaxing along a corresponding inner change.[13] We nurse a change from the outside in.

Contemporary psychological research on facial expression corroborates the intuition. Paul Ekman has long studied facial expressions and the army of muscles that go into making the furrows, wrinkles, and raised eyebrows of emotional expression.[14] At one point early on in his career, he and his collaborator Wallace Friesen were practicing facial expressions of anger and distress. After repeated sessions of making those faces all day, they realized they were both feeling emotionally stressed. Their conjecture was that facial feedback mechanisms had induced emotional change internally. To follow their hunch, they devised a test monitoring heart rate and body temperature—the bodily indices of anger, sadness, and fear—of two groups. One group was instructed to recall and relive a stressful experience. The other group was instructed to pose certain facial expressions on cue from Ekman. The second group, the pretenders who simply "assumed the position," as actors do, exhibited the same physiological functions as the first group. Similar results have been reproduced by a German team of researchers under the lead of F. Strack. In this experiment one group of students was instructed to read the funnies while mouthing a pen between their lips in such a way that the major smiling muscles were constricted; another group read the funnies with pencils clenched between their teeth in a way that forced upturned lips. The people who read the comics with upturned lips found them funnier.[15] Other studies confirm that overt facial expression can affect the intensity of emotional arousal.[16] Expressions of emotion thus seem to be sufficient to induce changes in the autonomic nervous system—that is, it indeed sometimes can work from the outside in.

Putting on a uniform might, in some ways, be like putting on a face. That is not to say there is any physiological feedback phenomenon of the sort suggested above. But in an attenuated way, something parallel can happen. More specifically, putting on a uniform can change one's attitude and self-perception, as well as how one is perceived by others. Some argue that this is precisely one of the functions of school uniforms, namely, to help set a tone of discipline and focus in the classroom, and to blur class and group distinctions that can lead to school violence.[17] The topic of the transformative aspect of wearing uniforms came up in a seminar I gave to an ROTC group at Wake Forest University in Winston-Salem, North Carolina, in April 2002. It was a wickedly muggy day, and students were not required to be in uniform. Aside from a few closely cropped heads, there were few signs that identified them as fledgling officers. But on their uniform day, they assured me, they were unmistakably labeled as ROTC candidates. I asked if wearing a uniform changed their behavior or their perception of themselves. Some answered that it was a clear source of pride; others said it was a stigma that they wished they could avoid. One male student said he felt kinder wearing the uniform, and in general more helpful and civil. He said he was more likely to do a good deed wearing it than not. Another said because his uniform attracted hostile stares, he went out of his way to convince people that he wasn't, in his words, "a heartless baby-killer," and this often meant taking on an attitude of enhanced civility. In these admittedly different ways, the uniform served as a reminder for these ROTC students of their responsibilities as military personnel and encouraged them to take their role seriously.

It is important to add here that for women, uniforms can raise a very different set of issues. Unisex clothing, despite its earliest advocacy by the Cynics as a way to put men and women on equal footing, is not a magic bullet for leveling the playing field in the military. A number of my female students at the Naval Academy expressed concern to me that men ridiculed them for the way the male-cut uniform trousers exaggerated their hips. Others felt that Navy whites were too revealing and that regulation-issue shoes designed for males simply didn't fit right. Women's attire was the subject of discussion at a mostly women's officer task force group I sat in on at the Academy. Senior officers were reviewing a request for women midshipmen to be able to wear non-regulation-issue underpants and to be allowed to buy their own dress shoes so that they could get a better fit. After much discussion of bloomers—plain and frilly, white and colored, brief and briefer—the underwear request was denied and the shoe request granted. Later I recounted this discussion to a family friend who at the time was a ROTC student at Holy Cross. She laughed and volunteered that she *was* allowed to wear underwear of her own choosing and that it was a definite comfort to her to know that when in that male uniform, in addition to her permitted bracelet and ring, she had on "something feminine!"[18] One obvious lesson here is that uniforms, if they are to transform from outside in, must first make reasonable accommodations for gender differences *and* for a sense of gender identity.

Dress, like posed facial expressions, can be a form of self-exhortation, but also a way to create good appearances before others. Indeed, for those in leadership roles, appearing to do wrong can be almost as bad as actually doing what is wrong, in that others take their lead from such examples, even if they misconstrue them.[19] Military leaders know the point all too well. In the post-Tailhook era, senior military men often go out of their way to avoid any chance that their actions toward women in integrated units might be misconstrued as sexual.[20] As leaders, they must be "above suspicion," mindful of how actions might be construed *and* misconstrued. The point was not lost on me in a personal way. The captains and colonels who taught with me at the Naval Academy were using my book *Making a Necessity of Virtue*. The dust cover, I discovered, made some squeamish. It features a photo from the Louvre of Canova's statue of a nude, "Psyche Brought Back to Life by Amor's Kiss." One officer joked that he would have to carry the book to class in a brown wrapper. The joke may have been a tip-off to his own prudery or, as Freud would invert it, to his voyeurism. But I think the real issue for him was how he would be perceived by the impressionable midshipmen. How would *they* take the cover? Was its eroticism pornographic to them? And would he be seen as endorsing pornography? For that matter, would I be seen as endorsing it? As one author who has written on the subject puts it, "Being good is sometimes a matter of looking good."[21]

So far we have argued, in a general way, for the importance of decorum and for the place of pretense, or role-playing, within it. But even if we grant the contribution of good manners to good morals, we might still have doubts about aspects of the military model. Earlier I raised a worry about the compartmentalization of military and private roles. But we might also have the inverse concern—that military habits of comportment can pervade a military person's private life. The habits become ingrained and shape behavior where it is less appropriate. In particular, appropriate forms of respect become muddled. The point becomes clearer when we consider Robert Duvall in his classic role as the career officer in *The Great Santini*. Santini painfully discovers that he can be the military colonel to his wife and children at home only at risk of losing them. He takes the gamble because he knows no other way of being respected.

Santini's notion of respect is based on hierarchy and rank. Its species, we might say, is "deference respect." Outside the military, however, respect often takes a more democratic form (we might call it "dignitary respect"). Of course, parents, elders, and people with titles and status may be deserving of a kind of deferential respect. One plebe midshipman told me after returning from Thanksgiving break that he was confused at home as to how to address his parents. Should he call them "sir" and "ma'am," as he did his commanding officers, or just "Mom" and "Dad," as he always had? The appropriate form of deference respect had become fuzzy in his mind. Still, in principle such deference rituals, within the military and elsewhere, ought to be undergirded by modes of mutual respect due all persons, independent of age or status. This is something Santini fails to acknowledge, and something often obscured and dampened by hierarchical military structures. In Santini's case, the deference rituals, roles, and decorum that define military life have come to define his life in general. The enactment of these roles within his family poisons the life of the family.

In this section I have explored the emphasis in military training on things that are "outer"—appearances, decorum, deference rituals, and demeanor. In response to objections that decorum can be superficial and a matter of faking it, I have suggested that such rituals are a pervasive feature of many social interactions that do not necessarily deceive. Moreover, outward emotional demeanor can sometimes move inward and effect deeper changes of attitude. Pretense can bootstrap sincerity. Finally, I have warned that military modes of comportment and respect can be misplaced in other arenas, in particular the family. They can occlude the more basic respect that is due all people, even those in uniform who are subordinate.

In the two sections that follow I turn the discussion to Stoic texts and to the insights we can glean from Stoic theory on issues of decorum and emotional demeanor. The first discussion draws on Cicero's *On Duties* and his transmission of Stoic views about the decorum associated with different roles or personae we wear. The second discussion draws on Seneca's *On Favours* and the theme of emotional demeanor as central to how we show kindness toward others. In a telling way, both accounts recognize our propensity for emotional expression and our reasonable expectation of it as part of respectful social exchange. Military demeanor, needless to say, is not known for emotional expressiveness. There may be all sorts of good reasons for this: a show of emotional warmth can breed misplaced familiarity, an acknowledgment of fear can undermine command, or anger can be read as lust for war. But stolidness as a ubiquitous response can be deeply damaging to both self and others. Hearing this from the Stoics themselves carries important weight.

CICERO ON DECORUM

Cicero offers a philosophical defense of decorum that is unparalleled in the ancient world. A major theme he develops is that decorum is part of the aesthetics of morals: decorum is "completely blended with virtue" in the way that true "bodily loveliness and beauty cannot be separated from healthiness."[22] The analogy underscores the notion that decorum (the term is Latin; *to prepon* in Greek) concerns the outward or appearances. As Cicero puts it, decorum is a "perceptible" aspect of every virtuous act; "it is not seen by esoteric reasoning, but springs ready to view."[23] It has to do with what is in the "public eye" and what meets with public approval.[24] It covers anything that may affect appearance and standing:

> For just as the eye is aroused by the beauty of a body, because of the appropriate arrangement of the limbs, and is delighted just because all its parts are in grace-

ful harmony, so this seemliness [*decorum*], shining out in one's life [*elucet in vita*], arouses the approval of one's fellows, because of the order and constancy and moderation of every word and action.[25]

Cicero gives examples to help define the scope of the concept. He suggests that decorum concerns matters of "respectfulness" and "shame," not causing "outrage" or offense—taking care not to "neglect what others think about oneself."[26] How we joke and play, what we find funny, the kinds of pleasures we pursue, and the nature of our nourishment and care of our bodies are all subjects, he says, of decorum.[27] With a little tweaking, Cicero's remarks on jokes could easily find their way into a commander's directives to his sailors about appropriate behavior within gender-integrated units:

> We do not allow boys complete freedom, in their play, but only as much as is compatible with acting honourably; similarly, the light of an upright character should shine forth even from our jokes. . . . It is easy to make the distinction between a well bred and an ungentlemanly joke, the former, provided the time is right, as when one is relaxing, is worthy of even the most serious man; the latter, if the words are indecent and the subject dishonorable, are unworthy of any free man.[28]

I myself have heard similar words spoken in the context of behavior in the USNA's massive coed dormitory, Bancroft Hall, where the standards of behavior are meant to simulate good conduct aboard a ship.[29]

Cicero goes on to suggest that decorum is indexed, more or less, to fundamental roles or personae (literally, theatrical masks) that we assume in life. Following the broad lines of the taxonomy of an earlier Stoic, Panaetius, Cicero claims that there are four principal personae.[30] The first two, he says, "we have been dressed" for, "as it were, by nature." They are (1) who we are in virtue of our shared rational natures—a "common" persona, "arising from the fact that we all have a share in reason," and (2) who we are in virtue of our individual temperaments and spirits—"for just as there are enormous bodily differences . . . similarly there are still greater differences in men's spirits." To this he adds (3) who we are by "chance or circumstance" and (4) the persona "we assume for ourselves," "as adulthood is approaching," "by our own decision," in the sense of "deciding who and what we wish to be, and what kind of life we want."[31]

In this view, then, our identities are complex composites that blend shared and individual natures with the accidents of fortune and history and with the career and life choices we willfully make. We moderns tend not to think of natural temperaments or shared reason as "roles" we assume, but Cicero is conceiving of them as elements of our natural lottery that we must "enact" well and in ways that properly fit with and are constrained by other roles we take on. The notion that we are actors in a play is a recurrent Stoic theme. Epictetus famously says: "Remember that you are an actor in a play, which is as the playwright wants it to be . . . what is yours is to play the assigned part well."[32] For Epictetus, the seminal point is that what we value most is making the best of ourselves, whatever the constraints of our roles. Cicero, we can assume, is voicing a similar theme.

It is also worth noting that Cicero's illustrations of career choices are un-abashedly autobiographical—"philosophy," "civil law," and "oratory." But he is quick to concede that different individuals "prefer to excel in different" vir-tues, and here we can find ample room for the warrior, a role that he himself mildly endorses, so long as it is not conceived as a quest for glory.[33] We fulfill career choices in the most "seemly" ways, he says, where there is natural talent and where we have taken due care to choose roles that are "most suited" to our constitutions and temperaments.[34] His insistence on taking adequate time to know one's own nature in making these choices is striking and as much a lesson for the youth of our own time, caught in the throes of educational and career choices, as for Roman youth of centuries ago. What is equally striking is that despite the clearly Stoic (and Roman law) notion of shared universal na-tures (the first of the four personae listed above), he often accents individual difference (the second persona in the list) and its role in the design of a chosen adult life (the fourth persona). He warns, with a kind of homespun wisdom, that we should never underestimate the difficulties here. It is all too easy to feel the pressure "to imitate our ancestors" and to "copy someone else's nature and ignore your own."[35] And late adolescence, just when one's "counsel is at its very weakest," is the time when we must make these deci-sions.[36] We are imbued with "parents' advice," the pressures of "customs and manners," and the pull of what seems "most glittering to the majority."[37] To choose the right role in life is, in essence, a dramaturgical choice of choosing the right part in a play.[38]

There are two further features of this account of roles and decorum that are especially pertinent to our concerns. The first again concerns individual tem-perament—this time, though, not explicitly with respect to career choice but rather in regard to what we might call varieties in leadership style and moral constraints on those styles. Here the relevance to military matters will become apparent. The second concerns the material elements of decorum, especially emotional demeanor, bodily comportment, and tone of voice. These too, as we shall see, have important implications for military conduct.

Just as differences in talent and temperament make specific career choices more or less appropriate, so too, within the same career arenas, do individuals establish their distinctive styles and signatures, often as an expression of their individual temperaments (their second personae). We might say that tempera-ment puts pragmatic constraints on leadership style. Moreover, Cicero sug-gests that, within limits, diametrically opposed styles can be equally fitting expressions of excellence in career roles. In this way, Cicero is keen to appeal to personality and temperament differences within civilian and military leadership roles as part of an implicit criticism of cookie-cutter views of what is fitting or in line with decorum.

His roster of examples draws from the lives of public leaders: Some, such as Socrates, are able to cultivate a sense of pretense and irony; others, including Pericles, the great Greek general of the Peloponnesian War, have authoritativeness without an ounce of levity. Certain leaders are distinguished for their cunning and craftiness, as are the Spartan military figure Lysander and also Solon, who "in order both to make his own life safer and the more to assist the republic . . . pretended that he was mad." Others, such as "Callicratidas, the next commander of the fleet after Lysander," are more "straightforward and open; they think that nothing should be done through secrecy or trickery, they cultivate the truth and they are hostile to deceit." And we should contrast Ulysses, who could suffer trial upon trial with patience and constancy, with Ajax, nicknamed the "bulwark of the Achaeans," who "would have preferred to seek death a thousand times than to endure such things." Some, like Catulus, "manage to appear in conversation to be one among many" despite their great power, while others of comparable stature are "not at all affable in conversation" and keep their distance from the minions. Cato, a paragon of austere self-discipline and constancy, seemed justified in committing suicide in the face of a tyrant, while others, "more gentle" and "easygoing" in their overall behavior, have less reason to do so even in the same external circumstances. Thus Cicero insists that the range of appropriate and permissible leadership styles is broad: "There are countless . . . dissimilarities of nature and conduct, which do not in the least deserve censure."[39]

The point is an important one in the military, where there is a premium on uniformity, especially in the lower ranks. Some recognition of permissible personality differences is important to help stem the erosion of self-worth in an environment bent on cutting individuals down to size. Military call signs serve this purpose in some ways. They are at once a playful and faintly irreverent way of letting personality leak through. In Ward Carroll's comical Gulf War novel *Punk's War*, call signs announce the idiosyncrasies of the characters in the squadron. Rick, who "knows punk rock when he hears it," becomes "Punk." "Spud" is so baptized not because he hails from Idaho but because of his ramp strike (a botched landing on an aircraft carrier, where the aircraft strikes the angled rear of the carrier, below the level of the landing strip) and the World War II term for it, "landing in the spud locker"—the potato storage area below the ramp.[40] And then there are Fuzzy, Smoke, and Einstein—let your imagination make the associations. The deeper point is that appropriate comportment needn't demand absolute conformism. It is no good to try to "copy someone else's nature and ignore your own," warns Cicero. That only introduces a kind of "unevenness," he suggests, which is itself "unseemly."[41]

But Cicero nowhere implies that breadth in style is without constraints. To bring it back to the military, a leadership style that plays to an individual's personality traits—say, spite or arrogance—can still be morally objectionable. And it can be so on the Ciceronian grounds that it fails to express a deeper persona one wears, namely, the core humanity and rational nature we share with others. Cicero reminds us in this same section of *On Duties* that in virtue of that shared persona, "we must exercise a respectfulness towards humans, towards the best of them and also towards the rest."[42] We can think of that shared persona as the ground of our dignitary respect toward all persons.

Consider a concrete case that helps make Cicero's point vivid. A number of years ago I was called in as an expert witness in a Coast Guard case. The case involved a female officer who was being turned down for promotion on the nominal grounds of failing to disclose the truth to a commanding officer. The case was complex. She, along with another female officer on the ship, had been sought out in confidence by an enlisted woman who had become suicidal after an affair with an enlisted man. At some later point one of the senior women agreed to report the information to the CO, but in order to protect the confidence of the suicidal woman, she misrepresented the source of the information, saying that she had heard the information on the mess deck. When the CO learned that she had misrepresented her source, she was severely punished and her career was threatened. The treatment, the female officer argued, was unjust and vengeful. The CO had many times before criticized her publicly, and he routinely made sexist jokes in her company. He himself was a scorned leader who commanded little respect from the hands on board. Many viewed his punishment of her as a desperate way to prove his rank. Here is a case where individual leadership style fails to meet the constraints of dignitary respect placed on any leader in virtue of recognizing others' humanity, women subordinates included. This CO's choice of jokes, his abuse of power, and his interest in catching a woman in dereliction of duty when she was in fact trying to counsel a suicidal junior shipmate in the most humane way possible are, on a plausible reading of Cicero's account, failures of appropriate fulfillment of role duties, both in one's chosen career as an officer and morally, in terms of one's humanity, as a person.[43]

Decorum or "seemliness" is linked to conduct appropriate to one's various roles in life. Cicero goes on to lay out the specific material elements of decorum—in particular, how we convey appropriate appearances through bodily comportment, facial demeanor, and tone of voice. The message is recurrent: "seemliness" or a sense of propriety "can be seen in every deed and word, and indeed in every bodily movement or state." So we must take care that "our standing, our walking, our sitting and our reclining, our countenances, our eyes and the movements of our hands" all express a proper sense of decorum. In this regard, we are not to adopt languidness in our gait, lest we look like "carriages in solemn procession," or show a kind of frantic haste, lest it betray (or encourage) a lack of equanimity within. Moreover, a careful observer can read into our characters "from a glance of the eyes, from the relaxation or contraction of an eyebrow, from sadness, cheerfulness or laughter, from speech or from silence, from a raising or lower of the voice, and so on."[44] "Voices," "faces," "gestures," "postures"—all are part of the aesthetic of character.[45] The study of duty and morality is impoverished, Cicero implies, if we view our moral relation to others in terms only of more explicit action and choice. In much subtler ways, our bodies and faces and tone of voice communicate to others the depths of our character, as well the depths of our respect or concern. "Character," the ancient Greek Stoic Zeno said, "can be known from appearance."[46] The communication of those appearances is a part of the glue of human fellowship.

Consequently, how officers address their troops can be an index of character and excellence. A tone of voice that is stern but not abusive, objective and authoritative yet still compassionate, is a way of commanding (deferential) respect and showing (dignitary) respect. It is a sign that can reveal a leader's good character and sensibilities. Again Cicero is instructive:

> Sometimes it happens that it is necessary to reprove someone. In that case we may perhaps need to use a more rhetorical tone of voice, or sharper and serious language, and even to behave so that we seem to be acting in anger. However, we should have recourse to this sort of rebuke in the way we do to surgery and cautery, rarely and unwillingly. . . . One ought for the most part only to resort to mild criticism, though combined with a certain seriousness so as to show severity while avoiding abusiveness.[47]

As Roman statesman and orator, Cicero brings to bear the specific lessons of his trade—and its biases as well. The voice, whether in speeches or in conversations, should be "clear and attractive." Good speech demands precise enunciation and a voice that is neither too sonorous nor muffled. Conversation aimed at learning should be "gentle and without a trace of intransigence"; it should be "witty" without being arrogant or sounding like a "boastful soldier." It should be neither "abusive" nor "insulting," whether to raise a laugh or to scorn.[48] It is easy to get mired here in the local conventions of class and history, but the spirit of Cicero's remarks, about character conveyed in voice, could not be more important for any leader commanding and training troops through the authority of a voice. The character and tone of one's voice are part of the example one sets. True, not all are gifted orators like Pericles, who gave a funeral oration for Athenian troops that came to define the species for all of history. But all have an obligation to find ways of commanding with seriousness and resolve, and with a respectfulness that still lets subordinates know who is in authority. Again, to use Cicero's notion of roles, the roles we assume when we express individual temperaments and fulfill professional duties must ultimately be constrained by the fundamental role that stems from our shared humanity.

There is one final note to this discussion of decorum and role duties, and my earlier comments about Cicero's prejudices help to introduce it. Decorum as the "aesthetic of character" focuses on appearances as indexes of depth. But some forms of those appearances can be highly cultural. They can reflect the mores and customs of locales, as well as roles specific to those locales. How do we avoid offending those whose customs are different from our own? At what point do we criticize those customs? The questions are hardly academic for military men and women deployed around the world. Do American or British women soldiers stationed in Saudi Arabia who drive military vehicles or walk about with their heads uncovered fail to show due respect to their host country? Are they arrogant or insulting, even if they are legitimately celebrating their own freedom of movement? Or what if within her own community a soldier or sailor objects to chivalry on grounds that it doesn't take her own equality seriously—whether it be the gesture of holding a door open or the more substantive issue of being barred from submarine duty or hand-to-hand combat? These questions hang on redefining roles, and reassessing who can participate in them and what the nature of that participation looks like. One factor that ought to weigh heavily in such discussions is, again, the Stoic notion of the fundamental persona we are all "dressed for by nature," namely, our shared humanity. Recognition of the import of this, and of the unfair disadvantages that can arise from the accidents of gender (or sexual orientation, or race, or religion—the personae "of chance or circumstance," in Cicero's terms), is crucial to ensuring fairer and more enlightened opportunity, choice, and fulfillment of career roles. These kinds of examples give insight into how Cicero's account of role duties offers powerful tools for framing difficult contemporary questions, however unrehearsed these questions may have been by Cicero or his fellow Romans.

In the final section, I turn to Seneca and to the import of his remarks on appearances and emotional demeanor for military conduct. In significant ways, his remarks strengthen Cicero's views on the notion of an aesthetic of character.

SENECA: EMOTIONAL DEMEANOR MATTERS

The notion that virtue is exchanged in emotional expression is, in the world of ancient philosophy, most often associated with Aristotle. Aristotle reminds us repeatedly that we must hit the mean in action as well as emotion. By emotion, he means not just inner motives and feelings, but outward emotional attitudes—how and in what way and to what degree character is manifest through our emotions.[49] Cicero, we have seen, develops this theme concretely, in the notion of decorum and the demeanor of virtue: Emotional demeanor is part of how we fulfill our duties and roles well. Seneca also develops the theme in his treatise *On Favours*. Though he is not specifically interested in military demeanor, his general remarks about the expression and concealment of emotions have important implications, I suggest, for military conduct.[50]

In the forward sweep of history, Seneca's discussions point toward Kant, who in his later moral writings also lays stress on the role of manners and demeanor, despite his underlying commitment to a leaner, inward morality. Indeed, in a significant way, Kant's view in *Anthropology from a Pragmatic Point of View* sets the tone for understanding Seneca:

> No matter how insignificant these laws of refined humanity may seem, especially in comparison with pure moral laws, anything that promotes sociability, even if it consists only in pleasing maxims or manners, is a garment that dresses virtue to advantage, a garment to be recommended to virtue in more serious respects too. The *cynic's purism* and the *anchorite's mortifications of the flesh*, without social well-being, are distorted figures of virtue, which do not attract us to it. Forsaken by the graces, they can make no claim to humanity.[51]

It is easy to dismiss this garment as mere decorative flourish. But Kant himself, at times even more austere than the Stoics, insists that this is not his intent.[52] Full virtue requires fully human ways of being responsive to the dignity of moral persons. Seneca, whose writing Kant was steeped in, seems to pave the way.

Seneca's *On Favours*, written between 56 and 64 CE, is addressed to one Aebutius Liberalis, about whom we know little more than his name and its appropriateness for the occasion.[53] Seneca's treatment follows ancient views in including under a single heading topics we moderns might find disparate—gift giving, gratitude, and kindness. His own examples of favors include "large kindnesses," such as gifts of large sums of money, emancipation, saving a life, and so on, but also "small kindnesses," including gifts of clothing and books, as well as what we shall focus on here: the emotional expression of kindness and gratitude conveyed in looks and gestures. He will stress that it is not necessarily the grand or heroic acts of kindness but the small ones, conveyed in gesture and facial expression, that weave the fabric of community.[54]

Still, *On Favours* might seem an odd book for a Stoic to write, for orthodox Stoicism urges the self-sufficiency of individuals and detachment from external goods such as health, good fortune, and material wealth—in general, the kind of conventional goods that are part and parcel of giving and receiving favors. As I have said in earlier chapters, the doctrine allows that favorable externals are things to be "preferred" (*proēgmena*) rather than "dispreferred" (*apoproēgmena*) as selective advantages congenial to our natures. But those selective advantages are themselves regarded neither as genuine goods nor as proper constituents of happiness. In this sense, they are "indifferents" that do not bear substantively on true flourishing. The project of moral cultivation is one of coming to appreciate, emotionally and intellectually, that what lies beyond the exercise of virtue, including the material virtue works up or is expressed through, is neither a genuine good nor a genuine evil. The exchange of material goods, as important as it is in the practical world of social interactions, seems to undercut Stoic doctrine about what is really good to have and to hold.[55]

Here it is important to remember the decidedly practical thrust of much Stoic writing, both ancient Greek and Roman. Seneca's own campaign, through epistle and essay, is to influence the moral novice who takes relatively seriously the project of moral improvement but who is unlikely ever to reach the rarefied heights of sagehood. (Certainly Nero, to whom he was tutor in residence and to whom the essay *On Mercy* is addressed, had little chance of approaching that status. But this notorious case aside, it was commonly acknowledged that true sages would arise only as frequently as the phoenix.) Still, the sage remains the moral ideal for all those who are trying to make progress. (In a similar spirit, Epictetus, whose counsels can be uncompromisingly severe, cautions his students against thinking that their actions can ever be error-free in the way requisite of a sage: "So is it possible to be altogether faultless? No, that is impracticable; but it is possible to strive continuously not to commit faults. For we shall have cause to be satisfied if, by never relaxing our attention, we shall escape at least a few faults.")[56]

Thus the audience for *On Favours* is imperfect human beings, who rely on each other for goodwill not in some abstract sense but concretely, in its material and emotional conveyances.[57] And while the treatise is sensitive to the nuances of Roman moral decorum (with its stress on gift giving and gratitude, patronage and clientship), the focus of *On Favours* is on revision of Roman practices and attitudes, though not the outright deprecation that is the Cynics' hallmark.[58] In the foreground is the practical reality of individuals who routinely need external goods replenished and restored, who depend upon friends to be sensitive to what is needed and when, and to what is useful or pointless:[59] no one should give "winter clothes at midsummer" or "a present of gladiators or animals for the arena when the show has already been put on,"[60] "books to a country bumpkin or hunting nets to a scholar or man of letters."[61] But also we should give presents to others that "bring us to mind whenever he [the recipient] comes into contact with it,"[62] that "endure," that are "imperishable," that can't be "used up," "that stay in existence, cling to my friend, live with him."[63]

This last remark underscores the palpable tension in this work: gifts are to encourage precisely the sort of attachment (to gift and giver) one would expect a Stoic to be admonishing against. Seneca himself tries to mitigate the tension, reminding the reader to distinguish, along technical Stoic lines, the inner, mental act of doing kindness from the material deed, "which is neither good nor bad."[64] "What we can hold or look upon, what our covetousness fixes on, can be taken away from us by misfortune or malice. The favour, even when its vehicle is lost, remains. It is a right action [*recte factum;* in Greek, *katorthōma*] and no force can undo it."[65] "A favour cannot possibly be touched by the hand; the transaction takes place in the mind."[66]

Yet as we read the treatise, these points fade into the background. In the foreground is attention to the details of what is given, and how and when. The *choice of vehicle*—that is, the decorum of gift giving—is precisely Seneca's concern here, in the same way that decorum and aesthetic seemliness were central to Cicero's concerns. True, as recipient (and as giver as well) we may be misled by the "outer," by "what strikes the eye," by the "trace and mark of a favour," by holding on to something outward rather than inward.[67] Still, the good person aims to convey her good intentions through a careful choice of the "outward," be it via the material gift, the timing of the gift, attunement to the recipient,[68] emotional gesture, or body language.[69]

But we should not entirely dismiss Seneca's doctrinal appeals to the intention (or *animus*) of donor and recipient. There is little doubt that he means to criticize the excessive materialism of Roman rituals of gift giving and to breathe a new spirituality into the practice.[70] Outlining an acceptable form of gratitude that conceptually separates thankfulness and reciprocation from the strains of a matched, material recompense is thus an important step. But even if Seneca is at pains to deemphasize the materialistic aspect of the exchange (especially in terms of a material quid pro quo for a gift), he is not at similar pains to deemphasize its aesthetic aspects. Indeed, he seizes on demeanor and appearance as crucial to how we project our good intentions, respect, and deference. These are resources we all have, whatever our material status. Thus the question of *how* we show our concern, interest, appreciation, and thanks does not retreat. Nor does the importance of an embodied intention. We are still to deliver palpable and carefully chosen goods to others. Ghostly but good intention is of little interest to Seneca.[71] The intention must be tethered to manifest, expressive attitudes. That is part of the gift.[72]

This is to say, once again, that the aesthetics of character matter. As Seneca puts it, in words that echo Cicero, how to play "*the role* of the good man" (*partes boni viri*) becomes key.[73] Creating the right appearances and doing so through outward emotional expression of attitude emerge as central themes in Seneca's essay. External conduct matters. The point has a corollary that figures as a more general Stoic thesis: we fulfill duties (*officia*) or do what is appropriate (*kathēkonta*) even when we lack the right motives (those a sage would have). In the same vein, manifesting certain looks and appearances are ways of acting appropriately even when the corresponding inner states are absent. Sometimes that is all we can muster. Of course, it is better if outer conduct matches inner virtue. But when that can't be achieved, the appropriate outer expression itself is ethically important. The emphasis on the appearances is captured well in this passage:

> No gratitude is felt for a favour which has long stuck to the hands of whoever granted it, which he seemed unhappy to let go, giving as though he were robbing

himself. Even if some delay should intervene, we should do everything to avoid the *appearance* of having had to think whether to do it [*ne deliberasse videamur*].[74]

In a similar spirit, we are to contrive to make favors *appear* as if they have been unsolicited, whether or not they have been: "to give the impression not of having been asked [*ne rogati videamur*] [to perform some action] . . . we should make an immediate undertaking and prove by our very haste that we were on the point of acting, even before we were approached."[75]

Playing the role of the good person thus has to do with sensitivity to how much information, candor, nuance, masking, and so forth is requisite for showing respect or due regard. It has to do with socially sensitive behavior—how we convey to others interest, empathy, respect, and thanks through the emotional expressions we wear on our face (or exhibit through our body language and voice). Seneca is emphatic here. We create ingratitude when we do favors with a plaintive attitude and when we are "oppressive" and nagging in our demands: "We spoil the effect entirely, not just afterwards, but while we are doing the favour."[76] We spoil kindness also if our reluctance is betrayed in inappropriate "furrowed brows" and "grudging words." Nor should we give a gift in a way that is "humiliating" (*contumeliose*): "No one can feel gratitude for a favor haughtily tossed down or angrily thrust on him" or given with groaning or flaunting, with an "insolent expression" or "language swollen with pride," with "a silence that gives an impression of grim severity," or in a way that is simply "irritating." It is like giving bread with stones in it.[77] In short, gifts that are true kindnesses are bestowed with a look of human kindness, be it in the language of words, in voice, or in facial or bodily expression.[78] The same goes for expressions of gratitude. The look and feel of virtue matter. They indicate attitude, even if that attitude is at times feigned.

Underlying Seneca's views on gratitude is the theoretical point that material recompense is not the *moral* return for a gift, since material goods are (moral) indifferents. As he puts it, one may give some material recompense, "but that is not the missing part of a duty." Rather, on strictly Stoic grounds, the duty is fully performed if one has the right mental attitude; the material recompense is something supplemental.[79] That said, however, the *behavioral display of that attitude* is still a critical part of Seneca's focus; the appropriate *outward* expression of thankfulness matters in the conveyance of attitude. Thus the Stoic principle that goodness is a matter of inner virtue—a matter of the mental act—is simply too thin, according to Seneca. Kindness, respect, and other virtues need to manifest in comportment and demeanor.[80] And even when the outer doesn't fully match the inner (as it may not in the case of us learners), we still often get credit for the outer—for faking it, for playing our parts well.

A LESSON FOR THE MILITARY

The upshot of this last point for the military is significant, and it is a lesson that takes us beyond Seneca's specific focus on kindness and the theoretical fine points of that treatment. Seneca's claim is that displays of attitude in body language, facial demeanor, tone of voice, and so on are critical elements of doing what is appropriate, regardless of whether they faithfully represent what is inside. So the grunt may be annoyed with her commanding officer or worn out by endless drill, or a commander might be frightened by the risks that lie ahead, yet the aesthetic of the outer—what one projects to others—matters, whether it be the crispness of a salute, mission readiness spoken in body language, or a steely look of determination and reassurance. It matters to those who share in the ritual and to those who depend on those signs for instruction and confidence. And it may be important for oneself, as a way of coaxing inner change.

In future chapters, I shall revisit this theme of control of outer decorum. In particular, I shall consider it in the case of grieving, a subject Cicero and Seneca each take up. But for now, there are further related points to note. As psychologists have noted from Darwin through Ekman and beyond, we express and "pose" emotions through movements in facial musculature that are readily readable by others.[81] Seneca anticipates the idea. The face can both hide and disclose what is inside, and we are emotionally sensitive (and vulnerable) to its messages. That this comes from the Stoics, famous for marginalizing emotions in our lives, is both surprising and encouraging. More true to form, they do imply, as we have seen above, that we can and ought to control that outward expression, in facial and bodily decorum in general. As we proceed with our story, we shall have to ask just how much control they think we have, and moreover, how much control is a good thing. Is solemnity or a stolid demeanor, even if a way to curb warrior rage or lust, an adequate expression of grief?

One qualification is important here. There is no suggestion, at least in the works we have just studied, that a Stoic stance, however controlled, must be a uniform armor of stolidness or imperturbability. Rather, Seneca, in particular, suggests that emotional expressions of kindness, warmth, gratefulness, disappointment, and hurt are all part of a complex palette of morally mature and fitting responses. This point has obvious military implications. Military life is not only about the vertical line of command and the buttoned-up decorum that can characterize the roles of superior and subordinate. It is also about horizontal bonds of camaraderie, affection, and love, and the boundless gratitude for buddies who put their own lives on the line, shattering limbs and nerves, in order to save others. Being able to express this gratitude is part of that bond.

And what about when your warrior's anger goes home? What is it like with his wife and children? Is it useful then, too?

—Cicero, *Tusculan Disputations* 4.54 (Graver trans.)

[Bear Mercer] takes pride in the fact that he was never responsible for an artillery error that caused American casualties.

Sergeant Mercer did, however, see the results of the fires he called in on the enemy. His patrol found a Viet Cong, dying after his legs had been blown off by a strike Bear had called in. Over the radio, the CO refused to call a MedEvac for the enemy and ordered Bear to kill the wounded enemy soldier. Unwilling to order anyone in his squad to do it, he performed this mercy himself, and believes that the dying Vietnamese assented to it by gestures. Now in nightmares and flashbacks the color of his blood, changing from bright red to almost black after Bear cut his throat, comes back again and again, as does the evil grin of a man in his squad who crushed the dead man's chest with a boulder, drenching Bear with blood that squirted out of the severed neck arteries. Bear felt the enemy had "paid his dues" and is enraged at the disrespect shown by the other American soldiers.

. . . Any incompetence Bear encounters in civilian life arouses the same feelings of fear, rage, and grief. When he yanked his general supervisor at the post office across his own desk and screamed at him, he screamed exactly the same words he screamed at his incompetent CO.

—Jonathan Shay, *Odysseus in America*

Hugh Thompson, the American helicopter pilot who ordered his side gunner to open fire on the GIs if they blocked his attempts to stop the My Lai massacre, returned to Vietnam some thirty years later. A frail, aging woman who survived the massacre rushed up to meet him. She implored, "Why didn't the people who committed the murder come back with you . . ." She finished her thought without pause but the interpreter's translation lagged behind. ". . . so that we could forgive them." This was not how Thompson thought the sentence would end. At that point, he recalls, "I totally lost it. How could this woman have compassion in her heart for someone who was so evil? She's a better person than I am."

—From the author's interview with Hugh Thompson

4

A Warrior's Anger

A RUNAWAY EMOTION

Anger is as much a part of war as weapons and armor. The greatest of war epics, Homer's *Iliad*, is arguably about warrior anger—about the fury of a warrior such as Achilles and the injuries to honor that can lead to that fury. Anger "whets the mind for the deeds of war," says Seneca, reporting the conventional ancient view.[1] In modern terms, it is linked with the adrenaline rush that allows non-killers in civilian life to become killers in war. But unlike weapons and armor, anger, warns Seneca, is not easily thrown off after the battle.[2] It is a "runaway emotion," easy to turn on but hard to turn off. Combat veterans, including Bear, all too often live out that truth. They bring home a rage that has lost its targets and finds new ones that are far less appropriate. Recently the point was brought home in an all too ugly incident in Fort Bragg, North Carolina: four Army men in the elite Special Operations forces who had just returned from Afghanistan killed their wives in brutal fashion. The motives were assuredly complicated, but on the surface, at least, the combat anger button couldn't be turned off.[3] Anger that might have been adaptive in combat became sorely maladaptive at home.

The story is a familiar one repeated in many veterans' lives. Marvin Brenner served as a Marine in Okinawa during World War II.[4] The fighting during April and May 1945 was ferocious, with men typically spending fifteen days at the line, armed with bayonets, living on three to four hours' sleep, pumped with Benzedrine (an amphetamine) for campaigns in which they had to fight for forty-eight hours straight. Battle rage still visits Marvin—in anger at employers whose voice and attitude bring back the feel of being given military orders, or in mini-flashbacks that transform a car that cuts him off on the road into an enemy with a one-and-a-half-ton weapon out to hurt him. Recently Marvin was taking a walk in a neighborhood park when young boys on mountain bikes crossed his path. They weren't supposed to be riding in the park, and he bellowed out a threat to them: "Tomorrow I start target practice." When they left, he did an about-face and marched through the woods as if he were at the front again. At that point another cyclist came into view, and his fury surged. His body started to tremble, and he imagined his hand coming down on the boy's collarbone and breaking it. "That would immobilize him. Then he would be at my mercy." Battle rage had exploded a half century after the campaign.

In response to the excesses of anger, the Stoics propose their own extreme measure: to do away with anger entirely. They propose an *apatheia*—a freedom from passions in which there is no frenzy or rage, no annoyance or bitterness, no moral outrage. Anger in all its species is eliminated. The full, orthodox scheme is even more radical: other ordinary emotions, such as fear and grief, pleasure and sorrow, are also to be eradicated from the healthy psyche. And why? Not because they are passive events in our lives. On the contrary, as I have noted before, the Stoics hold that emotions are voluntary states to which we assent in fairly robust form. Even so, they are to be removed because they are excessive, and because they give us false information about the world. They are false informers, liars of sorts, about what we see and hear. They mislead.

For some who return from war, Stoic *apatheia* might sound almost too good to be true. It offers permission to forget the anguish and pain of war, permission to numb the anger and grief that haunts many combat veterans' waking moments and fitful nights. It even offers therapy by means other than drugs or alcohol. Indeed, the Stoics conceive of themselves as doctors of the soul.

The Stoic view resonates with many military men and women who learn, not just in war and after but before, "to suck it up," to endure, to put aside their feelings in order to get on with the mission. However, anger is not usually included in the category of emotions that show weakness or vulnerability. If anything, from our own contemporary perspective, anger tends to be seen as a macho emotion that displays toughness and a resolute sense of self-defense and self-worth. It is, we might think, an emotion par excellence for a Stoic warrior—what some have argued boys learn all too well as part of a code of stoic toughness.[5] It has been argued that for many serving in Vietnam, anger was viewed as the one emotion whose expression was acceptable, and so it came to silence others, such as fear, grief, and sorrow. (Some argue that permission to express rage, together with a loose interpretation of the rules of engagement in guerilla war, was a significant factor in the high incidence of atrocities in that war—many of which remain unreported.)[6]

Yet as Stoic and warriorlike as anger may seem, the Stoics themselves deny this. Ancient Stoicism regards anger as a sign of vulnerability in the same way that grief or fear is, for we experience each when we allow ourselves to become invested in things outside our own control. The angry person reacts to affronts to honor or respect, the grieving person to loss, and the fearful person to danger in a way that the Stoics argue threatens the self-sufficiency necessary for good living. Indeed, anger, in a way more obvious than fear or grief, reveals a defensive (and at times retributivist) posture that at its rawest often seems just an impulse to bite back at those who bite us. Seneca, whose essay *On Anger* will be a primary text for us, liberally helps himself to that bellicose imagery. Still, he insists anger ought not be the emotion of a Stoic warrior. Its defensive stance only indulges our vulnerabilities. The true warrior, he argues, must fight without anger's aid. And he must also detach from other emotions with their sticky investments.

To many readers, Stoicism's stance against anger may sound quite similar to Buddhist approaches toward negative and self-destructive emotions. I cannot undertake a full-blown comparison of Stoicism and Buddhism here, in terms of either historical cross-pollination or thematic overlap. Still, a few brief words are important. Very generally speaking, in Buddhist views, anger, along with other negative emotions such as hatred, lust, and vengeance, is a form of craving and attachment built on false ideas about the self and its importance. Through meditation and other forms of mindfulness and study, we are to detach from those ego illusions and come to realize that they are the cause of our deep suffering. Once liberated from that ignorance and narcissism, we can learn healthier forms of compassion and selflessness.

Stoicism, too, holds that emotions such as anger and hatred are based on false investments. But on the Stoic view, it is not that we wrongly invest in the self; rather, we wrongly invest in external goods—property, wealth, fame, honor, and so on. In so doing, we fail to appreciate what is of true value in our lives: our reason, in its perfected form as wisdom or virtue, shared with others (and God). True, psychologically an overinvestment in external goods has an effect similar to that of false investment in the self and its objects—we ingrain habits of craving and possessiveness, and we become anxious, restless, and desirous of more. But Stoic therapy requires renewed valuing of the self and its potential for reason and virtue; Buddhist therapy works toward a complex and non-nihilistic form of selflessness. While it does so through some forms of metaphysical study, its primary tools are meditative techniques for quieting the mind, with its argumentative and discursive habits. In contrast, Stoicism's primary tool is philosophical, discursive study. It is true that Seneca in particular proposes meditation at the end of each day, but by this he means careful review of one's habits and failings; for example, has one been overly harsh with one's servant today, or flown off the handle about something that is only a minor provocation? He is not proposing the kinds of techniques Buddhists recommend. Thus, though the goals of both Stoicism and Buddhism are a kind of quiescence and freedom from attachment, the path there and the metaphysical, moral, and psychological underpinnings of each are quite different.[7]

In this chapter I examine the Stoic view that anger is a dangerous emotion that can torment both its possessor and the human beings who are its object. My overall response is that while some forms of anger are little more than destructive, others are constructive and morally healthy responses to injustice and wrongdoing. In their absence, we cannot properly record wrongdoing or morally prepare ourselves for forms of repair and healing. I introduce the Stoic position on anger after a brief consideration of some earlier ancient views that serve as a backdrop for Stoic positions. Among the questions I shall be asking in the course of this chapter are: What is the role of anger and revenge in the healthy soul of a warrior? Is anger a necessary battle motivator? What is the role of forgiveness? In what sense is rage distinct from more constructive forms of moral anger? As in previous chapters, my primary interest is to develop a plausible conception of military character in response to both the explicit stoic aspirations of many contemporary military men and women and actual Stoic doctrine. But as before, the implications for those of us not in uniform are never far from the surface.

INSULT, INJURY, AND REVENGE

In the *Republic* Plato regards anger as the special province of the warrior class. It is the fire in a warrior's belly, or more precisely in the *thumos*, the spirited part of the soul. Sandwiched between the reasoning and appetitive parts (just as the warrior or auxiliary class is positioned between the ruler and artisan classes), *thumos* can do the bidding of either. But in the healthy and just soul, the alliance with reason prevails.[8] The spirited part will resist arousal should reason declare it not warranted, or it will submit to chastening if, in a momentary lapse, it unwisely succumbs.[9] Thus anger can listen to reason. In the famous metaphor of Plato's *Phaedrus,* even a wayward steed can be chastened by the commands of the charioteer.

In locating anger in a special function and seat of the soul (*psychē*), Plato begins to paint a psychological portrait of the notion of a warrior's rage familiar to every Greek through Homer's Achilles. Achilles is the angriest, "most violent man alive," proclaims Agamemnon.[10] But Achilles has much angry company in the *Iliad*, both divine and human. Famously, it is Agamemnon's own vindictiveness that sets the epic in motion. Apollo and his priest demand that Agamemnon, chief of the Achaeans, surrender to them his war bride, Chryseis, daughter of the priest, in return for a handsome ransom. Agamemnon will not have it. Chryseis is his war prize (*timē*), a sign of his honor and status; to snatch the prize is tantamount to stripping him of his medals before his troops. He dismisses the priest only to face Apollo's wrath in the form of nine days of relentless arrows that cut down his men "in droves." Finally Agamemnon relents, but he won't tolerate a full dressing-down before his men. He'll give up the girl, but not without a proper replacement. "Fetch me another prize," he orders, "else I alone of the Argives go without my honor."[11]

The pressures to surrender the symbols of military honor bring to mind more recent examples. In the spring of 1996 it was alleged that the "V" decoration that Admiral Jeremy M. (Mike) Boorda, chief of naval operations (CNO), wore (for valor in engaging the enemy in the face of combat) misrepresented his actual combat record in Vietnam. The facts surrounding the allegation are complex, but not insignificant was that Boorda had been appointed CNO in the wake of the Tailhook sexual abuse scandal in 1991, and many of the old guard within the Navy believed that the new leadership, including the new CNO, "had caved in to" new sexual politics after the pressure of Tailhook.[12] On May 16, 1996, Boorda committed suicide by shooting himself in the chest, in the very place where he once wore his medals.[13] It would be presumptuous to claim to understand the motives of any suicide, and in this case in particular it would be naive to think that the accusation of wearing an illegitimate medal was the sole or principal motive. Still, what is of interest, given our purposes, is the assumption within parts of the military community that honor, in some way or other, can be captured in external war prizes and that these can convey a sense of a warrior's real status and worth. The Stoics, like the Cynics before them, tend to be cynical about this kind of conventional coin. Even if the awards rightly signify something deeper, it is the deeper stuff that is less tangible and more intelligible—virtue and virtuous choices—that is the real mark of a warrior. True, demeanor, as we saw in the last chapter, may be a surface index of deeper virtue. But neither it nor virtue can be easily taken away, as medals and ribbons can be.

For Agamemnon, restoration of honor is a matter of a transfer of external goods—he'll replace his lost war bride with Achilles's bride.[14] This is the insult that unleashes Achilles's unrelenting fury. He digs his heels in and refuses to fight under Agamemnon's command. "Don't give me commands! Never again . . . will Achilles yield to *you*."[15] His refusal to join the cadre results in massive troop losses, and one must wonder if Achilles's anger, excessive as it is, would have been more acceptable to Homer were it directed primarily against the enemy. The captains of the war beg him for solidarity as brothers in arms.[16] But Achilles can't let go of a revenge that has become far "sweeter than dripping streams of honey."[17] Book 9 of the *Iliad* turns into a genre scene of anger, captured vividly by Fagles: "seething" and "mounting fury," "heartbreaking anger," a "rage" that "still grip[s] his proud, mighty spirit," an "iron, ruthless heart," warlords who keep on "blustering in their anger," wrath that comes "sweeping" over some men and "swells the chest of others," "blood so fired up," "smoldering, vengeful spirit," "cruel, relentless fury," "a heart that still heaves with rage," rage that cannot be "quenched," a rage that seizes his listeners with "stunned silence, struck dumb."[18] And all this venom, the Stoics will say, is because a sense of worth and virtue is falsely taken to rest primarily outside ourselves, in what can be torn from our grasp.

The plot that ensues is well known: While the hero stays home, Patroclus, Achilles's beloved comrade, disguises himself in Achilles's famous arms only to meet his death at Hector's hand. With this fresh and inconsolable loss, Achilles's wrath turns from Agamemnon to Hector. If Achilles's anger toward Agamemnon is a response to jealousy and competition, then his anger toward Hector is a response to both loss and survivor guilt—after all, Achilles yielded to Patroclus's entreaty to let Patroclus impersonate him by wearing his armor. The friendship of Achilles and Patroclus has become the archetype of the relationship between war buddies. We can speculate, as many have, whether this friendship was in addition a homosexual relationship of the sort the U.S. military demands be kept under wraps but which the Greeks welcomed as a fitting part of an aristocratic boy's development. The more pressing point, however, is that Achilles has in some real sense died with Patroclus. "My spirit rebels— I've lost the will to live." "The man I loved beyond all other comrades, loved as my own life—I've lost him."[19] Achilles experiences what many soldiers feel in losing their "brothers"—that it should have been themselves, that they would give anything to switch places. In Achilles's case, he would give anything to undo the original switch.

Revenge once again consumes Achilles, but this time it launches him into the war effort—to "fight in the front ranks" with a "soldier's strength and nerve."[20] We might argue that Achilles's revenge has finally found an appropriate object, for a warrior is entitled to some sense of restitution, even if we moderns bristle at the idea of a private vendetta, on the battlefield or off. But the revenge turns ugly quickly with Achilles's desecration of Hector's corpse by dragging it facedown around Patroclus's tomb. The poet's voice finally becomes decisive—Achilles's rage transgresses the decorum of war. Achilles, "that man without a shred of decency in his heart," outrages even "the senseless clay in all his fury."[21] Priam's tragedy, however, will be softened by the gods' intervention, which keeps Hector's body intact despite Achilles's brutality.

But not all soldiers' families are so lucky. I am painfully reminded of a conversation I once had with Sybil Stockdale, the wife of Admiral James Stockdale, the senior POW in Vietnam.[22] The husband of a close friend of hers had served in Laos and was listed as missing in action. Many years after the war, her friend received confirmation that her husband had been killed shortly after his capture. The news came from an officer who had served beside her husband and who had seen his severed head used by the enemy in a gruesome game of soccer. I don't know the specific circumstances of how the officer came to share this news with the widow, but I can imagine that it was only most reluctantly disclosed.

Here, as in Achilles's desecration of Patroclus, revenge knows no notion of dignitary respect of the body. Achilles, the archetypic archaic warrior, may have an excuse for not being guided by war conventions that view the enemy as an equal, whether alive or dead. But the modern warrior, given the history of just-war theory and international treaties about the just conduct of war, has no excuse.[23]

Hector's final words to Achilles are: "Give my body to friends to carry home again."[24] Over and over again, military men and women have stressed to me the importance of Hector's plea: should they go to war, they need to know that their bodies will be returned home. The Rangers, an elite Army unit, bellow out as part of their creed each morning: "I will never leave a fallen comrade."[25] The Marines make a similar pledge. The pragmatics of risking one's life to pull out a cadaver is, of course, another question, as is the wisdom of spending military dollars and lives on elaborate rescue missions. But part of what fuels such missions is the inconsolable terror of never making it back home and of one's body being desecrated by the enemy. This is Hector's terror, and Achilles plays havoc with it through his unbridled warrior rage.

In Achilles, Homer paints a complex portrait of traditional views of guilt, honor, and anger in a warrior. But Homer also editorializes. Achilles is the archetype of warrior anger gone amok. Still, Homer himself never gives up on the conviction that anger, and in particular revenge, has military utility. Properly restrained, it can be a reasonable combat motivator; it need not morph into rage and sadistic hatred. The Stoics, as we have anticipated, deny the claim. A soldier who relies on anger is a soldier who has surrendered control. Anger can never properly be contained, they will argue. And this is so for all forms of anger—not just rage and revenge but what some might view as more positive and constructive forms of anger, including moral outrage, indignation, and resentment. I shall raise objections against this blanket indictment of anger and argue that in some contexts expressions of certain forms of anger are morally justified and praiseworthy. To fail to express these emotions in those contexts is to fail to respect self and others as beings with dignity and a sense of worth. I shall come to this shortly. But I should also anticipate here a further point developed later in this chapter: the view that Stoic-like techniques for disarming anger, through attempts at elimination and dissociation, may in the end only cause those feelings to fester and become twisted into more toxic emotions of sadistic hatred and rage.

First we must turn briefly to Aristotle, however, for it is against his claims about the role of emotions in the virtuous life that the Stoics propose an alternative.[26] After this brief discussion, we can turn to the Stoic response.

ARISTOTLE ON ANGER

If Plato is the first to construct formally a psyche with *thumos,* or an angry part, Aristotle is the first to analyze anger (*orgē,* as he tends to call it) as part of a systematic study of the emotions, or *pathē.* The account appears in the *Rhetoric* and is intended for orators in the business of manipulating the emotions of a jury or assembly. But despite its practical aim, Aristotle's study is both deep and broad, offering a unified account of emotions unparalleled in the history of philosophy.

Roughly speaking, Aristotle proposes what psychologists (and many philosophers) today call an appraisal theory. (The theory is the reigning view of emotions in cognitive psychology and for the most part, in philosophy.[27] As we shall see, the Stoics put forth the view in radical form.) On such a view, emotions are constituted by judgments or appraisals about one's situation. To be more precise, an appraisal is an evaluation about the goodness or badness of some perceived or imagined event. Thus, anger requires an evaluation that one has been unjustly slighted by another, fear that there is present harm or danger or that something valuable is threatened, or grief that something valuable has been lost. In this sense, emotions are more like thoughts than brute feelings or sensations (or, as William James held, the proprioception of physiological changes in the viscera and musculature, such as knots in our stomach or tension in our hands). Aristotle never denies that most emotions have a certain kind of "feel." As he puts it, they are "accompanied" by pleasure and pain (and sometimes physiological feels, like the boiling of blood around the heart), but those feels cannot constitute the emotion independent of the thought content to which they attach. Moreover, it is the thoughts and not the feels that allow us to identify specific emotions. Thus although emotions may sometimes announce themselves to us through a physiological or psychic feeling (i.e., a knotted stomach or an uplifted, positive mood), those feels on their own are not determinate enough to convey just what emotions we are experiencing.[28] The same sort of knotted stomach can be part of fear or indignation, just as a feeling of uplift can be part of excitement or hope. In addition, Aristotle claims, emotions often include a reactive desire—an "action tendency," as contemporary psychologists call it—that motivates us to action or reactive behavior. Combining the elements, Aristotle says that anger involves an "apparent" (i.e., perceived, judged, or imagined) "wrongful slight to self or those near to one" "accompanied by pain" and issuing typically in a "desire for revenge," which can bring its own pleasure.[29] Contemporary philosophers tend to distinguish between anger as irascibility versus anger as a discrete outburst (i.e., emotions as dispositions versus emotions as episodes). Aristotle doesn't formally make the distinction, but something like it is often implicit in his remarks.

Aristotle's appraisal view entails that emotions "share in some way," as he puts it, in rational capacities.[30] But it is not just that emotions are in part cognitions. It is that they can be made rational. They can respond to reason, as a child "listens to and obeys" a parent.[31] In this sense, he upholds just what the Stoics deny: even an emotion such as anger can be expressed in ways that are apt and appropriate. It can "hit the mean." This does not require, as many interpreters from the Stoic period onward have insisted, that appropriate emotions must always be moderate, with no sign of either vehemence or mildness. Rather, as Aristotle explains, the person "who is angry at the right things and with the right people, and further, as he ought, when he ought, and as long as he ought, is praised."[32] Extreme anger may be exactly the right response in certain circumstances.

Or so it seemed appropriate for some peacekeepers in Bosnia constrained by rules of engagement that forced them to leave innocents to perish in areas slated by the Serbs for ethnic cleansing. The hands-off approach made them feel complicit in the cleansing, although their commanders insisted that to remove Bosnians from their homes would be a more direct act of complicity. We can think of their extreme anger at being commanded to let innocents die as a form of moral outrage. And we may think that in this kind of case, the expression of moral outrage is not only appropriate, in the sense of intelligible, but also morally justified. It seems a sign of the good soldier's conscience, and a sign of moral despair at being forced to leave in harm's way those whom they could have evacuated.

What seems perhaps equally intelligible, though not morally justified, was the extreme rage that some of the soldiers brought home with them after the war. Their anger and guilt would not abate, and it was displaced onto inappropriate objects. This is captured well in a BBC dramatized documentary, *Peacekeepers*. In one scene, a returning reservist lashes out at a whining child in a supermarket for making a scene: doesn't she know that children in war zones have something *real* to cry about? The mother of the child whisks her away from the raving man. Another newly returned veteran flies into a rage when the whirring motor of an earth tiller suddenly becomes enemy artillery. He attacks the person standing nearest to him—his girlfriend, eight months pregnant. War rage and "berserking," symptoms of war forms of post-traumatic stress disorder (PTSD), are manifest here.[33]

Now, Aristotle holds that to fail to be angry at the things one ought to be angry at is the mark of either foolishness or servility.[34] It is a deficit in virtue. But if one can't turn off anger, however legitimate its initial object, is it still servility to abstain in the first place? Might not abstinence, as the Stoics argue, ultimately be a better kind of wisdom?

Aristotle at one point says that anger "seems to listen to argument," though it often "mishears" it, like a hasty servant who "muddle[s] the order."[35] But he is optimistic that with a little rational guidance, we can straighten out that servant. The Stoics challenge the optimism and the metaphor. Isn't anger more like a disease that needs a surgeon than like a servant that needs a good talking-to? And even if emotions, like anger, are cognitive, as the Stoics agree they are, why should we assume they use reason *well*? With this as anticipation, we turn to the Stoics.

STOIC ABSTENTION

In a lesser-known dialogue by Plutarch, *On the Control of Anger*, Fundanus, the principal speaker, compares refraining from anger to learning sobriety.

Anger, like drink, is hard to control once indulged. It is best to give it up entirely and practice full abstention. Fundanus speaks from firsthand experience of this method. He himself first passed "a few days without anger, sober and wineless days, as it were," and then a "month or two" pure of the taint. Though he knows anger is the kind of disease that requires lifelong therapy, the cure seems to be sticking, at least for now: he is no longer angry toward his household slaves and in general is more "courteous in speech." Those he interacts with benefit from his new humane (*philanthrōpon*) spirit, but he himself is the greatest beneficiary.[36]

Plutarch, here in Stoic voice, rehearses the Roman and Hellenistic preoccupation with anger and its suppression. The wrath of Achilles is fixed in all minds. But so too are the atrocities of political and military leaders such as Caligula or Nero, and the abuses of lesser men—heads of household (including Fundanus), who, given the status system of Rome, exercise nearly monarchical powers over their slaves and dependants.[37] The shift in discussion is from an archaic warrior's anger as a kind of battle motivator on the ground to leadership anger and its potential abuses.[38] The havoc anger wreaks on others remains a constant theme, but perhaps even more so the havoc it wreaks on one's own soul.

These concerns strike a chord with the American military. Stanley Kubrick's notorious drill sergeant in *Full Metal Jacket* paints a picture of sadism with which few professional soldiers would wish to be identified. "You will be a weapon," he bellows at his Marine inductees at Parris Island. "But until that day, you are not even a thing." He screams louder, his eyes filled with fury, "I am hard, but the more you hate me, the more you will learn. Here you are totally worthless. Do you maggots understand that?" Then he barks, "Good night, ladies," sexism woven deep into his anger.

The portrait is a caricature. But that is not to say there aren't caricatures of the drill sergeant in the military itself. "There are some out there," Lieutenant Colonel Tony Pfaff told me one day. "But they are cartoons. And others keep an eye on them. I've had long and drawn-out arguments with some about the bully style of leadership. It may be a class of leadership. But the mean guy, the bully, has got limited resources." The challenge, he suggests, is to be hard without being mean.[39] "Military training depends upon breaking down a self and building it up again." But Pfaff insisted that you don't need hazing or the bullying drill sergeant to make that happen. We need to distinguish between rites of passage and hazing, he urged. "Hazing makes life in the profession of arms seem arbitrary," simply a matter of power and abuse. It strips the officer of his dignity.

But what is it to break down a self and build it up again? Presumably, part of what is meant is that boot camp experiences crush cockiness and selfish

Marine boot camp at Parris Island, South Carolina.

independence. More fundamentally, boot camp attempts to change the core values of a self, so that one is ready to sacrifice in a way uncommon in civilian life, and prepared as well to overcome the fear of and aversion to killing that is bred in the bone as a civilian (the latter is a topic I examine further in the next chapter). Some of these changes come to be motivated through horizontal bonding, even when ordered from the top down. A soldier such as Pfaff urges us to believe that the breaking down of a self does not depend upon bullying and a response of brute fear. A subordinate must trust that a superior is stripping neither himself nor his subordinates of dignity. We might flesh out the idea by arguing that guilt or moral anxiety comes to replace the fear of a coercer when subordinates can respond to demands and punishments as having legitimate authority, and to a commander as setting reasonable expectations and rules.[40] The commanding officer who is admired and emulated by his subordinates as a role model can still "break down" his subordinates, but it is done

through a process that involves respect for their capacity to assess the legiti-
macy of his rule.

Under this kind of enlightened command, bullying might not be fully ruled
out. But we can imagine it as a *mock* bullying that uses *mock* anger. Once again,
we can learn from Stoic writing here. Both Seneca and Cicero recommend
mock anger as a crucial part of motivational technique in oratory. The orator
may need to show the "guise of doing harm," says Seneca, without actually
feeling anger.[41] Real anger is superfluous, they argue, contra the Aristotelians
(or Peripatetics, as they come to be called). The drill sergeant, like the orator,
may get the job done by "faking it." So recruits at boot camp may need to feel
the palpable pressure of a cruel punisher whom they can fear during a training session, even though they know in the back of their minds that the commander is no sadist. They play his game for their own advantage. They feel real
fear toward him—they are not playacting that—but it is real fear that is manipulated by fake anger. And it is fear not only of the drill sergeant but of the
real possibility of failing. The drill sergeant plays on those fears.[42] His role is to
make recruits buy into the system and be frightened of "screwing up."[43]

(This line of Stoic argument is an important one in *On Anger*. One of Seneca's
most powerful arguments against the Peripatetics is the reply he makes to their
argument that, in effect, what needs doing will never get done without the
motivational force of anger.[44] Seneca's reply, like that of the enlightened drill
sergeant above, is that sometimes "faking it" suffices. This, too, is Seneca's view
with respect to kindness, as laid out in the previous chapter: sometimes faking
kindness and gratitude suffices. It will reemerge in the discussion of decorum
in grieving: one may have to put on a cheerful face even when one's heart is
heavy with grief. But while faking it, in the case of the drill sergeant, may get
the job done with little damage to self or others, feigning cheer in the face of
profound grief may have graver costs, as we shall see. Here the Peripatetic
counterargument—that full-fledged ordinary emotions can, at times, be appropriately expressed—may seem more compelling. This discussion will especially bear on the military leader whose response to troop loss sets an example
for others.)

Pfaff gives us some insight as to what it is like to be on the receiving end of
the drill sergeant's barks. He is a graduate of Ranger School, by most accounts
one of the most grueling Army programs. However, he takes it as significant
that it wasn't in Ranger School that he encountered the screaming drill sergeant, but rather in three weeks of airborne school, while training to become a
paratrooper. There his commander did call him "dirtball" and worse. On his
telling, the screaming was not because the tasks were difficult or failures frequent. He parodies the drill: "You climb up, you fall off. You climb up, you fall
off. It is the same thing over and over. It's not challenging in the way Ranger
School is," where the deprivations are extreme and the requirements of stamina

and resourcefulness enormous.[45] Still, to be "ready to jump, you really have to want it," he notes, adding, "Mock anger may be necessary to get you to take the task seriously and have the nerve to jump." Those in airborne school probably have the unconscious thought "If you can't handle this big guy yelling at you, how are you going to handle the fear of jumping?" In this case, as Pfaff explains it, mock anger is a motivator to shame soldiers into success and competitive performance.

Still, few military educators underestimate the temptation to engage in *real* bullying and scapegoating. At the Naval Academy, a handful of entering third-year students, or "second class," as they are called, are selected each spring to become squad leaders for the incoming freshmen or "plebes" during "plebe summer." They will be junior drill sergeants, in effect, marching their troops in formation around the base, toughening them with grueling physical fitness regimens, and in general overseeing their initial indoctrination into military life. It is easy to overstep the boundaries of this job, especially when the indignities of one's own suffering during plebe summer are still fresh. Annapolis summers can be blisteringly hot, with humidity that often brings the heat index to well over 110 degrees Fahrenheit. In the old days, punishment for a slacker in the unit might have consisted of the entire squad doing remedial push-ups into the high double digits, without any break for water afterward. These days, this is on the banned list as a blatant form of hazing. True, hazing of this sort may be one way to break down the self and mold individuals into group creatures, responsible for the whole. But it does so at the cost of instilling anger that then turns into festering resentment at one of its members. The scapegoat may feel that the only way to extirpate his shame is to become the abusive squad leader next time round.

From our discussions thus far, it is easy to see how some leaders might confuse stern leadership models with angry and abusive forms and allow mock anger to devolve into the real thing. Similarly, it is easy to appreciate how midshipmen or cadets might think that the proper attitude to adopt to prepare oneself and one's troops for war is a kind of warrior rage. However, with respect to the latter, Marine colonels and Navy captains with whom I taught often took it as precisely their mission to knock the "Rambo" out of their young charges. "They have simply watched too many Rambo movies," one officer lamented to me. They are too ready to flare up, he complained, in the name of warrior glory. Others worry that some of their students may not themselves be Rambos but will end up in the cockpit next to one who is all too eager to use his trigger finger—very much like what happened to Einstein, the brainy radar intercept officer in Ward Carroll's novel *Punk's War.*

In the back of some officers' minds at service academies and ROTC programs are the careers of Lieutenant William Calley and Captain Ernest Medina, principals in the My Lai massacre, and the atrocities to which warrior rage can lead. Many of the midshipmen I taught had initially only a perfunctory grasp of the events that unfolded in My Lai. But on the base were a handful of Vietnam veterans, in particular Marines who had struggled hard in Vietnam, often at great cost to their own troops, to make the distinctions that Calley and Medina failed to make between combatant and noncombatant among an enemy who often deliberately blurred that line. In their minds, as military educators, Stoic abstention from warrior anger was a way to avoid another My Lai. They took seriously the example they, as senior officers, set daily of military leadership as stern but neither abusive nor bullying. Anger in the form of rage on the ground or in the form of real bullying as drill sergeant was not viewed as fitting for a professional soldier. In this sense, they were in line with Stoic teachings.

In the next section we shall put forth in greater detail the Stoic view on anger as Seneca details it. The Stoics may be right to think that faking anger can in some cases be a more effective and morally and psychically healthy response than the real thing, and this, as we have seen, has important implications for military leaders. But what of occasions that we might intuitively think warrant anger in the form of moral indignation or outrage? Here, feigning is beside the point, for we are trying not primarily to goad others into action but, more fundamentally, to express our hearts. Through that outrage, we are trying to restore ourselves or others from the injury that comes with being wrongly victimized. Can the Stoic blanket proscription against anger accommodate these intuitions? This is a question we should keep in the back of our minds as we continue in the next two sections with the Stoic story. And it is a question that, again, has significant implications for the person in uniform.

THE IRRATIONALITY OF ANGER

Seneca dedicates On Anger (De Ira) to his elder brother, Novatus, who served as governor of Achaea in 51–52. Although Novatus himself apparently did not need lectures on overcoming irascibility (indeed, he is remembered by some for his "sweetness"), the essay, which is addressed to him, stands as a bold teaching to those who do need exhortation.[46] Seneca opens the essay with a voyeuristic glimpse at the face (and body) of anger.

> Eyes ablaze and glittering, a deep flush over all the face as blood boils up from the vitals, quivering lips, teeth pressed together, bristling hair standing on end, breath drawn in and hissing, the crackle of writhing limbs, groans and bellowing, speech broken off with the words barely uttered, hands struck together too often, feet stamping the ground, the whole body in violent motion . . . the hideous horrifying face of swollen self-degradation.[47]

Like theatergoers watching at a safe distance, we often find fascination in the gruesome, and Seneca's portrait may be intended, in part, to feed our appetites. But however titillated we may be, few among us would wish to be on the receiving end of such a hideous face, nor to be wearing one themselves. What can the mind be like if the image is so foul? What is reflected on the face is only "a tiny fraction of its true ugliness."[48]

The look of anger, Seneca says, can terrorize in the way a hideous mask strikes fear in a child.[49] Indeed, the face is a mask we read all too well. Research confirms the point. We are exquisite readers of faces, and anger is one of the faces we read instantly, from early childhood onward.[50] But it is what we *do* in anger, not what we communicate through our eyes or mouths, that Seneca worries about most. Anger, Seneca declares, is responsible for far too many of the atrocities to which Romans have grown accustomed:

> No plague has cost the human race more. You will see slaughter, poisoning, charge and sordid counter-charge in the law-courts, devastation of cities, the ruin of whole nations, persons of princely rank for sale at public auction, buildings set alight and the fire spreading beyond the city walls, huge tracts of territory glowing in flames that the enemy kindled. Look and you will see cities of greatest renown, their very foundations now scarcely discernible—anger cast them down; deserts, mile after mile without inhabitant—anger emptied them ... look upon gathered throngs put to the sword, on the military sent in to butcher the populace *en masse,* on whole peoples condemned to death in an indiscriminate devastation.[51]

Seneca could just as well be describing the anger that underlies many of the atrocities of our own time—the butchery in Rwanda, the desolation of Kosovo, the inferno at the World Trade Center, car bombs in Baghdad. The horrors of war, whether the result of just actions or unjust ones, Seneca suggests, are the work of unrestrained rage. Seneca's style, here and elsewhere, is hyperbolic. But more than any author, he outlines for us the futility of anger and the inherent difficulties of keeping a lid on its excesses. And with a can-do attitude familiar to the military, he insists that eliminating it is a practical possibility. We shall have to ask whether, indeed, vice lurks in all or even most species of anger and whether trying to root it out is, as Seneca insists, the best way to "cultivate our humanity."[52] But in order to assess Seneca's specific claims about anger, we need to understand the Stoic conception of emotions in greater depth. (The remaining part of this section reviews in greater detail Stoic theory of emotions. Readers who are interested in the theory should continue; those less interested should proceed to the next section.)

Anger, Seneca tells us, is a "departure from sanity."[53] But all ordinary emotions, on the Stoic view, are such departures. More specifically, as I have said earlier, they are perverted cognitions.[54] So Seneca claims that anger, like emotion in general, "cannot . . . come into being except where there is a place for reason." All the same, it is "the enemy of reason."

In viewing emotions as cognitive, the Stoics follow Aristotle. But they take their leave from him in holding, as I have said before, that emotions are completely determined by their cognitive nature. They are uncompromisingly opinions or beliefs in a psyche that is itself undivided and homogenously cognitive. In this way, a unitary, rational mind comes to replace the bipartite and tripartite psyches of Aristotle and Plato. Given that emotions are perverted or false opinions, the task of Stoic enlightenment is to submit to a radical therapy (*therapeia*) that will cure us of ordinary emotions and their habits.[55] The underlying assumption is that it is possible to have dominion over our emotional lives.

Elaborating on the voluntary nature of emotions, Stoics claim that emotions are opinions or beliefs insofar as they are voluntary assents to appearances or impressions regarding goods and evils.[56] As Seneca explains, "Anger is . . . set in motion by an impression received of a wrong. But does it follow immediately in the impression itself and break out without any involvement of the mind? . . . Our view is that it undertakes nothing on its own, but only with the mind's approval."[57] Emotions, however spontaneously experienced, are mediated by an appraisal, conscious or unconscious, that is voluntary in the sense that while we may be "struck" by impressions, we accept or "assent" to those impressions—for example, in the case of fear, that something in our midst is threatening. In addition, we assent to a further opinion that certain reactions or affective responses (e.g., fleeing or trembling) are appropriate.[58] The overall claim is that emotional experience is, in a substantive way, voluntary.[59]

The view runs counter to much ordinary thinking about emotions. Emotional language is filled with passivity. We are "bowled over" by love, "overcome" with grief, "paralyzed" by fear. And while emotional experience doesn't always leave us helpless victims, there is often a lag before we are able to take charge. The Stoics, too, suggest we are seduced by impressions, but they maintain that we give those our assent, however unreflectively. The Greek word for emotion, *pathos*, underscores the sense of passivity. It derives from the verb *pathein*, meaning "to suffer or endure," and our Latinate term *passion* preserves some of that gloss. The Stoics, however, demand that we cease to view emotions as events that merely happen to us. Though we may feel possessed by emotions, in truth we are the possessors, ultimately in charge of our experience. Undoubtedly the Stoics once again push their claim too far. But their views nonetheless give us insight into ways in which we *can* take responsibility for our emotions.[60]

The ancient Greek Stoics hold that all emotions can be classified into four basic types that divide along two major axes: they are about either goods or evils, and they are focused on either the future or the present/past. So desire (*epithumia*) is directed at the appearance of a future good in the offing, fear (*phobos*) at the appearance of a future evil. Pleasure (*hēdonē*) is judgment of a good in the present or past, and pain or distress (*lupē*) is a judgment of evil in the present or past. All other emotions are conceived as subspecies of these four generic ones.[61] So, for example, the Stoics, fixing on the revenge motive often linked with anger, classify anger as a desire, alongside sexual appetite and love of wealth and honor.[62]

Emotions, then, are assents to a mistaken conception of what is good and evil. The Stoics stipulate a further point: that emotions are by definition excessive. They are "excessive impulses," in Zeno's original formulation. Angry feelings are especially excessive, in Seneca's view. They are like "bodies in free fall" that "have no control over themselves."[63] They drive the mind "headlong." Chrysippus's metaphor is apt here: imagine a runner whose pace doesn't allow him to stop suddenly. In a similar way, emotions rarely proceed at a walking pace; they exceed the measure of natural reason.[64] Furthermore, excess leads to other evils of irrationality. Anger, Seneca insists, can waver in its judgments, like a serpent whose fangs become innocuous once the venom is dried out. And it can be capricious, leading us to treat individuals in arbitrary ways.[65]

It is hard to understate the historical impact of this negative picture. Until only the past few decades or so, the overwhelming view of emotions, within and outside the academy, was that of disruptors and distorters of reason— "mist on the mental windscreen," as one philosopher whimsically put it.[66] Kant, in a clear way, helped to preserve Stoic biases in his famous Enlightenment notion that morality must be grounded in reason, not emotion, lest moral motivation be held hostage to blind and capricious inclinations. But while Kant, at least in his most well-known writings, subscribes to much of the negative view, he resists the more tenable Stoic piece, namely, the descriptive, cognitive view that emotions are essentially judgments.[67] In his own view, ordinary emotions are brute feelings like itches and tickles; their irrationality—indeed, their pathology—has to do with their stupidity. They are merely dumb feels, not judgments.

The Stoics, like Kant, will make significant concessions. The sage, along with Kant's paragon of moral virtue, is not impervious to all feeling. The sage will experience cultivated "good" emotions (*eupatheiai*, not *pathē*), just as Kant's moral paragon will feel "practical," not merely "pathological," emotions. In both cases, cultivated emotions are the products of mature virtue, "garments" that "dress virtue to advantage," as Kant puts it. In the case of the Stoic sage, removing ordinary emotions will involve removing the excessive emotions that come with overestimating the importance of external goods in one's life. With more accurate calibrations of danger, wealth, and the like (as indifferents and not proper good and evil), reasonable, "good" emotions come to replace the old ones. True, a sage may still feel shadows and scars of older feelings—bites and gnawings, as some of the texts put it.[68] These may be the emotional residues of a former life, moments when he is caught off guard and feels the stirring of an emotion, what Seneca calls emotional preludes (*proludentia adfectibus*). However, if he is truly a sage, then there will be no risk of backsliding. If he is not yet a sage, the fate of most of us, then these moments may threaten regression. "Thus it is," concedes Seneca,

> that even the bravest man often turns pale as he puts on his armour, that the knees of even the fiercest soldier tremble a little as the signal is given for battle, that a great general's heart is in his mouth before the lines have charged against one another, that the most eloquent orator goes numb at the fingers as he prepares to speak.[69]

The genuine sage will resume control almost instantly. He will refrain from assenting to impressions and will be able to catch himself before the stirring grows into a full-blown emotion. But those who yet fall short of sagehood, even the bravest, may not catch themselves in time.

From a non-Stoic perspective, we might think of an emotional prelude as a useful signal to take tighter control; it is a kind of "affect signal," as Freud came to characterize anxiety and the subconscious way it can alert us to take up defense.[70] Or we might think of these preemotional phenomena as the sort of "enactments" trained psychotherapists say they experience: fleeting emotional responses, such as a momentary wave of guilt or retaliative anger, that briefly interrupt a therapist's more neutral posture.[71] In the case of the listening therapist, these enactments are, more often than not, informative. They record something the therapist finds salient in the patient's story or in her own resonance to it.

But we need to be careful here. While from the perspective of psychotherapy or other contemporary views we might think of emotions and preemotional experiences as potentially informative, Stoics must resist the move, for on their view, emotions and their precursors give nothing but systematically false evaluations—they misinform. What we might think the Stoics *can* concede, however, is that the appearances that we assent to give us information about *preferred* and *dispreferred indifferents*. This may be. But if we go on to have full and ordinary emotional responses as a result of these assents, then we are in fact not evaluating the circumstances *as indifferents*. We are viewing them as genuine goods and evils and are thus still in the grip of the old picture.

These remarks give us some insight into the extreme nature of the Stoic position on an emotion such as anger. It may be one thing to restrain abusive wrath on the ground or in command, but quite another to feel no trace of anger when one loses one's limbs in a war one believes is unjust or to experience no moral outrage when one witnesses genocide. This may be a kind of equanimity that not only is hard to come by but undoes what we hold as our essential humanity. We get a better grasp of the radical nature of the view when we examine Seneca's full indictment of anger in the next section.

SENECA AND THE RAVAGES OF ANGER

Seneca paints a picture of all anger as incipient frenzy and cruelty. Its natural course is to turn into a thirst for bloody revenge. It is an urge to "lash and lacerate," to seek retribution not for its own sake but for pleasure.[72] It is a "raging malady," a "sheer brute force that rushes" on a person, "a butcher" of the innocent and those "dearest," a force "to sink what cannot be drowned unless he himself drowns with it."[73] In short, anger terrorizes others as it torments us. Excessive by definition, it becomes impossible to moderate. These characterizations are meant to apply not just to malicious anger or hatred but to all species of anger. Indeed, Seneca takes principal aim at the type of anger that may seem to us most justified—namely, moral indignation at culpable wrongdoing. In what follows, I analyze dialectically Seneca's arguments, raising objections to his condemnation of moral indignation and to the related claim that retributive anger amounts to an untenable form of revenge.

Seneca begins his remarks (in Book II) by noting that wrongdoing in the world is legion. If the wise person habitually reacted to it, "his entire life would be spent in bad temper and grief."[74] He would become a ranter and raver, not so different from those whose lives are filled with petty malice and spite, who, although "out of military dress," are "still at war with each other," bickering and fighting as if in a "school of gladiators."[75] This is no life for a sage, or for even one who aspires toward virtue in more modest ways. Moral indignation robs one of a life of equanimity.

Seneca is right to warn of the self-destructive and obsessive character of anger. As Aristotle pointed out before him, it is easy to deviate from the mean in anger and become bitter, on one hand, or choleric and explosive, on the other.[76] Moreover, with time and repetition, those responses can become hardened into deeply habituated patterns that we reinforce by exaggerating the degree or severity of the moral injuries suffered.[77] But Seneca's response to the slide toward excess and abuse is extreme—we are to abstain from all moral anger. Resentment, indignation, moral outrage, retribution, and revenge, all angry attitudes of moral disapproval and protest, become suspect. Instead, we are to learn to ignore, endure, or forgive. We may assess, punish, and reeducate wrongdoers, but we are to do so without any angry feelings.

We need to be fair here to Seneca's insights. He is surely right that moral anger or righteousness can take on a life of its own that bedevils its possessor. And the urge toward forgiveness and reconciliation, in some cases independent of a change of heart by the wrongdoer, may be a response to one's urgent need to find moral health and wholeness. It may be time to move on and heal, even if those who have committed the wrong have not repented for their sins.[78]

But the need for this sort of repair and calm does not obviate the moral need for another kind of repair that may come only with allowing oneself, for example, to be angry at rather than afraid of a violent aggressor or to protest a wrong publicly rather than through silent suffering. If calm is a moral psychic good, then so too, at the right moment, may be righteous indignation; moreover, it may be the means to a secure calm. It may be curative and restorative, whether as part of a private narrative (for a victim of rape, for example) or as part of public protest (say, against a reign of state torture). Too, there may be moral outcry on behalf of others whose voices may be silenced, or on behalf of the dead by their survivors. A relentlessly just assessment of right and wrong and a determination to act on it needn't preclude these sentiments. Nor need these sentiments be conflated with the violent rage, hatred, or abuse to which they may be responses. A battered wife should not think that forgiving her husband is the only way to avoid meeting his brutality with her own.[79] A Holocaust victim need not hold that unless he grants forgiveness to a penitent Nazi torturer he will be consumed by the same kind of hatred that fueled Nazi atrocities.[80] A victim of genocidal rape during wartime ought not think that retributivist sentiments will put her on a par with her assailants.[81] Meaningful forms of vindication and moral outrage are possible without us morphing into the brutal aggressors we condemn. Some involve appeal to legal redress, war crimes tribunals, or a process of bearing witness. Moreover, public and legal forms of vindication need not replace the need for private anger or the appropriate expression of anger in public places. Nor need it replace the ongoing personal work often required to find a way to be angry that destroys neither others nor ourselves.

Now, Seneca may be arguing not that a rational assessment of wrongdoing *precludes* sentiments of moral protest but that it can do the *same job* as those passions, and that it can do it without the added risk of wreaking psychic havoc on an agent. As in the case of the drill sergeant's mock anger, you don't need to have the real thing to get the job done. The point is well taken in that context. The drill sergeant is motivating troops. Anger that can arouse a bit of shame or humiliation may bring out a fighting spirit that otherwise lies dormant. Moreover, faking it may be better than the real thing, insofar as it enables one to stay in control the whole time. In an arena where sadistic abuse of power is all too easy, playacting may be the safer route. Perhaps, too, faking it works well in arenas that lay emphasis on decorum, as discussed in the last chapter. Putting on the right face may be just enough of what is required for some of the conventions of social exchange, whether it be military deference or polite gratitude.

But responses to wrongdoing and violations of dignity are a different matter. Here the point is not to take up a persona that manipulates others or to observe a surface convention. Rather, it is to sincerely protest and record a moral violation. It is to defend the value that makes the action wrong and to show the damage the action inflicted. It is to express one's heart. Seeking fair assessment and punishment are compatible with moral outrage, but they do not have the same expressive function.

Seneca might reply to us that moral outrage is simply not an emotion that a sage will feel. Its expression does not have a place in the sage's reformed emotional vocabulary. He himself does no wrong, nor is he undone by others wronging him. But in this respect at least, the sage offers a model that is not simply revisionist but too far removed from human moral experience to offer adequate guidance for us non-sages. We need guidance precisely in feeling moral anger that is constructive but does not fester and that takes seriously others' capacity to injure our dignity.

The spirit of Seneca's remarks brings to mind the phrase "forgive and forget." But that phrase is misleading at best. We can't forgive if we forget, for forgiving requires remembering the moral injuries we suffered and making a conscious decision to forswear for the future (or at least the immediate future) our resentment or rage.[82] To forgive is to move beyond or overcome punishing anger for *moral* reasons—because the wrongdoer has repented, or because we see other redeeming features in the person untarnished by the wrongdoing, or because we are ready to readmit the shunned wrongdoer back into the moral community. In forgiving, we neither renounce nor repress the protest that our anger registers; instead we decide that it is time to move beyond it on moral grounds. Forgetting, in contrast, is something that *happens* to us over time, and as therapeutic as it may be, it is not something we *do* for moral reasons. Forgiving may achieve some of the peace that forgetting brings, but in a way that doesn't magically erase our memory. Moreover, even if we think of forgetting as first requiring forgiving, the point is not that we forget the earlier protest. We remember it, but it may no longer be a burning preoccupation or an all-consuming source of pain.[83]

Nor is forgiving condoning. In a passage from the *Doctrine of Virtue*, Kant reminds us of this important point:

> Men have a duty to cultivate a *conciliatory spirit (placabilitas)*. But this must not be confused with *placid toleration* of injuries . . . , renunciation of the rigorous means . . . for preventing the recurrence of injuries by other men; for in the latter case a man would be throwing away his right and letting others trample on it, and so would violate his duty to himself.[84]

In this passage Kant directs us to the wrongdoer and to the cost of condoning his actions. To condone, as a routine response to wrongdoing, undermines the very notion of holding individuals responsible for their actions and responsible for respecting others through constraints they put on those actions. Seneca warns that anger "casts out all sense of human solidarity from the mind."[85] But the absence of moral anger in the face of villainy or evil can just as easily tear the social fabric.[86] And without being able to trust that decent-minded persons will protest violations of dignity on behalf of others, there is little chance for social fabric in the first place. Kant does not overlook the moral costs to self either. To let others trample on our rights is a failure of the duty of self-respect. It is a way of letting oneself become servile.

In fairness to Seneca, he rightly reminds us that moral injuries come in different shapes and sizes, and minor provocations (being spat at is a favorite he invokes) might best be left ignored.[87] But he also says that a calm demeanor might be the most beneficial response to the grossest sorts of violations, such as being forced to bear witness to the torture and murder of our own children.[88] His example is important. Seneca retells a story from Herodotus in which the Median king Astyages punishes his advisor Harpagus for a piece of unwanted advice. His punishment was to be served up his own children for dinner, complete with their heads on the serving dish. Did he like the seasoning? he was asked repeatedly. "Words did not fail the poor man, his lips were not sealed. 'Dinner with a king,' said he, 'is always delicious.' What did he achieve with this flattery? He was spared the leftovers." Seneca warns about misunderstanding his point:

> I am not saying that a father should not condemn anything that his king does, I am not saying that he should not try to punish such monstrous ferocity as it deserves; I am just proving, for the moment, that even anger generated by enormous affliction can be concealed [*abscondi*] and compelled to use words that express the opposite. . . . It is necessary to bridle your indignation in this way, especially if your lot is to have this sort of life and be invited to the royal table.[89]

Again, the story is about faking it, about demeanor that is within our control and which, in this case, might spare us a worse tragedy. To Seneca's credit, with this story he is not exhorting suppression of moral indignation itself. It is not clear that he thinks that it is even humanly possible. But he does think that putting on a good face is. Even in this "slavery," "the way lies open to freedom."[90]

However, the example leaves important questions unanswered: Ought there be a public or even private venue for the indignation? Can it not have its own kind of benefit? Can there be a controlled way of being morally angry and of expressing it in a way that has both social utility and personal reparative benefit? In striking ways, we shall see the Stoics take up similar positions with regard to demeanor in the case of grieving. Cicero in the *Tusculan Disputations,* in Stoic voice, urges that we can put a wedge between our public persona and our private, inner feelings. And while the point is well taken—that we ought not underestimate what we can control in our outward appearance—it is not clear that we accomplish all that is required morally or psychologically when we put on a good face.

The military, as we have said many times, is an arena in which putting on a good face—a face of calm, a face of solemnity, a face of deference—is important. It is an arena in which control of emotional expression matters, in part because of deference rituals such as Harpagus engages in. However, this discussion of Seneca's text shows that it is easy but wrong to move from the value of external emotional control to the elimination of specific emotional feelings themselves. In the next section I speak more expansively to the question of anger and military experience.

Two other points are worth mentioning in Seneca's objection to forms of moral anger and outrage. The first is the claim that we can more effectively change others through therapeutic reform than through retribution. We should take up the "kindly gaze of a doctor viewing the sick" and get on with the business of cure rather than moral protest. [91] We are better off viewing wrongdoing more as pathology than as evil. Our souls are like leaky ships, Seneca continues: "Surely a man whose ship has timbers loose and leaking badly will not be angry with the sailors or with the ship itself?" Sufficient help is what is needed.[92] Seneca implies that even an impersonal protest that is not defiant—one that focuses on a moral mistake (and not the victim's injury) and defends the *value* that makes the action wrong—is misguided.[93]

On a sympathetic note, we may agree that retributive punishment, properly understood and designed, is not just a way of redressing wrong but also a way of educating the wrongdoer.[94] Still, it would be unreasonable, however revisionist, to suspend all ordinary personal interactions of resentment, indignation, or moral protest at wrongdoing in favor of a medical model of pathology, management, and treatment. Tellingly, the therapeutic model that Seneca must ultimately recommend lays great stress on the rational powers of the patient to develop enlightened attitudes about what is truly good in her life. It is *Stoic* therapy, "rowing the oars of dialectic," as Cicero earlier put it: "a medical science for the mind does exist: it is philosophy."[95] But if the engagement of reasoning is crucial in therapeutic treatment in general, then it is not clear why we should regard the "sick" person as exempt from the reason-based responsibility that attitudes of resentment and indignation presuppose. To this, Seneca might reply that moral treatment *does* presuppose reason-based responsibility. It is just that resentment and indignation have no function once dispassionate and fair methods of holding people accountable are in place. But I have argued above that resentment and indignation do not serve the same expressive function. Nor, I can add, need they stand in the way of those proceedings.

The second point, worthy of note, is Seneca's claim that retaliative anger is a primitive bite-back defense. As such, he argues, it is counterproductive and ultimately undermines our mature well-being.[96] That is how "an animal, struggling against the noose, tightens it."[97] We're better off if we give up biting back like a dog and "agree to go easy on one another."[98] "To bite back is the mark of a wretched little man; mice and ants, if you put your hand near them, turn their jaws towards you; anything weak thinks itself hurt, if touched."[99]

Seneca here touches a raw, modern nerve. The revenge component of anger makes us queasy. "Getting even" or "demanding payback" strikes us as thug or vigilante talk, perhaps glamorized in *The Godfather* or *The Sopranos* more recently, but not something we are keen to hear out of soldiers' mouths. We bristle at the vengeance of Achilles, but more so at his modern counterparts: "This was a time for us to get even. A time for us to settle the score. A time for revenge—when we can get revenge for our fallen comrades." This is Sergeant Kenneth Hodges's recollection of Captain Medina's orders to Charlie Company on the fateful night before the My Lai massacre.[100] In context, and given the consequences of this order, it is hard not to think of revenge here as barbarous and part of a false code of military honor.[101]

It is worth reflecting, tangentially, that vengeance that is part of a divine prerogative makes us no less uncomfortable. Consider the narrative in Exodus 6–13, in which God punishes Pharaoh for the enslavement of the Jews. Recall that God has installed Moses and his brother Aaron as prophets to help liberate the Jews. Although he has armed Moses with a bag of tricks to outwit Pharaoh's magicians, even rods that morph into burning bushes and into serpents that devour other serpents fail to convince Pharaoh of a power greater than his own. His heart hardens, and he grows more stubborn in his enslavement of the Jews. Finally God visits plagues upon Pharaoh and the Egyptians, with each plague an escalation of terror. The raining of plagues becomes something of a publicity act for God, to let his power be known before all and to show that in the contest of strength between Pharaoh and himself, he is the stronger.

Now, there is something morally unsavory about this punishment of the Egyptians, and it is not just that redress or retribution can hurt and indeed, as in this case, be extraordinarily severe. Nor is it that we see God taking malicious pleasure in infesting a land with pestilence or locusts or in slaying the firstborn, for he doesn't. Rather, it is that God seems caught up in a pissing match with Pharaoh that protracts the Jews' enslavement. Though Pharaoh hardens his own heart in the beginning against the Jews, as the story continues God intervenes to stiffen Pharaoh's heart (even after Pharaoh repents).[102] And in response to that newly stiffened heart, God unleashes yet stronger punishments. It is this extra turn of the screw, the making of Pharaoh more evil than he need be, that has the touch of vindictiveness, of crossing the moral line.[103]

But must revenge always cross that line? Is it *necessarily* immoral or irrational? On the conventional view, revenge is the disreputable cousin of retribution. It is thought to involve a *malicious* satisfaction on the part of a victim in inflicting suffering on the person who wronged her. It is associated with excess, private retaliation, and the caprice or subjectivity of a victim's response to wrongdoing.[104] Retribution is the demand that wrongdoers get their just deserts proportionate to the suffering inflicted, without the feelings of moral anger or hatred toward the wrongdoer, or the excesses, vigilantism, and sub-jectivity of revenge. The Stoics themselves will assume that a just moral re-sponse is possible without revenge. What is required is calm rationality in the prosecution of justice, where again there is no need for passion if you have relentless rational determination.

But if we resist from the start identifying revenge with private retaliation, with illegal activities such as those at My Lai, or with unconstrained vindic-tiveness, then it is not so clear that it is the taboo it is made out to be. What may be problematic for some is the notion of satisfaction in getting even. Sen-eca urges that we must resist that pleasure. To want to get even is just the urge to bite back like a dog. It is a primitive response, perhaps like that of the infant the psychoanalyst Melanie Klein depicts who bites back instinctually at the breast when it returns from its withholding.[105] Klein would argue that humans are primed to view deprivations, both deliberate and unintentional, with a touch of paranoiac rage. With developmental maturity, we give up some of the para-noia but not all of the anger. Toward those whom we trust and love, we learn to integrate love and hate, but toward those who willfully and actually harm us in severe ways, hatred and anger are not mere persecutory fantasies.

There is something to be learned here: we may, in healthy ways, retain our feelings of moral anger as we go on to hold others accountable for their willful injuries of us. This is not to say our anger should be boundless or prevent us from seeing any good in those who wrong us. Nor do we want to make the mistake of viewing our natural and psychological development as one with our moral development. This said, however, many of us would argue that ex-cising moral anger or outrage from our human repertoire is not a mark of moral maturity. To feel outrage in bearing witness to torture, massacre, or rape is a fundamental response to human violation, and a fundamental way we protest the shame and abject servility that violence inflicts. These responses are a part of our humanity to cultivate, not excise.

THE CHANGING SHAPE OF ANGER ON THE BATTLEFIELD

I have been talking about moral anger in somewhat abstract terms. In this section, I assess Seneca's indictment in a more concrete way by turning to the testimony of those who have seen the face of war.

In 1991 Tony Pfaff (whom we met earlier) served as a platoon leader within the 82nd Airborne Division when they secured landing sites with the Marines for the first stages of Operations Desert Shield and Desert Storm during the Gulf War.[106] Pfaff describes the anger that frames a combat soldier's mind-set as he prepares for war. He focuses on the professional soldier, not the

conscript, and on a war that the soldier by and large views as a justified response to unjust aggression:

> I'll start with maybe the Persian Gulf War, which for me is a little bit cleaner
> example [than Vietnam]. What were any of us angry at? Most of us genuinely
> believed that Kuwait was unjustly aggressed against. And so you're angry at the
> aggressor for bringing you over here, for making you have to go, to leave your
> routine that you're comfortable with, and place you in this awful place to do
> these awful things, or at least have the prospect of doing these awful things. It's
> a little easier for the professional soldier to deal with it, because he's built a life
> out of practicing for this kind of thing. So his feelings are more ambivalent. A
> lot of time you feel like the basketball or football player practicing for the big
> game, hoping he never has to play. It's just a weird sort of feeling that's kind of
> hard to reconcile. . . . You're feeling really excited about going to play in the big
> game, and horrified and scared out of your mind that you have to play the big
> game at the same time.

"Horrified exactly of what?" I asked.

> That you could get killed. And you get asked to do things that you really don't
> want to do. I don't know many serial killers in the Army. Most people just really
> prefer not to have to kill anyone if they don't have to.

Pfaff describes a baseline resentment at being dragged into war because of
an unjust provocation. But in addition, there is the resentment at being forced
to use one's deadly skills and at being exposed to those of others. The irony, of
course, is that this is the point of professional war training—to become a warrior not just notionally but actually. The commitment is to put oneself in harm's
way if necessary. Is it rational to resent having to honor that commitment?
The best answer comes from Aristotle, and it is a simple one: the truly courageous, unlike the merely daring, feel pain and anger because they know the
terrible cost of self-sacrifice.

> And the more one is possessed of excellence in its entirety . . . the more one will
> be pained at the thought of death; for life is best worth living for such a person,
> and he is knowingly losing the greatest goods, and this is painful. But he is none
> the less brave, and perhaps all the more so, because he chooses noble deeds of
> war at that cost.[107]

Resentment becomes the backdrop against which other forms of anger associated with war mingle. Irritability, anger, and frustration mount with the
countless deprivations brought on by war. In this context, the endless waiting
that is part of war becomes no small irritant. It fuses with anxiety about losing
one's battle edge and anxiety about extended deployments. Any deployment
pits the role of soldier, sailor, airman, or marine against that of family person.

Fear of loss of family and the dread of separation can easily morph into anger at the enemy for forcing those conflicts. "You begin to think," reflects Pfaff about the first Gulf War, that

> Iraqi soldiers, conscripts or not, are fighting for an unjust cause, and this unjust cause is disrupting our lifestyles in a very, very personal way, keeping us away from our families and the rest. . . . Everyone's really irritated. By the eighth month people's families are starting to collapse. The first month of our return, there were two hundred divorces in a division with roughly two thousand married.

The soldier's view of the enemy in all this is complicated. Some project their frustration and anger onto the individual foot soldier who is their counterpart. But Pfaff insisted that most within his unit resisted the move. From what he could tell, the enemy was, by and large, not demonized in the way it often was in Vietnam. "You have an anger at the enemy, but you also have this kind of appreciation for the enemy soldier as being just another schmuck like you." Personalized anger, he said, was for the most part reserved for those responsible for the war, in this case Saddam Hussein. (Pfaff did not himself address the issues of uncontrolled rage that can come home with veterans after the war, as discussed earlier in this chapter.)

Pfaff's sentiment about reserving anger for those responsible for war was echoed at the funeral of the philosopher John Rawls. One of his sons said his father never spoke much of his experience in World War II, but he did share one story with his family. He said he harbored no anger against the Japanese foot soldier, and in one instance, when face-to-face with his counterpart, both he and his opposite chose to retreat rather than fire. But he did have contempt for the Japanese authorities responsible for the war. At the close of the war, he volunteered to be part of a search contingent walking for several days in the treacherous and still enemy-held jungles of the island of Luzon to capture General Yamashita and bring him back for a formal surrender.[108]

A tolerant view of the enemy soldier can quickly change, though, if he becomes a cheater. Ilya Shabadash is a distant cousin of mine who fought in World War II on the Russian side. Throughout the war, he harbored deep background anger for Hitler, though by and large, like Pfaff, he found himself respecting his opposite number engaged in the daily business of battle. What outraged him, though, even sixty years later in the retelling, was the trickery of a German peasant woman who hitched a ride back to town with his unit. She was carrying a basket of food and offered the hungry Russian troops some produce. Those who took her up on the offer later fell deathly sick. They had been poisoned. The survivors exploited the incident as an opportunity to rail at the Russian brass for underfeeding the troops. But that was just displaced anger, Ilya insisted. The real anger, he said with pique still in his voice, was at the enemy, who cheated by using a civilian to do their bidding.[109]

Enemy mischief adds a new level of culpable wrongdoing to the equation. In the old language of just conduct of war, such actions as Ilya suffered are violations of chivalry. The word betrays the origin of rules of war in a medieval culture that mixes brutality with the gallantry of knights.[110] Yet the term doesn't easily capture for us the gross violations of humanity posed by terrorism and weapons of mass destruction (nuclear, biological, and chemical). Nor does it capture the anger and moral anguish decent-minded soldiers must contend with when the enemy uses its own innocent citizens to do its bidding. Retired general Roméo Dallaire, in charge of United Nations forces in Rwanda in 1994, fought back tears as he recalled at a recent breakfast talk, almost ten years after the massacres started in Rwanda, how the enemy combatants routinely placed children in the middle of the road in Rwanda as shields between their troops and the approaching UN trucks. The children knew they would be shot at if they tried to escape. The UN troops knew they would take heavy losses rather than shoot. Whether by the rules of morality or chivalry, they would not accept the enemy's terms for the fight.[111]

Perhaps some in the military become desensitized emotionally as they bear witness repeatedly to the atrocities of war. They have learned by means, very different from Seneca's, to detach emotionally. They have learned how to create a "bulletproof mind."[112] No doubt some desensitization is part of the psyche's survival system for facing gruesome evil up close. It is an adaptive way of coping with horror. The Stoic appeal to apathy invokes different means *and* different grounds. Its means I address later, in the final section. Its rationale, as we have said before, is that ordinary emotions misinform us about genuine evil and that we can do all we need to do morally without their input. Those who suffer from psychic trauma would argue otherwise, for often they suffer precisely because emotions have revealed to them all too clearly what they take to be genuine human evil.

Dallaire himself, whose pleas to the superpowers to intervene in Rwanda fell on deaf ears, returned to Canada with his experience of the genocide stuffed away mentally. It stayed there for two years until, as he says, he couldn't "keep it in the drawer any longer."

> There are times when the best medication and therapist simply can't help a soldier suffering from this new generation of peacekeeping injury. The anger, the rage, the hurt, and the cold loneliness that separates you from your family, friends, and society's normal daily routine are so powerful that the option of destroying yourself is both real and attractive.[113]

Dallaire, now retired from the military, heads up a unit in charge of posttraumatic stress disorder education for veterans in Canada.

Seneca well appreciates that the rampage of emotions can unravel a soul. But his argument that the goods and evils that they characteristically respond to are not genuine parts of human well-being is something that Dallaire would dispute. Tragically, in Rwanda in the spring of 1994 more than the outcry of a general in charge was needed to check what he took to be real and catastrophic evil.

Hugh Thompson was perhaps luckier than Dallaire.[114] On the morning of March 16, 1968, as a twenty-five-year-old reconnaissance helicopter pilot with the 123rd Aviation Battalion, he happened to be circling above a small hamlet called Tu Cung by the Vietnamese and My Lai 4 by the Americans. In the bubble were also his eighteen-year-old door gunner, Lawrence Colburn, and his twenty-two-year old crew chief, Glenn Andreotta. As they hovered, at times only four or five feet off the ground, they began to see a swath of devastation and a ditch filled with bodies. They had just flown over the area an hour earlier with no sign of enemy action and no reports of Americans being hurt. His mind began to go places it didn't want to go. Relating the events some thirty-five years later, Thompson recalls, "I guess I was in denial. You've got to understand, we were ready to risk our lives to save these American guys on the ground." And so he began to construct for himself alternative scenarios. Maybe the carnage was from the early-morning aerial artillery prepping of the area. But why then the ditch? So he tried out another scenario:

> When the artillery started coming, the enemy ran out into the ditch and a lucky artillery round got them. But I'm thinking, "Every house has a bomb shelter in it. When artillery starts coming in, are you going to leave this safe bomb shelter and take a walk in the park? I don't think so." So I threw that out. So I said, "Well, when the Americans came through, they did the humane thing and put all of the bodies in the ditch that was going to be a mass grave." Well, then you look in the ditch and there's live people in there. Everybody isn't dead. Wait a minute. We don't put the living with the dead in a grave. And then I just finally said, "These people were marched down in that damn ditch and murdered." . . . The thought was there the whole time, but I was trying to justify it.

Thompson then radioed for help in evacuating a wounded girl, but shortly afterward he saw an infantry officer (later identified as Captain Medina) prod her with his foot and then shoot her. Minutes later, after again asking for help with the wounded in the ditch, Andreotta heard a barrage of machine-gun fire coming from a soldier near the ditch (later identified as Lieutenant Calley). Tears came to Thompson's eyes as he remembers the horror of believing at the time that his pleas for help had somehow gotten garbled and were misconstrued as warnings about a threat, and so resulted in more killing. These days, he no longer believes the messages were mangled. The killing of innocents was deliberate, just as the earlier killings had been. But he still holds himself morally responsible for being a link in a causal chain that may have led to murder. "I'm responsible for their deaths now. . . . If I had kept my mouth shut, then maybe they'd [the soldiers] have walked away and they [the Vietnamese] would have lived."

Thompson next saw the Americans approaching a bunker, and figured to himself that the people inside had about fifteen seconds to live. "I said, 'Dammit, it ain't gonna happen. They ain't gonna die." . . . I was hot. I'll tell you that. I was hot." Those who received his radio message that day got a taste of his outrage: "His voice was choked with emotion. He swore obscenities, cursed, and pleaded with the aerocrew to come down and help rescue the civilians."[115] At this point Thompson had had enough. He landed his aircraft, instructing his crew to fire on the GIs—"open up on 'em and kill them"—if they shot at him as he tried to rescue the people in the bunker. He gave the GIs one last chance, asking for help in getting the civilians out. The reply was "We can get them out with a hand grenade." Thompson's reply was: "I think I can do better than that. And I've already told my people to kill you" if they tried to stop him. The rescue was successful, and the civilians were evacuated by aircraft shortly after.

Thompson raised enough hell at headquarters that day to get the operations, scheduled to last for four days, to cease. Some 350 persons were massacred that day, but his interventions may have stopped the massacre of more than twenty thousand more who were living in the My Lai area at the time: "There was nothing to make me believe that the same thing wasn't going to happen everywhere." But once he filed his report, he did his best to forget the day and to numb the pain. And he continued to forget until the story broke and the court-martials of the Charlie Company officers took him to Washington to give testimony. Once the trials were over, he tried again to put My Lai behind him until a British documentary crew drew him out in the late eighties. In the spring of 1998, after some thirty years of their own silence, the Army belatedly decorated Hugh Thompson, Lawrence Colburn, and Glenn Andreotta (posthumously) with the prestigious Soldier's Medal for their valor at My Lai.

Over the years, Thompson has found comfort in his own version of emotional detachment. "Numb is good," he once told me. He wanted to forget My Lai, but he also wanted others to forget, especially those who viewed him as a traitor and made death threats to him. Like many Vietnam veterans who have kept their war experiences to themselves, he returned home without telling his family what he saw and did that day. Undoubtedly the Army's belated acceptance of Thompson has made it easier for him to own his own past. These days he is no longer silent or numb. The outrage he felt that day in My Lai is palpable in his voice and in his eyes. And there is still anger in his self-reproach for having caused the death of innocents in his first botched attempts at helping. "Don't make me break down," he warned as we began our interview. He didn't break down. He was controlled but emotional. He bore his emotions with a soldier's grace and dignity. Like Shakespeare's Roman warrior

Coriolanus, his eyes "sweat[ed] tears of compassion." Through projects he is involved with in My Lai to build a school and a memorial, he is trying to give back a small bit of what Americans took that day. Contrary to Seneca's warnings, in Thompson's case at least, keeping anger alive turns it into neither frenzy nor chronic embitterment. True, he cannot forgive, unlike the My Lai survivor who wished Thompson had brought Calley and Medina back with him so that she could forgive them. He cannot forgive them because, as he maintains, the evil was simply too great. But even if that woman was ready to forswear her anger, she had not forgotten what happened or lost her pain. "Why," she begged Thompson tearfully, "did they kill my family? Why were they different from you?" Seneca exhorts us to believe that anger is a mistaken judgment—we perceive as trespasses and violations actions that aren't really so, that don't really violate our human core. Yet who among us would venture to tell this Vietnamese woman that what she and her family endured was not a violation of the human soul?

Grief can address genuine violations of the soul that affect happiness. Granted, to say this is not the same as to rescue a place for retributivist anger or indignation at genuine wrongdoing. And this Vietnamese woman, unlike Thompson, does let go of such anger. But if she couldn't let go of it, or if—even more minimally—she couldn't feign such a face, few of us, I dare say, would think her anger misplaced or misinformed.

THERAPEUTIC STRATEGIES

I bring this chapter to a close by reflecting briefly on the relationship of Stoic therapy to more modern variants. Some of Seneca's techniques for the prevention and treatment of one's own anger seem fairly homespun and moderate: "postponement" allows anger to abate;[116] suppressing facial expressions that "inflame the eyes and alter the countenance" can short-circuit internal feedback responses;[117] "putting ourselves in the place of the person with whom we are angry" can shift our judgments; taking stock daily of our habits can help curb our impulses.[118] Meditate at the end of each day, as Seneca says is his own wont ("when the light has been taken away and my wife has fallen silent"). Replay all your interactions and "conceal nothing" from yourself—ask yourself whether you lost your temper at the party, whether you spoke "too pugnaciously," whether when you were the butt of a few jokes you forgot to "stand back and laugh."[119]

But however moderate these techniques, the underlying aspiration—to eliminate all anger—is nothing if not radical. Seneca describes the goal using a mix of quasi- medical and military metaphors. On the medical side, we are to "cut out" (*exsecare*), "exclude" (*excludere*), "remove" or "eliminate" (*tollere*).[120]

Emotions are pathological, noxious toxins that need to be isolated (*diducere*) from healthier parts of the soul. On the military side, "the enemy must be stopped at the very frontier"; we are "to beat [it] back" (*spernere*) and "resist" (*repugnare*) before it "has invaded and rushed on the city gates."[121]

On the Stoic view, anger is a disease because vulnerability is our enemy. Anger reveals us as vulnerable to others' attacks—in particular, vulnerable to their deliberate wrongdoings and slights. But there is an interesting modern way of restructuring the problem that sheds light on Seneca's solution. On a psychoanalytic view, it is not so much anger or emotional investments that are the irritants, but the *conflict* that emotional investments can bring. We don't tolerate ambivalence well. We worry consciously and unconsciously that any angry feelings we allow ourselves may overtake our kinder motives, that our militant side may persecute our softer parts, that hostility toward a child or parent will swallow up our love. At times Seneca himself worries about anger in these terms: if reason starts to mix with anger, then anger may prevail in a way that prevents reason from "ris[ing] again." "How can it free itself from the chaos, if the admixture of baser ingredients has prevailed?"[122] To allow the mixing and mingling of motives is to run the risk of being muddled and conflicted or, worse, overtaken by motives that we don't fully endorse. Better to be resolute and staunch and keep countervailing desires well at bay. Vowing to eliminate anger, or any emotion that can oppose reason's control, is a way of wishing for self-sufficiency. But it is also a way of wishing to be rid of conflict.

Of course, the irritant of psychic conflict is not really a modern problem. Plato and Aristotle carve up the soul largely to account for conflict. If order rather than conflict is to prevail, then the top of the soul must whip the bottom into shape. Desires must know well their hierarchical rankings. Only then can we have psychic well-being. The Stoics resist dividing the psyche, making all mental functions products of the same mind-stuff. But this, they acknowledge, does not do away with conflict or oscillation. Anger can resist reason, and one emotion can quarrel with another, even if each is made of the same cognitive stuff.

Seneca's cure for the disease of emotional vulnerability (and psychic conflict) is elimination. We are to root out all conflict, similar to how we might chemically or surgically remove a cancerous tumor. But while elimination may capture the body's self-healing process, it does not really describe what we do when we resolve psychic conflict. In this vein, consider a contemporary discussion by philosopher Harry Frankfurt on becoming "wholehearted," a state not so unlike Stoic resoluteness. He too considers the notion of psychic elimination:

> When the body heals itself, it *eliminates* conflicts in which one physical process (say, infection) interferes with others and undermines the homeostasis, or equi-

librium, in which health consists. A person who makes up his mind also seeks thereby to overcome or to supersede a condition of inner division and make himself into an integrated whole. But he may accomplish this without actually eliminating the desires that conflict with those on which he has decided, as long as he dissociates himself from them.[123]

In this picture, psychic repair requires not the elimination of a conflicting desire but a "dissociation" from it, or, as Frankfurt says more forcefully elsewhere, "a radical *separation*" in which it is "extruded entirely as an outlaw."[124] Though Frankfurt is not writing with Seneca in mind, his remarks shed light on Seneca's model. In warding off an unwanted emotion, Seneca would concur, we fight it as an enemy, banish it from our borders, resist all alliances with it. We build tall city gates to keep the aliens from invading.

It was Freud who made famous in his case study of the Ratman the convolutions of one who struggles with his ambivalence.[125] The Ratman case, which Freud undertook in 1907, involves the treatment of obsessional neurosis. Ratman is a young man of university age who seeks Freud's help because he has obsessive and paralyzing fears that, as Freud put it, "something might happen to two people of whom he was very fond—his father and a lady whom he admired."[126] In addition, he is plagued by sexual fantasies and self-destructive impulses that he compulsively tries to ward off with tormenting prohibitions and sanctions. One such imagined punishment is that rats are boring their way into the anus—hence the pseudonym "Ratman."

At the heart of the Ratman's ambivalence is a love/hate conflict with his father. The conflict took many guises, but among them were repeated fantasies, including two in the months and then days before his father's death, that the price of his love for a woman he wished to marry was his father's death. That he loved his father was unquestionable to him. That he might punish his father in this way was an intolerable thought that he warded off through a web of defenses and obsessive behaviors. The case is complex and the twisted logic of the obsessions at times bewildering. But what is significant for our purposes is Freud's diagnosis of the Ratman's problem as not his ambivalence but his struggle against it. The extreme "splitting" and "disintegration of his personality"—the very dissociation and isolation from unwanted emotions that Seneca (and Frankfurt) views as a cure—Freud diagnoses as the disease.[127]

Freud explains that in the case of those who are close to us, we "wish our feelings to be unmixed," and consequently, as is "only human," we "overlook . . . faults, since they might make" us dislike the loved one. We often ignore the faults as though we "were blind to them."[128] The Ratman's undoing is in failing to tolerate this ambivalence, with the result that the conflict deepens and his defenses harden: "His hostility towards his father . . . though he had once been acutely conscious of it, had long since vanished from his ken, and it was only in the teeth of the most violent resistance that it could be brought back into consciousness."[129] Obsessive behaviors are invoked to ward off punishments (including the dreaded rat punishment) that have now become stand-ins for his repressed hostility.

To be sure, Seneca does not postulate a way of keeping emotions at bay that amounts to their repression in the unconscious.[130] And Frankfurt also largely focuses on conscious forms of dissociation—of "making one's mind up," "deciding" to identify with certain emotions and not others. His idea of "taking responsibility for the shaping of one's characteristics" has the ring of Stoic notions of voluntary assent and control.[131] But however conscious the control, Frankfurt's "dissociation" and Seneca's "beating back" of unwanted emotions are, like repression and other unconscious defenses, ways we armor ourselves against vulnerability and conflict. And as happens with many defenses and fantasies that are not sustainable compromise solutions, chinks in the armor soon appear.

But what does all this have to do with the warrior? My suggestion is that Stoic aspirations for the warrior to treat anger as an enemy represent an unhealthy psychological phenomenon. It will be objected that warrior rage and revenge, an Achilles-like spirit of vindictiveness and frenzy, are precisely the emotions that a warrior needs to restrain. I could not agree more. And Seneca's *On Anger* provides one of the best places to teach that lesson. Seneca argues persuasively that unrestrained anger, whether of rage, bitterness, revenge, or indignation, are more often than not inappropriate. But Seneca insists that the way to guard against these excesses is to ostracize *all* anger from our lives, and we are to achieve that end through a robust use of defensive techniques that we today know as dissociation and splitting, or more popularly "compartmentalization." On Seneca's version of compartmentalization, competing desires don't mingle or mix, modify or moderate each other. There is no Aristotelian notion of unwelcome emotions becoming tamed by more congenial ones, or excesses in each direction finding more moderate forms by mutual adjustments. Instead, there is only containment.

Granted, compartmentalization of this sort may be for many soldiers an involuntary response to the rage of battle and to the twin traumas of gruesome loss and what can seem undeserving self-survival. How to integrate these experiences in the rhythm of ordinary life becomes a lifelong challenge. Marvin Brenner, with whom we opened this chapter, and others are still struggling fifty years later with (in Kay Jamison's language) the floods of battle memories, trying to rebuild sea walls around those memories, so they are both low enough and permeable enough to let in fresh seawater.[132] Seneca resists this sort of healing and integrating process, recommending instead that one build and maintain the sea walls high enough to fend off the brackish waters—to keep the bad away from the good lest there be contamination. In mixed Stoic and Freudian tones, he exhorts, "Fight with yourself . . . conquer anger"; "conceal" it and give it "no exit"; keep it "hidden and secret"; give the mind an advance directive that should anger erupt, the mind must "bury it deeply and not proclaim its distress."[133] Presumably Seneca, unlike Freud, rejects (or simply has not the perspective to reflect on) the view that demons, buried deep in the soul, can still rise. But those who must live with those demons know well that to bury is not necessarily to vanquish.

Frankly, if a commanding officer looks frightened, then his ship's company will be frightened. If the commanding officer looks not in the least bit wired and very content, then he will impart that to his people. . . . So in order to get the job done, there is actually quite a lot of pressure to be stoic.

—Interview with Admiral R. P. Stevens, former commander of NATO submarines forces in the eastern Atlantic

Like most of my generation, I was obsessed by a complex of terror and longings connected with the idea "War." War in this purely neurotic sense meant The Test. The test of your courage, of your maturity, of your sexual prowess: "are you really a man?" Subconsciously, I believe, I longed to be subjected to this test; but I also dreaded failure. I dreaded failure so much—indeed, I was so certain that I *should* fail—that, consciously, I denied my longing to be tested altogether.

—Christopher Isherwood, in Richard Holmes, *Acts of War: The Behavior of Men in Battle*

Trauma shatters one's most fundamental assumptions about the world, including beliefs about our ability to control what happens to us.

—Susan Brison, *Aftermath: Violence and the Remaking of the Self*

5

Fear and Resilience

———

STOIC ELIMINATION OF FEAR

For Christopher Isherwood, as for many before and after him, war is the ulti-mate test of undaunted courage. And undaunted courage, some would add, leaves little room for fear. It requires being tough, unflappable, and steady, even in the face of life-threatening danger and terror. In this view, to eliminate fear is to live up to the ideal of a truly wise, Stoic warrior. Epictetus makes the point without equivocation: "Dishonor [to aischron] does not consist in not having anything to eat, but in not having reason enough to exempt you from fear or sorrow."[1] Cicero rehearses the views, adding a military tone: "We want the happy man to be safe, impregnable, fenced, and fortified, so that he is not just largely unafraid, but completely."[2] Seneca embellishes the martial theme: "And what is bravery? It is the impregnable fortress for our mortal weakness; when a man has surrounded himself therewith, he can hold out free from anxiety during life's siege; for he is using his own strength and his own weap-ons."[3] But those who have fought in war know that all sorts of fears can visit the minds of even the toughest of warriors. And like Isherwood, they know that longing for the ultimate test can at once involve dreading its arrival. "YOU'LL BE SCARED," a Second World War pamphlet, *Army Life*, tells even the most eager soldiers. "You'll be frightened at the uncertainty, at the thought of being killed."[4]

The prescriptive Stoic view is that all fear is irrational. Like anger—indeed, like all ordinary emotions—fear misinforms us about what is truly good and evil in our lives. In particular, it elevates external dangers and threatened losses to genuine evils that can detract from our happiness. These, the Stoics argue against the Peripatetics, are not in fact genuine evils that can undo real happi-ness, for they lie beyond our control. What really threatens happiness—what makes it impossible, rather—is the absence of virtue, or vice. And while the sage will experience a kind of caution or wariness (*eulabeia*) in circumstances where ordinary people feel fear—caution that helps him guard against viewing those circumstances as truly fearful—ordinary fears will have no place in his life.[5]

This goal is austere and, as the Stoics themselves would be the first to concede, next to impossible to realize fully. Even they suggest that sometimes we must settle for just conveying the outer look. Still, it is easy to see the appeal of *aiming* at the deeper goal, especially for warriors whose business is "to survive and function in a world organized for one's death."[6] For those who must kill and risk being killed, Stoicism's tough stance seems the right philosophy for the job. Not surprisingly, a popularized stoic sensibility pervades military life.

The following excerpt, from an article that ran in the *New York Times* on Memorial Day 2003, captures the popular image of stoicism:

> Kevin Joyce got around so well in his wheelchair that his son and daughter did not think of him as disabled, even though he had stumps for legs. He did not complain about his frequent pain, or about the bits of shrapnel that popped up through his skin over the years, souvenirs from the day, July 15, 1968, that Specialist Joyce was nearly killed by a mine after alighting from an Army helicopter in Vietnam.
>
> "I'm sure he saw a lot worse," Brian Joyce of Watertown, Mass., said in explaining his father's stoicism.[7]

Here, being stoic means rationalizing a tough stance toward adversity. However, it is worth noting that both ancient Stoicism and popular views of stoicism within the military hold that prosperity as much as adversity pose challenges to those who care about virtue and character.[8] The challenges it raises have to do with wanting and having what is vulnerable to loss. To be indulged, to grow accustomed to luxury or simply a life of worldly possessions, can in obvious ways exacerbate feelings of need and the pleasures of attachment. Comfort and luxury threaten to corrupt the self just as severe material deprivations can. It is the corrupting effect of materialism that Epictetus in particular rallies against, having lived as a slave during the time of Nero and having discovered firsthand the kind of mental freedom that can be achieved in enslavement and which can be threatened by preoccupations with the conventional goods of freed men:

> What you concern yourself with is how to live with marbled walls, how to be served by slaves and freedmen, how to wear fine clothes, how to have a great number of huntsmen, harpists, and tragic actors.... But, on the other hand, have you concerned yourself with judgments, or even your own rational faculty? ...
>
> ... But as long as you occupy yourself with externals, you will have those, indeed, to an extent that no one else can match, but you will have this ruling faculty just as you want it, squalid and neglected.[9]

Underlying the caustic bite is the more fundamental claim that vulnerability is a matter of misplaced attachments and underestimates of personal autonomy. Put simply, we fail to appreciate just how self-sufficient our goodness is and how intimately tied our happiness is to self-sufficient virtue and its rational foundations. In Epictetus's phrase, which has a legacy in Aristotle, we fail to understand how much is up to us.

But even here, with regard to attachment and fear of loss, Stoicism presents us with a range of views. Or at least we can begin to reconstruct such a range from various remarks Stoic authors make. While an orthodox Stoic will argue that all attachments to externals and fear of their loss (including attachment to oneself as embodied) rest on false evaluations, a more moderate Stoicism might distinguish between trivial and tragic losses, and between trivial and life-sustaining attachments.[10] As we saw in the last chapter, Seneca concedes that Harpagus can only feel absolute horror at being served up his children, even if he is able to mask it to avoid worse punishment.[11] Seneca tells a similar story about Prexaspes, a servant of the Persian king Cambyses, son of Cyrus the Great. One evening Prexaspes advised Cambyses to drink a bit less wine. Enraged and drunk, Cambyses showed just how steady his hand was by ordering his critic's son to stand before him. The king "drew his bow and shot the boy through the heart," then asked the father "whether his hand had been sure enough." The father replied, "Not even Apollo . . . could have aimed better." Seneca himself is aghast at the flattery: "There he was praising something which it was too much even to have witnessed." But he retells this story from Herodotus to show that anger and grief can be masked, however much the heart rages: "Not cursing the king, he uttered not a word even of grief, though he felt his heart transfixed no less than his son's. You can say that he was right to choke back his words; expressions of anger would have denied him the role of father."[12] The critical point for us is that Seneca accepts the notion of some losses as tragic, even though he thinks that in such circumstances, control and "faking it" are still possible and prudent.

A more orthodox Stoicism would urge that we put all attachment to external goods on the same scale: witnessing the gruesome death of one's best friend in war or the torture and murder of one's child by a tyrant constitute no greater loss to one's well-being than the loss of a beloved object, perhaps an heirloom or a valued piece of jewelry. All these losses, to the extent that they are external to one's agency, are only apparent evils and do not themselves count against one's happiness. They are all equally indifferents. "Do not talk of the matter in a tragic strain," chides Epictetus. "To me" they are all "mere figs and nuts."[13] Children can scramble for them and fret about their loss, but not grown men and women. Even the most heinous of tyrants, he insists, ought not inspire fear in the eyes of the truly virtuous person: "What makes a tyrant frightening? His guards, someone says, and their swords; the chamberlains and those who would shut the door on people who enter?"[14] But if we hold that our virtue can remain intact, even under the cruelest acts of an oppressor, then we can learn to value its fine exercise, however constrained the instruments and circumstances through which we exercise that virtue. We learn, Epictetus says, what children know when they play games with potsherds they find scattered on the ground: what is valued is not the game pieces but the game and exercise of skill they make possible.[15]

We are at once attracted to and repulsed by this stance. Who among us doesn't want more resilience and fortitude at times? To witness or endure the most violent acts of humans with the assurance that one's own virtue will not be compromised would be a remarkable charm to own. Yet it is a charm, we worry, that would alienate us from our very humanity. At what cost to our humanity do we arm ourselves against terror and torture? If we are to prepare ourselves to see the loss of children and friends as little different from bidding adieu to a favorite crystal goblet that breaks,[16] then what is the point of building a life around family and friends, or of fighting for and beside men and women who come to be, in essence, family? This is the unacceptable face of orthodox Stoicism.

Seneca tries to soften Stoicism in other ways. We have seen (in Chapter 3) that he insists on the importance of emotional demeanor in performing kindnesses. In this chapter I will show how he argues in guarded ways for the reasonableness of certain kinds of fears, and, as we shall see in the next chapter, he proposes "respectable" forms of grieving that still acknowledge, to some degree, the loss of beloveds. Granted, the concessions are limited. But what I wish to underscore is that Seneca constantly struggles within his own writing to articulate a more supple form of Stoicism. In this spirit, we too need to see if there is a brand of Stoicism that prepares us for enduring the worst tragedies without compromising our fundamental humanity. That, it would seem, is a Stoic ideal worth supporting.

The more human face of Stoicism also emerges when we adjust our focus, as Seneca often does, to include not only the sage but also the advanced moral learner, or "progressor," to use the Stoic term. This is the morally decent yet morally imperfect adult whom Seneca addresses in many of his essays and letters. The work of exhortation is not for the sage, who has already arrived, but for those who are still aspiring. Although in strict Stoic terms anyone who is not a sage is a fool, Seneca's letters show the abundant room for moral growth that can preoccupy even a fool. Similarly, the Stoic notion of "appropriate" acts performed by sage and non-sage alike (in the case of the non-sage, with "well-reasoned" [eulogos] but not perfectly right motives) is evidence that good conduct is not an exclusive moral category, open only to the most morally elite.[17]

Those in the military who insist on the perfectionism implicit in a zero-defect policy have something to learn from this important Stoic concession.

Here we can do no better than to cite a now famous anecdote Colin Powell offers in his autobiography. At one point in his early years, he lost his sidearm, a fairly serious offense for a junior officer and one that under a zero-defect policy can be career-ending. But Powell's superior officer spared him. Powell (and others—I first read about it in an e-mail circulated at the Naval Academy) tells the story as a cautionary tale: too harsh a screening process can weed out some of the military's best. In addition to any moral implications, in sheer economic terms it can be too costly.[18]

With an eye fixed on articulating a gentler Stoicism, I explore in this chapter Stoic conceptions of fear and resilience. More specifically, in the next section I return to the discussion of the Vietnam War helicopter pilot Hugh Thompson and imagine what his emotional responses to the atrocities at My Lai would be were he cast as a Stoic sage. On pages 109–122, I invite us to think more concretely about a soldier's fear of killing and being killed. Both Seneca and Cicero, in quite different ways, shed light on understanding these fears. Beginning on page 122, I shift the focus to contemporary notions of war trauma and to the insights ancient Stoicism sheds on the nature of resilience in the face of extreme terror and stress.

THE EMOTIONS OF A SAGE

As Hugh Thompson witnessed the atrocities unfold in My Lai that sixteenth day of March, 1968, his mind swarmed with emotions. Once he became convinced that his GIs were committing a massacre, moral outrage and moral disgust raged. He feared that if he didn't intervene, more massacres would ensue in the neighboring villages. He also knew that treating GIs as potential "enemies" was a dangerous position to be in and that a court-martial might result. According to a folk psychology model to which many of us subscribe, we might say that some of those emotions disposed him to notice with urgency and quickness (in a way he might not have in their absence) salient features of his circumstances—that innocent women and children were in mortal danger, that GIs were threatening them, and so on. And they motivated Thompson's decision to intervene. On this view, emotions are epistemic and motivational. Emotional sensitivities central to Thompson's character—his capacity to feel outrage, compassion, and fear—predisposed him to take notice *and* to act.

The Stoics accept some of this descriptive picture of moral psychology. To review, they hold that emotions are assents to impressions or appearances that give us information about apparent goods and evils in the world. As some put it, the resulting opinions are "fresh" or "green"—that is, they have immediacy or urgency. Moreover, emotions are a kind of impulse (*hormē*), as the texts say, in the sense that they are the kind of response to the world we make when it requires that we react.[19] But note that this is the Stoic descriptive account. The Stoics argue *prescriptively* that reactions of fear and distress, of the sort Thompson manifested, have no role in the truly virtuous action of the wise person. Moreover, to rely upon them is to rely upon systematic *mis*information. Were Hugh Thompson a Stoic sage, and assuming what he did was truly right, he could and would act as he did without the kind of emotional sensitivity limned above. Perception and reason could do the job alone. Or at least if he had emotions, they wouldn't be the ordinary ones that we non-sages have.

The view is radical and meant to challenge ordinary assumptions. The point is to show, as I have said before, that the truly virtuous and wise can act without the vulnerabilities of ordinary emotions, and those of us who are not wise can still act like sages by not indulging our emotions—we can fake them when we need them (as with the drill sergeant's mock anger) or hide them when we can't fully get rid of them (as with the servant's prudent flattery in witnessing his son's murder). In these latter cases, the Stoics are eager to show just what forms of emotional control are possible for us non-sages.

Of course, the true sage is not just controlled but *transformed*, and this transformation manifests in a new emotional repertoire. More specifically, the sage's recalibrated view of what is truly good and evil in the world manifests in rational or equable forms of emotions, literally "good emotions" (*eupatheiai*). These replace ordinary emotions. The result is that the sage is not really emotionless but rather is moved by a new kind of good feeling, which is meant to retain some of the feel of ordinary emotions, though without their excess or misappraisals.[20] These "good emotions" are experienced as calm, equable, smooth, and fully rational or "consistent." The new feelings correspond in part to the ordinary emotions: in lieu of fear will be caution (*eulabeia*), described in some texts as "well-reasoned shrinking" or "avoidance" (*ekklisis*); in lieu of desire will be wish (*boulēsis*), described as "well-reasoned stretching" or "desiring" (*orexis*); in lieu of pleasure will be joy (*chara*) or "well-reasoned swelling" (*eparsis*).[21] Significantly, there is no correlate to distress in the new taxonomy. Why? Cicero suggests that the sage constitutionally can do no evil and so will never experience the sort of distress or dejection that comes with doing it.[22] In this sense, there is nothing parallel to a non-sage's regret, remorse, shame, and so on.

These new emotions are the exclusive achievements of a sage.[23] But for the sake of argument, let us imagine Hugh Thompson in the guise of Stoic sage; better, let us imagine that he has a sage twin, whom we may call Huey Thompson. What would Huey's emotional responses to the My Lai massacre look like? What would his moral psychology be like?

The extant Stoic texts are somewhat vague about the details of the doctrine of "good emotions."[24] But on one plausible reading, Huey's "good emotions" will be responses to *true* good and evil, in just the way that ordinary emotions are responses to *apparent* goods and evils. Given that true good and evil for the Stoics are virtue and vice, "good emotions" will be the emotional impulse behind striving to promote (or having strived to promote) virtue in oneself and others (in the case of wish and joy) and of striving to avoid vice (in the case of caution). On this reading, Huey, in surveying what he took to be the evolving massacre at My Lai, would have experienced *caution*—that is, a calm, well-reasoned feeling of aversion against doing anything that would lead to or promote (in himself and others) a vicious character. At the same time, he would experience a positive *wish*—a calm and, again, well-reasoned yearning to sustain his virtue. Once he and his gunners had done their best to save the innocents at My Lai, he would then experience a kind of *joy*—a gladness or contentment in perpetuating virtue.[25] But with virtue and vice as the sole objects of emotions, Huey seems remarkably removed from the actual events Hugh witnessed and from the kinds of emotions they inspired in him. Can the sage twin have emotional responses to the suffering of the villagers? Can he be moved by feelings to help them, and not just by feelings with respect to his own virtue?[26]

One way to respond to this objection is to recall that the sage's recalibrated values involve not just a new view of what is good and evil but a new view of the *old* goods and evils. What are goods and evils to ordinary folks—for example, health, welfare, security, safety, and their opposites—he now reliably sees as preferred and dispreferred indifferents. For instance, his caution would be not just an abstract aversion to the possibility of future vice, but experienced precisely on those occasions that give rise to fear in others and cause them to buckle. The caution warns him to steel himself against temptation in those circumstances where others do succumb to fear and view things like risk or danger of injury as real evils.[27] In this sense, Huey, like Hugh, is still caught in the fray of human emotional response. He is not insensible when he takes on the risks of My Lai. He is not naive to the potential harm. But instead of fear and flight, which would eventually lead to vice, he is wary of these very tendencies and cautious about not yielding. In the case of wish, to take another example, while he has the ongoing desire to promote his own virtue as an end in itself, those wishes have as their specific objective liberating the hostages. Thus Huey responds emotionally, just as Hugh does, to the same external set of circumstances, but he construes them differently—as things to go for, select, and care about, but not as choices whose outcomes can upset his calm or substantively affect his true happiness.

On this interpretation, then, the sage is allowed some emotional trafficking with the concrete circumstances of normal life. Still, significantly, what he is not entitled to feel is any notion of distress, dejection, or moral outrage. Even moral shame or distress at moral failure, an admirable emotion for most of us, would have no place in the life of one who was perfectly wise and good.[28] But what are we to say about emotional reactions to good and evil deeds that *others* commit? To take up the case at hand, what of the vicious atrocities that our sage twin witnesses? The Stoics will grant that those atrocities will inspire a certain kind of well-reasoned wish and caution, but not distress. In part this may be because distress, in the Stoic view, is not an emotion that postures one directly for action.[29] It is not inherently a striving or averting—it is more a reaction. Moreover, if moral anger is partially a wish for justice, then that aspect of anger, they can argue, will be captured by rational wish without any of the upheaval that distress brings.

But the response leaves unaddressed the objection that many of us will still have—that the emotions of distress, moral outrage, or indignation should be part of a wise response to atrocity. Thompson's response is not just a forward-looking wish to hold persons accountable. His response is to the present evil he sees around him, and it expresses his dismay, disappointment, and shock. Similarly, his fear is not just wariness about vice that may ensue but worry that innocent lives are being needlessly threatened now. In feeling fear, he feels others' vulnerability and anguish, and this moves him. Thus even though the sage twin is not affectless as he engages in the world, the emotions he expresses still leave out many we want reinstated.

But perhaps the Stoics can come back with a further reply, especially in the case of fear. In the previous chapter I talked about the notion of emotional preludes—preemotional phenomena to which even a sage is susceptible. In *On Anger*, Seneca tells us that the bravest man may turn pale as he puts on his armor, and the general's knees may tremble as he hears the clarion call.[30] He will feel emotional preludes that fall below the threshold of proper emotions. Another ancient author, Aulis Gellius, reports that even the wisest of sea captains turns white if he knows that his ship and crew are about to go under in a storm.[31] In a letter to Lucilius, Seneca explains that these phenomena ought not to be regarded as cases of fear proper, however much the bodily reactions look like those of fear, for unlike full fear, they are involuntary responses that arise without the intervention of reason, or assent:

> For there are certain emotions, my dear Lucilius, which no courage can avoid; nature reminds courage how perishable a thing it is. And so he will contract his brow when the prospect is forbidding, will shudder at sudden apparitions, and will become dizzy when he stands at the edge of a high precipice and looks down. This is not fear; it is a natural feeling which reason cannot rout.[32]

"Prefear," such as a startle reaction or peeing in one's pants when confronted with extreme danger, is, as we would say today, a sympathetic nervous system response often elicited during stressful experiences. In Seneca's terms, it is just "sensations of the body."[33] He has these physical sensations in mind when he writes, "I do not withdraw the wise man from the category of man, nor do I deny to him the sense of pain as though he were a rock that has no feelings at all."[34] Brave individuals, sages and non-sages, will experience these shocks at different moments: "Certain brave men, most willing to shed their own blood cannot bear to see the blood of others." Others "will collapse and faint at the sight of a freshly inflicted wound."[35] What characterizes the sage is that he will not assent to the impression that a shock embodies, and so will not experience an ordinary emotion in its wake.

The doctrine of emotional preludes is a way of holding on to some aspects of ordinary emotional phenomena while still being revisionist. And in doing so, the Stoics seem to be conceding something of the *adaptive advantage* of fear. But they don't concede it in the usual way. From the point of view of ordinary psychology, when we feel fear, a registered threat arouses the sympathetic nervous system and causes us to rush into a state of alert. Attention is heightened, focusing on survival through battle or flight, and perceptions can become altered, so one who perceives extreme danger may be able to disregard hunger, thirst, or fatigue.[36] In including prefear in the life of the sage, the Stoics may be suggesting that we are hardwired with something like this sort of early warning system for danger.[37] But if it has any adaptive advantage for the sage, it's that it warns about the selective and disselective advantages of *indifferents*.

In this section we have seen that the sage is no robotic creature, devoid of all feeling. He does have feelings ("good emotions"), and he is susceptible to shocks, startling, and trembling (preemotions). Still, these concessions are limited and show just how far the sage's emotional repertoire is from our own considered judgments of what good emotions involve. In contrast, we would expect that the most courageous individual would feel some fear (and not just rational caution) in the face of gruesome battle and might even break in the face of catastrophic stress. In the two sections that follow, I illustrate some concrete examples of fear in battle as a way of preparing us for Seneca's own "milder" strain of Stoicism. I introduce these examples with some words about Aristotle's views of fear and courage, for they capture some of our own notions.

BREAKING POINTS

The Aristotelian view of courage, which orthodox Stoics must reject, is that courage requires not entirely overcoming fear but "standing well" with regard to it.[38] That is, one has not suppressed all fear but stands up to it. So courage is a matter of doing what is noble *at a cost*, where the cost is *felt* in the exposure to danger and sacrifice. The person who is excessively fearless, Aristotle insists, would be "some sort of madman or insensible person," "immune to bodily and psychic pain." She would not be a candidate for real courage. But while courage requires experiencing and enduring fear, some dangers, Aristotle remarks, are simply too great to be humanly endured. There is a human breaking point—we might think of it as a "dose response" to toxic levels of terror: "What is fearsome is not the same for everyone; but there is a sort of thing we say it is actually beyond human capacity to endure. This, then, *is* fearsome to everyone—everyone that is, who has any sense or intelligence."[39]

It is unlikely that Aristotle is suggesting a shared breaking point to which we are all susceptible. More plausibly, his notion is that all sensible people will break at some level of catastrophic stress, though just where that breaking point is will vary from person to person. Thus resilience comes in different flavors and strengths. There is no one human standard for what is the limit. More generally, we can say on his behalf that courage requires not immunity from all fear or pain but endurance in the face of them.[40] And even in the very best of us, courage has limits.[41]

Aristotle invites us to think about this second point in more detail, and in a way that will ultimately return us to Stoicism. Courage, he suggests repeatedly, is not blind daring, but a kind of knowledge built on comprehensive experience, resourcefulness, and skill. Like sailors trained to endure the most dangerous seas, we can put up our strongest fights, Aristotle tells us, when we bring to bear relevant prowess and skill.[42] Of course, not all skills that sailors and soldiers bring to war may actually prove useful, and it may be precisely the skills one lacks that are requisite for courage in the circumstances in which one finds oneself. Captain Rick Jolly, a highly decorated Royal Navy surgeon who served in the Falklands War and in Northern Ireland and is now retired, reminded me of the point in a powerful anecdote as we talked one afternoon in his home in Cornwall.[43]

Jolly told me of a high-level parachute instructor who was taken down to the Falklands on the chance that he might be needed to teach special forces there. But as things turned out, he was put to work as an ammunition carrier instead. One night, as Jolly tells the story, the paratrooper was carrying ammunition for a fighting patrol when they came under fire.

> He was on the ground. There were no airplanes, there was no parachuting. There was no place for him to use his special skill. And he was very frightened. He was so frightened that his hands started shaking. He came back to my field hospital as a psychiatric casualty. And I didn't know what to do with this guy because I didn't actually have a psychiatrist with me. . . . And here he was. "I just can't go on," he said to me. Then I had a bright idea and I said, "That's interesting. Come with me."

Jolly proceeded to take the paratrooper to the back of the hospital
where a bomb, planted by the Argentineans, was sitting in the refrigeration
compartment. "This is an unexploded
bomb," Jolly said calmly.

"Fucking hell, boss," shot back the
paratrooper. "Why are you bringing
me here? Jesus Christ!"

"I am happy to be in this building
with this unexploded bomb," Jolly
said, "because I know that it has got
the kind of impact fusing device that
won't detonate unless another bomb
goes off somewhere near it. So I'm
kind of happy to be here. Now, would
you jump out of a balloon that is floating at eight hundred feet?"

"Balloons?" the paratrooper said.
"Yeah. I've got no problem with that."

"Right," Jolly said. "I wouldn't do

Captain Rick Jolly in his home in
Cornwall.

it. Well, maybe to save your life or
maybe if someone like you were to dispatch me and then go with me. But I'm
just not interested in doing it otherwise."

At this point the paratrooper got impatient. "Where are you going with
this story?"

Jolly, a man who likes to tell stories, answered by appealing to a now famous metaphor of Lord Moran, a World War I field medic and later Winston
Churchill's private physician. Moran pictured courage as a bank account.[44]
Courage, like money, either can be withdrawn in one fell swoop, as happens to
those who are suddenly attacked, or just trickles away. In talking to the paratrooper, he puts his own twist on Moran's analogy. We have different bank
accounts with different kinds of courage, he tells him:

> "You've got dollars. I've got sterling. You are a man who does something most of
> us would point-blank refuse to do—jumping out of an airplane at night with
> oxygen. And I am happy to work here with an unexploded bomb.... I don't think
> you are 'psychiatric.' I don't think you have battle shock or anything like it. You've
> just been overdrawn in something that is not part of your normal." And he looked
> at me and said, "Yeah, boss, you're right." And his tremors disappeared.

The story is about breaking points, and about an acknowledgment of the
kinds of fears that can grip a soldier in the course of duty. In this paratrooper's
case, fear makes way not for courage, as Aristotle outlines, but for a paralysis

that prevents him from carrying out his responsibilities. However, Jolly's intervention allowed this soldier to find a way to "stand well" in the face of his fears. And he does this not by arguing that the fear is ungrounded or that a better soldier would stand his ground but by showing the soldier that he too, a senior officer, would break in circumstances in which he felt, in some comparable way, unskilled and unprepared, or simply depleted of strength. His strategy is to empower his subordinate through a candid disclosure of his own vulnerabilities and by acknowledging the role of skill in mustering courage.

In a curious way, there is something Stoic in the message here: the idea of empowerment. Jolly's therapeutic tack is to respect what this soldier can and cannot change, and to suggest that his agency begins there. He urges neither resignation nor retreat, but reflection about what it is to hit one's limits (as in the prospect of Jolly parachuting from an airplane) or to feel supremely confident and in control (as in the prospect of the same descent for the paratrooper). And like Seneca or Epictetus, he is exhortative, though he adds to the Stoic's standard tools of exhortation and example a heavy dose of empathy. Jolly's style recalls Seneca's less well known teaching to Lucilius: "The first thing philosophy undertakes to do is to give fellow feeling with all men—in other words, humanity and sociability" (*humanitatem et congregationem*).[45] The episode is an apt capsule of Jolly's style, for after the Falklands War, he was decorated for his humanitarian kindness not only by Britain with an Order of the British Empire but by Argentina with that country's equivalent decoration for having treated their wounded alongside his own troops. (In one three-week period in the Falklands, he had more than seven hundred British wounded in his unit as well as three hundred Argentineans. When asked afterward whom would he treat first, the British or the Argentinean, "the reply is simple," he said. "The one who is most severely wounded.")[46] After receiving the Argentinean honor, Jolly wrote to Queen Elizabeth to ask if he was permitted to wear the metal on his uniform alongside his British one. Permission was granted.

In the section that follows, we listen again to soldiers' voices about the fear of killing and being killed, and we turn to Seneca and Cicero for help in framing the conceptual issues.

CONCRETE FEAR AND A "MILDER" STOICISM

When we think about war and fear, we tend to think of the fear of being killed, captured, or abandoned on the battlefield. In its traumatic forms, we might think of this as a form of annihilation anxiety. Or we think of a soldier's terror of inadequate first aid on the field, or inadequate medical and psychiatric care afterward. But many combat soldiers fear not only being killed but killing. As Seneca observes, some "meet the sword-strike more readily than they see it dealt."[47] Alfred de Vigny makes a similar point in writing about the Napoleonic Wars: soldiering requires being ready to be both victim and executioner.[48] In what follows, I consider both a soldier's fear of being killed and fear and aversion to killing.

Fear of Being Killed

In the *Iliad,* Hector's final words to Achilles are "Give my body to friends to carry home again."[49] In modern times, dog tags are a response to a soldier's concern to have one's body or body parts repatriated. American dog tags come in pairs—typically, one is worn attached to the boot lace, another hung around the neck. Some soldiers accumulate multiple tags, hoping that the more they have, the less chance they have of dying. They become charms, sacred amulets to ward off death. Anthony Swofford, who served in a scout/sniper platoon in the Marine Corps during the first Gulf War, writes in *Jarhead,* his irreverent memoir of the war, of the mystical faith a soldier can invest in his tags:

> The comfort of dog tags is surrounding yourself with and disbursing so many pairs that there is no way you could possibly die, because your goddamn dog tags are everywhere: in your boot; five pairs hanging from your neck; in your mom's jewelry box; in your girlfriend's panties drawer; buried in your backyard, under your childhood fort; discarded at sea; nailed to the ceiling of your favorite bar ... There's no way a jarhead with that many dog tags—his name and SSN and blood type and religious preference stamped into so many pieces of metal, spread so far and wide—will die.
>
> This is the only true religion.[50]

But not all modern armies afford their troops the solace of reliable body identification. Argentinean troops interviewed after the Falklands conflict of 1982 told of their terror of wearing makeshift dog tags, essentially slips of paper taped onto a small aluminum disk. After a few days of heat and sweat, the writing would run, and the identification would be wiped away. Others, who counted themselves "less lucky," were left to write their names and addresses on their arm in ballpoint ink. Still others wrapped letters from home in plastic and shoved them deep in their pockets, hoping that even if they didn't survive, at least the return addresses on the envelopes might. Fear is still audible in this interview with a veteran: "*Señora,* do you know the terror that it means to a person to think that they will die and no one will know where you are buried? Your mother will never know. Your body will never go back home and no one will ever visit your grave."[51]

This Argentinean's terror of vanishing without record must mark a recurrent theme in the history of warfare. For dog tags are a relatively new phenomenon, with more long-lasting types emerging only during the two world wars and used today by only those countries that can afford the luxury. It is worth recalling that American Civil War soldiers, much like the Argentineans more than a hundred years later, went into battle with their names and addresses written only on paper pinned onto the back of their coat. The slightest amount of mud, blood, or rain could wash away an identity.[52]

Here I vividly recall one of my earliest introductions to the Naval Academy—a "hail and farewell" party for arriving and departing members. As my host, Betsy Holmes, a Navy captain and clinical psychologist, was to explain to me many years later, such events are a ritualized way of "honoring absence and presence" within the military. They are a reminder that despite the frequency of those cycles in a military person's life, absence and presence are never to be taken for granted. In a powerful way, this Argentinean soldier reminds us that *permanent* absence must be honored as well, and he also reminds us of the powerful fear that can attach to leaving this world without markers.

In a significant way, Seneca shows some sympathy with the point. While he will hold that full moral perfection requires facing the inevitability of death with equanimity, he nonetheless maintains that this may be too much to ask of the moral learner, even in advanced stages of moral progress. In this regard, Seneca self-consciously opts for a strain of Stoicism "milder," as he puts it, than orthodox doctrine: "For it is our Stoic fashion," he writes to Lucilius, "to speak of all those things, which provoke cries and groans, as unimportant and beneath notice; but you and I must drop such great-sounding words" and speak "in a milder style."[53] Here, the issue of how to apply Stoic ideals to less than perfect moral beings is clear.

Seneca proceeds to distinguish between what he takes to be an idle, anticipatory fear about future uncertainties and what is, in his view, a more reasonable fear of clear and present dangers. Of the first he observes: "We are in the habit of exaggerating, or imagining, or anticipating sorrow." We let our imagination run wild, and we conjure up "false shapes of evil when there are no signs that point to any evil"; we "twist into the worst construction" some remark we hear. We "catastrophize" events, bringing upon ourselves "unlimited sorrow."[54] We would do better instead to emulate beasts, who simply avoid dangers they see, and put them out of mind once the dangers have passed.

Seneca's point is rhetorical but not without appeal. We do fret about the future in unproductive ways that leave us, and those around us, more anxious than prepared. With respect to war, there is no finer tale of this than that told by Stephen Crane in *The Red Badge of Courage*. The setting is the Civil War, and a youth (whose name is Henry) awaits with anxiety and doubt the decisive moment when he will finally be measured:

> His emotions made him feel strange in the presence of men who talked excitedly of a prospective battle as of a drama they were about to witness, with nothing but eagerness and curiosity apparent in their faces. It was often that he suspected them to be liars. . . .
>
> In his great anxiety his heart was continually clamoring at what he considered the intolerable slowness of the generals. They seemed content to perch

tranquilly on the river bank, and leave him bowed down by the weight of a great problem. He wanted it settled forthwith.[55]

The youth's anxiety turns into a metaphysical inquiry, conducted amid cannon and rifle fire, of whether or not he has the stuff of manhood. World War II bombers experienced what were perhaps less metaphysical versions of this doubt when they faced protracted delays between briefing and takeoff. One Royal Air Force doctor, treating men during that period, reports: "No one who has seen the mask of age which mantles the faces of these young men after a period of continued standing by punctuated by inevitable false alarms, is likely to forget it."[56]

The RAF doctor's remarks are grist for Seneca's mill: anxiety about the future can derail agency. Still, we may object, insisting that some level of anxiety can be adaptive. Current psychological research gives credence to both sides: while *traumatic* levels of stress often impair memory,[57] *moderate* levels enhance it.[58] Moreover, many of us would argue on intuitive grounds that some forms of anticipatory fear, contra Seneca, can lead precisely to the sort of assertive attitude that enables one to plan for and take charge of one's life. Indeed, to have neither fear nor hope about the future, however narrowly that future is defined, is a recipe for powerlessness. It is to take a decidedly non-Stoic stance toward one's agency. In this regard, POWs during World War II reported that although thinking about the distant future was often unbearable, reducing the future to the next hour or day became a way to regain control.[59]

Still, Seneca himself is intent on brightening the stripe between anticipatory fear of the future and fear of present danger. He suggests that the former is futile and idle, the latter more adaptive. And of the latter, he claims, what we fear most are clear and present threats from "the violence of the stronger." More specifically, it is the "visuals" that accompany threatened torture—its "spectacle" and "paraphernalia"—that most engender fear. The "bluster and heralding" of war equipment, the "shock of terror to the eye and ear," can cause dread in a way that the evils of "want and sickness," which "steal upon us silently," typically do not. We might object that the former stimulate *anticipatory* fear, for they symbolize future harm. But Seneca views them as evidence of an imminent threat. The worry is not an idle what-if. The torturer is present with his barbarous equipment. We are at his mercy.

> Picture to yourself under this head the prison, the cross, the rack, the hook, and the stake which they drive straight through a man until it protrudes from his throat. Think of human limbs torn apart by chariots driven in opposite directions, of the terrible shirt smeared and interwoven with inflammable materials, and of all the other contrivances devised by cruelty.... It is not surprising, then, if our greatest terror is of such a fate; for it comes in many shapes and its paraphernalia are terrifying.... Other troubles are of course not less serious;... they

are, however, secret; they have no bluster and no heralding, but these, like huge arrays of war, prevail by virtue of their display and their equipment.[60]

Seneca's remarks are a salvo to his countrymen on the "cruel contrivances" to which Rome has grown accustomed for sport and entertainment. But the cultural polemic aside, his observations help us begin to understand why some objects of fear, in war or peacetime, can traumatize. Certain threats and encounters with violence are traumatic, Judith Herman writes in her landmark 1992 book, *Trauma and Recovery*, "because they overwhelm the ordinary human adaptations to life."[61] Here Seneca makes a similar point. "Displays" of imminent and intimate brutality "coerce and master the mind," leaving us powerless. They overwhelm the human capacity for coping. The brute and violent images—"the disembowelled entrails of men," "human limbs torn apart by chariots," "the cross," "the rack," "the hook," "the stake"—all are meant to convey that human sensory and reactive capacities can absorb only so much before shutting down.

"No man is an iron man," Jim Stockdale reminded me, just as he had reminded his subordinates during seven and a half years of captivity in North Vietnam. At some point, one breaks. S. L. A. Marshall, the World War II military historian, reiterates the point: "There is no such person as the soldier who is dauntless under all conditions of combat. There is no such unit as the company that stays good or the company that is shockproof; there are only companies which are more resolute than others and less likely to break in the face of unexpected emergency or surprise."[62] We have seen that Aristotle insists on this point. This is not surprising, given his embrace of conventional views. But more significantly, so does Seneca in the above passage. It is a point torturers, whichever side they belong to, bank on.[63]

We have seen that Seneca carves a distinction within the category of normal fear between what he views as idle fear of uncertainties in the future and the more justified fear of imminent danger. He goes further: fear of death itself, he argues, is not only natural but, given habit and socialization, not totally misplaced. At the very least, our fears cannot simply be dismissed as trivial worries, nor can they be cured, as the orthodox insist, by rehearsal of syllogism and argumentative tactics. Rather, we must acknowledge the power of the fear and understand how, for the majority of us who are not perfectly wise, violent death may still bear a "semblance" to real evil.[64] In this way, Seneca once again demonstrates that Stoic moral theory must focus not just on the perfectly wise but also on the non-wise individual trying to act in virtuous ways in the face of what most human beings regard as worth fearing:

> But how can you prove to all these men that death is no evil? How can you overcome the notions of all our past life,—notions with which we are tinged from our very infancy? What succor can you discover for man's helplessness?

What can you say that will make men rush, burning with zeal, into the midst of danger? By what persuasive speech can you turn aside this universal feeling of fear, by what strength of wit can you turn the conviction of the human race which steadfastly opposes you?[65]

Seneca goes on to frame the issue in terms of how a military leader can motivate his troops for a charge that both he and his men know will end in certain death:

When a general is about to lead into action an army prepared to meet death for their wives and children, how will he exhort them to battle? . . . They have no hope of victory, no hope of returning. The place where they stand is to be their tomb. In what language do you encourage them to bar the way with their bodies and take upon themselves the ruin of their whole tribe and retreat from life rather than from their post?[66]

Not, Seneca says, by reciting syllogisms about death not being an evil.

Seneca himself has no simple answers. But he does hold that wit and "hair-splitting logic," the "subtleties" of the dialecticians, need to be replaced by examples that can inspire and lead.[67] In his own case, he appeals to Leonidas, the Spartan king who marched on Thermopylae, and who was of such character, according to Seneca's report, that he was able to rally his men simply by saying, "Fellow-soldiers, let us to our breakfast knowing that we shall sup in Hades!" And, says Seneca, the men "eagerly" accepted his invitation.[68] Still, we are not to expect that examples like this are likely to make deep changes in the moral psychology of the non-wise. They may motivate "appropriate" action, but they are unlikely to get the non-wise to see harms and dangers to their life precisely as the wise do—not as things to avoid through *fear*, but as things to be *cautious* of just because most humans do find them fearful and can be tempted by them to act in wrong ways.[69]

Given the overwhelming grip fear has on the non-wise person, Seneca urges that we take measures to fortify ourselves against it. At the top of his list is a frequent and thorough rehearsal of likely future events, which for a soldier would presumably include one's own violent death. For the inexperienced, "a large part of evil," he explains, "consists in its novelty." But "if evil has been pondered beforehand, the blow is gentle when it comes."[70] Continual reflection on the unfamiliar, no matter how imposing the evil, makes for a kind of bulletproofing.[71]

As a prophylactic, prerehearsal of evil has its merits, and there is an obvious application to the military. In this spirit, when Captain Rick Jolly, whom we met earlier, was aboard a ship headed for the Falklands, he showed film clips from his medical work with troops in Northern Ireland. The point was to prepare the units for the sight of the mangled and bloodstained. (With military black humor, the show became dubbed "Doc Jolly's Horror Show.") Still, realistic simulation is no match for firsthand acquaintance with the gruesome. And as much as we may try to inoculate ourselves against stress and fear, preparation can only go so far. Surprise and uncertainty are simply the hallmarks of war. As military leaders are wont to say, "No military plan survives the first shot," and this presumably goes for both tactical plans *and* mental preparedness. Anthony Swofford makes the point from the Marine grunt's perspective:

> What we are about to accomplish, our first combat patrol, will void every training cycle we've participated in, every round we've fired at a paper or twisted-metal target, every grenade thrown at iron dummies. When you take the initial steps of your first combat patrol, you are again newborn—no, you are unborn—and every boot step you take is one step closer to or further from the region of the living, and the worst part is you never know which way you're walking until you're there.[72]

In a later encounter with a fragmentation grenade, Swofford's life stretches before him in a flash. He knows grenades all too "intimately." Indeed, several hang from his body at that moment. But *ticking* bombs are something different. Ultimately, he detonates the grenade without injury. But the moment is one in which he loses his life and then regains it: "If I continue my forward motion I will trip the trap and die horribly. I realize all of this not in the length of that sentence, but in the length of my life, my life strung out thin along the wire."[73] As we picture the scene, it is hard to imagine the toughest among us being in Swofford's shoes without registering some fear.

But if that is so, then the question recurs: how should we understand the Stoic didactic appeal to the wise person who has learned to feel no fear? What can that person teach us? It is important to be clear here. As I have noted, it is not that the wise person wouldn't recognize this as a situation in which most persons do feel threatened. It is precisely because he does that he exercises caution (*eulabeia*) lest those things unnerve him or paralyze him and render him unable to perform right actions. But unlike Aristotle's courageous person, the sage doesn't experience them as actually threatening in themselves. In this sense, he does have a certain kind of insensibility, as Aristotle might charge, even though his cautiousness, in the face of the same circumstances, expresses its own kind of emotional involvement in the fray. However, to return to our question, perhaps the important lesson to learn is the one Seneca himself repeatedly suggests. We shift between two standpoints as Stoic moral aspirants: that constructed by the "great-sounding words" that invoke full perfection and that constructed by "milder" notions of appropriate actions and fulfillment of duties (in Greek, *ta kathēkonta*; in Latin, *officia*). We need both if we are to be committed to a life of ongoing moral improvement.

Fear of Killing

For some soldiers, the greatest threat of war is not their own death, or even that of their friends, but having to kill others. Becoming a killer is what's evil, even if sanctioned by wearing a uniform. We might worry that too thorough-going a Stoicism, if it can really inoculate against fear and aversions such as this, goes too far. Put differently, we seem reassured of the humanity of a soldier when we read in memoirs, by Robert Graves and others, that a soldier finds himself relieved that an enemy (perhaps because he is naked and bathing or squatting to take care of body functions) is not at that moment offering himself up as a target.[74] Might truly effective Stoicism deaden a warrior's soul?

The fear of losing one's soul in war is real, felt over and over again by those who wear a uniform. Rabbi Arnold Resnicoff, a retired Navy captain and se-nior chaplain assigned to General Wesley Clark in the European Command during the war in Bosnia, told me of a colonel who sought him out while serving in Bosnia. "Chaplain," he said, "the Army trains me to kill people and break things. Your job, chaplain, is to keep me from ever getting to a point where I like doing it." The late philosopher Richard Wollheim told me of a similar piece of advice given to him by a commanding officer he deeply ad-mired for his courage on the battlefield: "Never, but never, get to the point where you like war."

The concern is as old as the Old Testament.[75] In Exodus 30:11–16 we learn that each soldier who goes to war must pay a half-shekel to God for ransom on his soul, and in Numbers 31:50 that each warrior who returns must ask for expiation. For Resnicoff, the take-home lesson is that we need to prepare sol-diers better for the role transitions from civilian to warrior and warrior back to civilian.

> I think there should be more of a ritualized coming to terms when the war's over or when you come back, saying that you've done things that would never have been sanctioned in peace, and maybe even you've been part of things that shouldn't have happened in war, but war is not controllable all the time. But let's make the transition. I think that's one of the things that . . . happens in post-traumatic stress—there's no transition back, there's no break back.[76]

While at the European Command, Resnicoff proposed the notion of "spiri-tual force protection," a spin on the buzzword at the time, "force protection"—the minimization of risks in order to bring troops home. In retrospect, he is critical of the principle of force protection—the military went overboard at the time, he says, going for "risk aversion" or "risk avoidance" when it should have gone for "risk management." But he stands by the spiritual version of the principle: "We don't want our people just to come home physically; we want them to come back close to the human beings they were before they went in." That, as the biblical texts suggest, "is not something that you can wait and just start afterwards. It's something that you do before."

We might speculate that one way for the warrior to preserve humanity is simply to hold on to some of the civilian's fear and repugnance at killing. But clearly this doesn't make for battle-ready forces. The point has been borne out in recent history: in a report written in 1947 that would influence decades of subsequent American military training, military historian and retired brigadier general S. L. A. Marshall argued that fear of and repugnance toward killing swept through the American infantry lines during World War II. He claimed that of the infantrymen he interviewed shortly after the war, fewer than one in four reported that they discharged their rifles at the enemy when under fire. The methodology behind Marshall's famous "fire ratio" has since come under heavy fire itself.[77] Still, his general assumptions have been upheld: training needs to meet the natural and strong aversion to killing, and this requires fear and stress inoculation gained through more realistic and rigorous drill. Indeed, from Marshall's time onward, and notably for Vietnam troops, more realistic training has meant target practice that uses pop-ups with human-shaped heads, live ammunition, simulation of likely climatic and terrain conditions of battle, and exposure to the stresses of food and sleep deprivation and of sudden change and unpredictability. (The Marine crucible, the forty-eight-hour final hurdle of Marine boot camp, incorporates many of these training principles. Inductees must don the cumbersome gear they will wear in campaign, such as gas masks and bioterror suits. Sleep- and food-deprived, slithering in muck and mud and enduring an inhospitable climate, they must perform grueling tasks in record time, "leaving no Marine behind.")

Military historians other than Marshall have pointed to the fear of killing that can inhibit the trigger finger. Some note the number of loaded weapons that were salvaged from the battlefield at Gettysburg after the battle. (One author cites some twenty-five thousand muskets as being recovered from the battlefield, 90 percent of which were loaded and 50 percent of which in turn were loaded more than once.)[78] Stephen Crane fictionalizes a related Civil War scene in *The Red Badge of Courage*: Henry, the protagonist of the story, himself had no rifle. But if he wanted one, "rifles could be had for the picking. They were extraordinarily profuse."[79] Crane also makes clear that in war, responses to fear include not just flight and fight but "posturing."[80] The youth is an expert at posturing. He stays close enough to the edge of battle to seem to be a participant; he mingles with and gives aid to those who have fought and are taking their last breaths; he even suffers his own vicarious war wound, a head contusion for which he is tenderly treated by a member of the regiment. In short, he engages in a mock battle, not so much to fend off the enemy as to stay in the war without facing its risks.

Consider a slightly different form of mock battle I learned about at a conference I attended in Santa Barbara, California. After hearing a lecture on some of the themes of this book, a member of the audience approached me and told me about his brother, a graduate of the Naval Academy who served in Vietnam as a Navy SEAL (a member of an elite special operations unit). One skirmish changed the direction of the war for him: the moment he killed a fourteen-year-old boy, himself armed and poised to kill first. The incident soured him on killing, and from that day on, he exercised "his right to miss." Others quietly joined his conspiracy, and his unit soon gained a reputation for being "unlucky." Indeed, despite all its show of gunfire, it kept scoring low body counts. True, in the case of these soldiers, "unsuccessful" fire was probably less a function of fear than of a principled aversion to killing in a war they could not in any way justify. But in other, more popular wars, fear may be the more intuitive explanation for retreat and/or mock battle.

Earlier I suggested that some residual aversion to killing, even in uniform, might be a healthy sign of the humanity of the soldier, and I was concerned that taking too seriously Stoic lessons on inoculation against fear might deaden that humanity. In some sense, the problem is one of role transitioning: how to overcome one's aversion to killing while in uniform but then regain it in the return to civilian life. Put this way, a Stoic text explored earlier, in Chapter 3, is relevant and insightful, and it may serve as a partial response to the worry that Stoicism is dangerous in its focus on inoculation against fear.

Recall that in *On Duties*, Cicero, following the Stoic Panaetius, proposes four roles or personae we routinely take up in life: our shared human nature (for a Stoic, this means our shared rational natures), our individual temperaments, our accidents of history and circumstance, and our chosen careers.[81] In the career of soldier, certain actions and attitudes are fitting (*to prepon*, in Greek) that would not be so in the circumstances we face as civilians. And though we may come to that role of soldier with temperamental differences in regard to levels of fear or anxiety, still, certain attitudes and types of conduct befit the soldier, however difficult those may be to adopt or to shake when our roles change.

On this view, role switching requires flexibility and control, as well as perhaps a certain amount of genuine role playing. This is a point, as we have seen, that the Stoics emphasize often, especially when it comes to the emotions. But in one's role of sharing humanity with others—the most basic role, on Cicero's view, for which "we have been dressed, as it were, by nature"[82]—an underlying aversion to killing humans may very well persist even in the role of soldier. And, as in the quote from Graves earlier, it may be at moments when one's opposite number herself seems most clearly to suggest the shared role of fellow human that the underlying aversion is felt most strongly. A good soldier may allow his humanity to prevail at such a moment, though he is ready to revert to the role of killer the moment his opposite more clearly takes up the role of target. And similarly, a good soldier leaves behind the very role of killer when she takes off her uniform and returns to the career paths of civilian life. This is not to say that any such role switching is easy or that we want a soldier in war ever to become too comfortable with the role of killer. The moral challenge of war is always to hold on to one's humanity, especially as one kills. There are just and non-just ways to kill in war, in terms of who is a legitimate target and what is a legitimate weapon. These are meant to protect not just others' humanity but our own. Our humanity is always a constraint on our role as warrior.

Thus Cicero's notion of the multiple roles we assume in life tidies up the thought that duties and personae in one station of life ill fit those in another. And his notion of the shared persona of common humanity anticipates the modern notion that all soldiers are equals, whichever side they fight on.[83] As we have just seen, this notion has deep consequences for how soldiers justly conduct themselves in war. But the metaphor of assuming and shedding masks is limited. It cannot capture the enormousness of the psychological and spiritual challenge involved in the role shifts. How could it? For assuming roles is just that. To take on a role doesn't begin to address how one lives out one's life in that role with authenticity and calm. One of the most moving accounts of the challenge of reintegrating into civilian life after war is told by Erich Maria Remarque in his World War I novel *The Road Back*. His story is one of broken German soldiers tied to each other and to a war that has been lost, of men severed from their fathers and mothers and wives because the latter have no idea of what it is to live for years in trenches, with souls shattered by the sound of shells and the smell of burning flesh.

The story is an all too familiar one—of men and women who have fought in war with bravery and then have returned home with broken souls. It is time to ask some hard questions, using our own contemporary vocabulary: What is psychological trauma? What is resilience? The questions are modern, but I ask them with an eye on Stoicism. For in rather surprising ways, certain Stoic notions anticipate contemporary ideas about empowerment and resilience.

TRAUMA AND RESILIENCE

"Without warning, Prior saw again, the shovel, the sack, the scattered lime. The eyeball lay in the palm of his hand." In *Regeneration*, Pat Barker's remarkable World War I novel, set in Craiglockhart, the wartime psychiatric hospital outside Edinburgh, images of the eyeball keep intruding in Billy Prior's life. A benign mark on the door turns into a large veined eyeball, "an eye in the door," staring out at him with accusation. An innocent gaze turns into a "gob-stopper." The eyeball, he now finally remembers during hypnosis with the pioneering psychiatrist W. H. Rivers, belonged to one of his buddies. Prior had been on trench watch, finally enjoying a lull in the battle after a bombardment that had gone on for seventy hours. As he patrolled, he chatted with Tower for a moment while Tower and his trench mate fried up some bacon for their breakfast. One moment later "he heard the whoop of a shell" and turned back to find Tower's trench reduced to a conical black hole with little else recognizable. As he began to shovel out the trench, pouring the charred flesh and blackened bone into a sack, Tower's eyeball stared back at him from the debris. Prior delicately reached for it and rolled it into the palm of his hands. His hands started to shake, but "the shaking didn't seem to be anything to do with him." "'What am I supposed to do with this gob-stopper?' he blurted out."[84]

Prior, like the other trauma victims in this novel (which features the British World War I poets Siegfried Sassoon and Wilfred Owen as well as Rivers), relives his trauma through intrusive thoughts, flashbacks, hyperarousal, and nightmares.[85] But he also avoids it through emotional numbing, voluntary and involuntary forgetting, avoidance of circumstances that cue painful memories, and dissociation, which in the extreme becomes a form of multiple personality disorder. So Prior sometimes experiences Jekyll and Hyde moments, where in one role he becomes amnesiac about what he has done in the other. For some, dissociation is not just a post-traumatic symptom but an analgesic for coping with the acute stress of the actual traumatic event itself. Brian Ahearn, a hostage during the invasion of the American Embassy in Lebanon in the early 1970s, reports having survived his ordeal by disassociating himself from the identity of the victim: "it is not me suffering this," he convinced himself.[86]

By the time of Vietnam, the shell shock or neurasthenia of the First World War had come to be known as post-traumatic stress disorder. More specifically, in 1980, with the American Psychiatric Association's inclusion of PTSD in its *Diagnostic and Statistical Manual of Disorders, Third Edition*, PTSD formally became a diagnosis.[87] The diagnosis melded together insights from two rather separate communities—those who were at the time observing traumatic stress in rape victims and those who saw similar responses in returning Vietnam vets.[88] While PTSD still tends to be associated with Vietnam vets, it is,

The anguish of a recurrent nightmare.

as its early history suggests, a disorder specific neither to that population nor to combat exposure in general. It is diagnosed in men, women, and children, Western and non-Western groups, and individuals at all socioeconomic levels. Even so, Vietnam veterans have been among those most studied. The National Vietnam Veterans Readjustment Survey (conducted 1986–88) estimates that the lifetime prevalence of PTSD among American Vietnam theater veterans is 30.9 percent for men and 26.9 percent for women.[89] An additional 22.5 percent of men and 21.2 percent of women have had partial PTSD symptoms at some point in their lives. Thus more than half of all Vietnam veterans suffer from "clinically serious stress reaction symptoms."[90]

In an unprecedented early assessment of war-related psychiatric disorders in the ongoing wars in Iraq and Afghanistan, Charles Hoge of the Walter Reed Army Institute of Research found the prevalence of PTSD among those returning home from combat in Iraq to be 15.6 to 17.1 percent, and 11.2 percent in those back from Afghanistan. The assessments were made three to four months after the veterans returned home. Among soldiers and Marines who had been deployed to Iraq, the prevalence of PTSD increased linearly on the basis of the number of firefights the service member had experienced. One expert commenting on the study warned, though, that these early estimates may be conservative. A previous study of Gulf War veterans suggests that the prevalence of PTSD may increase substantially during the two years after veterans return from combat deployment. Also, on the basis of a study of military personnel returning from Somalia, there is reason to believe that a shift in the way war is prosecuted, from a campaign of liberation to guerilla fights with insurgents, is likely to lead to an increase in psychiatric disorders.[91]

But however new PTSD is as a diagnosis and area of research, the disorder itself is far from new. Descriptions of the phenomena are in the ancient literature we have already reviewed. Achilles's unbridled rage and survivor guilt after the loss of Patroclus might well be an early description of PTSD and its secondary symptoms of excessive anger, shame, and guilt. And certainly Aristotle and Seneca's acknowledgment that some horrors are too great for humans to endure is early testimony to the possibility of psychic breakdown in the face of extreme stress.

In its early days as a diagnosis, PTSD was generally thought of as a "normal response to abnormal circumstances." The normalcy of the response is a crucial acknowledgment of human vulnerability—an acknowledgment that goes against Stoic orthodoxy. But Matthew Friedman, executive director of the National Center for Post-Traumatic Stress Disorder, views the second part of the definition as the problematic bit. PTSD, he insists, can no longer be viewed as exposure to "*unusual* events." Traumatic exposure is simply not that unusual. He cites a major epidemiological study in which it is estimated that 50 percent of the American population will be exposed in their lifetime to traumatic stressors, with the estimated lifetime prevalence of PTSD among adult Americans at 7.8 percent.[92] In countries with post-conflict settings, such as Algeria, the PTSD rate climbs to 37 percent. "Stress is a part of life, like death is a part of life," he soberly reflects. If it is a kind of disease, then we should immunize against it, or at the very least fortify resilience. And if we do it right, he insists, we should formulate a national policy about exposure to traumatic stressors (be it war zone exposure, rape, or the events of 9/11) in the same way as we have thought about other dangers (e.g., anthrax) or epidemics (polio or rubella). On this view, resilience and coping rest in no small measure upon being prepared.

In a certain way, the Stoics take on a similar advocacy for resilience. Their preoccupation, after all, is to find equanimity in the face of life's vicissitudes. But would an enlightened psychiatrist endorse any aspects of the Stoic project as part of a reasonable conception of resilience? To ask a different but parallel question, could an enlightened commander, psychologically sensitive to human frailty, in good faith draw on Stoic notions of resilience and strength?

To each of these questions I would say both no and yes. Recall that for the Stoics, the way to fortify oneself is by beginning to devalue the impact of externals on one's conception of happiness. In contrast, what is distinctive about contemporary research on PTSD is that it does *not* minimize the external. Indeed, PTSD is unique among psychiatric disorders in that the etiological agent is viewed as lying outside the individual. There is simply no diagnosis of PTSD without exposure to an external event that in some objective sense is considered a traumatic stressor.[93] In this regard, PTSD requires a clear reality factor. Of course, few within the psychiatric community would deny the Stoic point that stress is to some degree a matter of individual perception and that reactions will vary depending upon, among other things, individual thresholds and attitudes toward anxiety and stress. But still, they insist, the presence of traumatic stressors is a necessary condition for PTSD, even if not sufficient. Catastrophic, external circumstances can derail the best-lived life. Moreover, and this is key, researchers insist that PTSD is a normal and reasonable response to extreme stress. It is a function of neither moral weakness nor mental pathology. So to the extent that an orthodox Stoic would deny this and would hold that what most of us would consider catastrophic circumstances *ought not* (in a moral and psychological sense) occasion traumatic fear or stress, the Stoic and the enlightened psychiatrist part ways.[94]

But what of how they might agree? PTSD, according to the latest revision of the *Diagnostic and Statistical Manual,* is a reaction to traumatic events where one experiences "intense fear, helplessness, or horror."[95] Traumatic events here paradigmatically include "actual or threatened death or serious injury to self and others," but they are not limited to these, in that events that are not life-threatening or injurious can be traumatic stressors that elicit intense fear and helplessness.[96] Losing a home to fire or flood comes to mind. Generalizing, then, the defining features of a traumatic event are lack of control over what is happening, the perception of the event as a highly negative experience, and suddenness or unpredictability.[97]

Now let us consider a Stoic text. In reporting the position of the ancient Greek Stoic Chrysippus, Cicero strikingly singles out the three criteria above (though he reverses the order and notes internal conceptual connections). Distress has as its object events that happen suddenly, that are evaluated as having a serious negative impact on one's life, and that one believes oneself incapable of preventing:

> [Some] hold that distress rises when something 1) unexpected has occurred, and at no other time. And as I said before, suddenness is indeed a major contributor. Chrysippus is of the same view, I know: what is unforeseen strikes us with greater force. But there is more to it than that. It is true that a sudden assault of the enemy creates rather more confusion than an expected one, and that a sudden storm at sea strikes more fear into those on shipboard than if they had seen it coming.... But if you were to study such events carefully and scientifically, what you would find, quite simply, is that when things happen suddenly, 2) they invariably seem more serious than they otherwise would. There are two reasons for this. First, there is not enough time to gauge the seriousness of what is happening. Second, we sometimes think that 3) if we had foreseen what was to happen, we might have been able to prevent it, and then our distress is keener because compounded with guilt.[98]

The passage is prescient and must be one of the earliest documents to show with such insight and systematicity the psychology and logic of what we would call traumatic stress. Cicero concludes by even calling attention to the guilt survivors often feel in not being able to foresee and prevent disaster. "Our distress is keener because it is compounded with guilt" (*culpa*), by the thought "I should have been able to prevent it." If we return to our earlier question of whether there are elements of Stoicism on which the contemporary psychiatrist and psychologically enlightened commander can draw, the answer has to be yes.

Cicero's remarks focus on the cognitive conditions necessary for the negative condition of trauma or severe stress. Underlying the view is the fundamental *positive* Stoic point that well-being depends upon a sense of control and agency, a sense that even in the most constrained circumstances we are not entirely powerless. Virtue represents the true form of that agency, and it is fortified through rehearsal of likely future scenarios. Anticipation thus becomes a way of inoculating against the unknown, a way of strengthening agency against circumstance. The strategy seems quixotic, but not entirely. Skill, foresight, and experience *do* help us face disasters in ways that we couldn't if we were unschooled. Moreover, researchers such as Friedman and his colleagues argue that simply knowing that PTSD can occur in the face of catastrophic events is itself a form of emotional preparation that can leave one more resilient: "Knowing that certain kinds of reactions are normal, that this is not an indication that you are 'losing it' is a critical coping strategy."[99]

Of course, the Stoics do not have preparation of this sort in mind. It is not that they deny that many will respond to catastrophic events in this way and so, in a sense, that the response will be statistically normal and even expected. It is that more often than not (with perhaps Seneca's "milder" style as an exception), they take the exhortative stance, with the sage as the definitive benchmark.

But given this benchmark, the congruence with contemporary researchers on what is key to resisting distress or fear is all the more striking. Both Stoics and contemporary PTSD researchers concur on the transformative power of the belief that one can carve out some domain of control even in the most constrained of circumstances. In the case of Vietnam POW Jim Stockdale, cultivating an Epictetan sense of agency meant that he constantly set himself the task of devising ways to make his torturer work for the information he demanded. Even at his breaking point, Stockdale could still assure himself that tomorrow was a new day, another opportunity to put challenges in the path of his captor.[100]

For others, the agency on which resilience hangs may be less a matter of cunning than the bringing to bear of specialized skills and knowledge. Consider the following vignette told by a PTSD researcher:

> The second author once worked with a group of rafters who had been caught in unexpected rapids in which equipment had been lost and young children had nearly fallen overboard. For the four experienced adult rafters, all of whom could swim well and believed that the team's joint skills were adequate to master the rapids, the experience was negative and arousing, but none showed PTSD symptoms afterward. Of the three inexperienced rafters, who trusted neither the capacity of the team nor their own capacity if thrown in the water, two had severe and one mild traumatic symptoms.[101]

Of course, it is naive in the extreme to expect that even the most experienced and skillful can ever be fully armed against the future. In the case of battle, whatever one's level of readiness, there will always be the fog of war. Still, one cannot do without the psychological and physical protection that skill brings.[102] Both contemporary research and Stoic thought agree on this.

There is one final set of issues to consider in thinking about the light Stoic doctrines shed on contemporary notions of resilience and stress. This is the Stoic view of emotions as constituted by evaluations or judgments and, correlatively, the notion of effecting emotional change through changes in these constitutive evaluations. Central in the successful treatment of PTSD patients has been cognitive behavioral therapy.[103] The approach is multi-pronged. One prong is exposure therapy that aims to undo avoidance symptoms. According to this model, a patient is typically "flooded" with a conditioned stimulus that cues her to painful memories (perhaps of a rape or captivity) that in the past she has avoided through numbing, disassociation, depersonalization, or the like. Now, in the context of a supportive therapeutic relationship, where she can tolerate the painful stimuli without immediately fleeing, the patient revisits and relives and, most important, reintegrates the traumatic experience into her life.

A second prong of cognitive behavioral therapy has more explicit affinities with Stoic practice. Here the core notion is that of cognitive restructuring.[104] That is, patients are encouraged to revise the automatic and erroneous thoughts that ground traumatic symptoms. Imagine a rape victim who later, both during sex and in moments of reliving her trauma, has the recurrent belief that she is dirty and has voluntarily sinned by being a victim of rape.[105] Or imagine a veteran who suffers PTSD after he accidentally kills a buddy in a friendly-fire incident. The survivor is tortured by thoughts that he is incompetent and guilty and that he "should have known better." Moreover, he believes that the world is an overwhelming place, one in which he has come to feel helpless much of the time. Those thoughts reinforce avoidance behavior and a retreat from constructive action. In such cases, the goal of cognitive therapy is to bring the patient to correct distorted beliefs and to renarrate the story in a way that more accurately reflects the limits of the sufferer's control and knowledge.

Stoic antecedents for this kind of therapy are easy to find, and in the next chapter I shall be considering some in detail. Briefly, the Stoics insist that we can transform emotions by modifying the opinions that constitute those emotions. Exhortation, persuasion, and dialogue are the tools used for such restructuring.[106] Though the Stoics substantively worry about the falsity of exaggerating the importance of externals in our lives, the formal point is one that contemporary cognitive therapy works from, namely, that our evaluations of situations ground our emotional responses to them, and that modifications in evaluations make possible emotional changes. The Stoics go on to suggest that evaluations are "chosen" and that we are responsible for our emotions in so far as we voluntarily assent to the judgments that constitute them. Cognitive restructuring proponents might plausibly resist this aspect of the account and endorse a different view of responsibility—perhaps one that looks not to the volitional *history* of an emotion but to its here-and-now links with beliefs we explicitly and implicitly hold. In this model, our responsibility for emotions becomes closer to the notion of responsibility for judgments in general. For example, the rape victim who is in cognitive therapy would be asked to take responsibility for the judgment that she has sinned, in light of her other beliefs and commitments. If she cannot rationally defend the view, she may be motivated to modify it, so that it ultimately better reflects her overall commitments. But this is a complex matter, and to delve further would take us too far afield.

In this chapter, I have touched on many aspects of fear and its control. I have assessed the notion of replacing fear with a sage's rational caution, and the cost in terms of acknowledging human vulnerability. I have discussed the stern side of orthodox Stoicism, but also Seneca's milder strain and his acknowledgment of the fears that a moral aspirant could appropriately and honorably experience. I have considered both the fear of dying and the fear of killing and the challenge of transitioning from the role of soldier to civilian. Finally, I have taken up contemporary notions of trauma and resilience and Stoic notions that might be seen as congruent with them.

But what I have not yet said anything about is perhaps the most commonsense point of all—that camaraderie can fortify a soldier against fear of death and killing. Let us listen again to the voice of the youth, Henry, in *The Red Badge of Courage:*

> He suddenly lost concern for himself, and forgot to look at a menacing fate. He became not a man, but a member. He felt that something of which he was a part—a regiment, an army, a cause, or a country—was in a crisis. He was welded into a common personality which was dominated by a single desire. For some moments he could not flee[,] no more than a little finger can commit a revolution from a hand.[107]

The image is one Marcus Aurelius, the great Roman general and Stoic author, also invites us to consider. We are social beings, he insists, constituted almost organically for fellowship: "If you have ever seen a dismembered hand or foot or a head cut off," you will have an image of what a person makes of herself if she cuts herself off from others.[108] In the next two chapters, we will take up the critical role of solidarity in a warrior's life—in Chapter 6 in the context of grieving and in Chapter 7 in the context of the competing aims of self-command and attachments to community.

When I am alone all my conversation is with books, but it is interrupted by fits of weeping, against which I struggle as best I can. But so far it is an unequal fight.

—Cicero, *Letters to Atticus* 12.15

Sergeant First Class Paul Ray Smith was killed in battle during an Army push to take the international airport in Baghdad on April 4, 2003. Moments before his death, he killed, on his own, twenty to fifty Iraqis, allowing the safe evacuation of wounded soldiers and saving an aid station and some one hundred lives. In those last moments, he told one of the men in his units, "We're in a world of hurt." His wife, Birgit, and son, David, now cope with that world of hurt. Birgit worries about their son: "I haven't seen the boy cry," she said. "I'm afraid sometimes he doesn't let it out." She remarks that his father, Sergeant Smith, was like that. He cried only once, she recalled, in their ten years of marriage. They were watching a documentary about the first war against Iraq in 1991, a war in which Sergeant Smith had also fought. He never mentioned the crying incident again.

—Adapted from Steven Lee Myers,
"Medals for His Valor, Ashes for His Wife,"
New York Times, September 23, 2003

And, sir, it is no little thing to make
Mine eyes to sweat compassion.

—William Shakespeare, *Coriolanus,* Act 5, Scene 3

Permission to Grieve

——————

STOIC AMBIVALENCE ABOUT GRIEF

During World War II, the *Queen Elizabeth I*, Cunard's luxury liner, was reoutfitted as a floating hospital, bringing a thousand American soldiers back and forth from Europe on a crossing. From 1940 to 1944 my father, Seymour Sherman, served as an Army medic on board, making some thirty-two round trips. The outward-bound ship served as a prep ward, for inoculation, morale boosting, and training. The homeward-bound ship bore the stain of war. Loss filled the space, with quiet tears for torn-off limbs and for buddies left behind. It was "a butcher shop," my father says, fighting back tears; the men's raw arm and leg stubs looked "like fresh cut meat hanging from a butcher's hook":

> On a nice day, during the summer, the surgeons would line the wounded on the deck, wrapping them up in blankets on their litters. And they would go through their rounds: "You're going to lose a leg, but in eight weeks, you'll have a prosthesis; the war is over for you." And to another: "You will lose an arm and a leg."[1]

"Anyone who tells you war isn't hell," he lectures me, father to daughter, "has got it wrong." The taste of World War II is still in my dad's mouth, though it took him over forty years to tell me his story, and for me to ask.

Grief, on the Stoic view, is a form of pain or distress, and thus in principle it is to be eliminated. More precisely, like other ordinary emotions that are derivatives of pleasure, desire, fear, and distress, grief is directed at circumstances beyond our control. It is directed at the kinds of goods toward which we ought to be indifferent, in the sense of not craving them as part of our happiness. That is, we must be neither appetitive nor possessive with regard to the conventional goods that lie beyond our full dominion (such as health, wealth, and the continued life of family members and friends) and, conversely, neither fearful about losing them nor distressed at their loss. Bereavement, no less than friendship and love, requires a kind of Stoic equanimity. Thus Seneca says that we should cultivate toward friends and loved ones the attitude that "I have had them as if I should one day lose them, and I have lost them as if I still have them."[2]

The recommendation sounds like wishful thinking. It is one thing to bear the memory of another, and something entirely different to live as if the past were no different from the present. And yet many a reflective person, amid grieving, has sought solace in Stoic doctrine. Cicero himself, distraught over the death of his most beloved child, Tullia, in childbirth, immerses himself in Stoic consolatory literature and then writes his own consolatory letter to himself (in a work now lost). His extant *Tusculan Disputations,* to which we will turn in this chapter, is itself a consolation of sorts, written just six months after Tullia's death, with death and grief still explicitly on his mind. Though not a Stoic himself, Cicero remains attracted to Stoic doctrine, and his exposition in the *Tusculan Disputations* of Stoic therapy is one of the finest ancient treatments we have on the subject. His commitment to exploring philosophy as medicine for the soul is announced in the beginning of that work and then again toward the end: "Let us therefore look to see what remedies philosophy has to offer for the sicknesses of the mind. For there must surely be some curative art. Nature would have had to be very unkind . . . to invent so many means of cure for our bodies, and none for our minds."[3] In the hands of the Stoics and their expositors, philosophy becomes psychotherapy, a way of healing the mind by rowing with the "oars" of dialectic.[4]

Seneca, writing a hundred years later in letters to Lucilius on the bereavement of his close friend and to Marullus on the loss of his son in childhood, also prescribes Stoic psychotherapy for the abatement of grief. But these consolatory epistles (63 and 99), like Seneca's epistles taken as a whole, are as much directed at Seneca himself as at his correspondents: "Listen to me, therefore, as you would if I were talking to myself." Seneca is at once the Stoic "doctor" and the patient "lying ill in the same hospital."[5] The epistles become a pretext for self-therapy. In Epistle 63, he concedes the conceit: he is one of those overcome by grief, he says, referring to the death of his friend Serenus.[6] Anguish and grief are all too familiar to him. Like all of us, and despite his most ardent Stoic efforts, he remains a patient, a progressor, a non-sage.

Indeed, this is part of the attraction of reading Seneca (and Cicero, in his Stoic moments) on grief. Each is caught in the fray and knows intimately not only the anguish of human sorrow but also the aspiration to be in control. As we have said before, Seneca, in much of his writing, flip-flops between palpable empathy for human suffering and a zealous drive to find rock-bottom resilience. It is tempting to mock this as some version of moral weakness, intellectual waffling, or simply hypocrisy: with regard to the latter, he is no former slave, as is Epictetus, who can preach having lived firsthand through the very deprivations the Stoics and Cynics urge. In stark contrast, Seneca sits in the innermost circle of a massive imperial court in the center of Rome. He is Nero's tutor and political advisor, his spin doctor and publicist. He will suffer the loss of loved ones as well as political exile to Corsica, but an Epictetan life of slavery is not in the cards for Seneca. Moreover, the ascetic habits he seems to maintain from adolescence into older age—sleeping on a hard bed, refusing to eat oysters and mushrooms—began as a matter of choice rather than necessity.[7] Still, I suggest that we can frame Seneca's conflict sympathetically as an honest struggle for self-reliance and inner virtue in a world that is by and large outward-directed and socially dependent.

This tension we find in Seneca between the conceptions of ourselves as at once self-sufficient *and* socially dependent are all too familiar to military men and women. Be "an army of one," the new U. S. Army recruitment slogan reads. Promoters say it is targeted at Generation Xers, but the ideal of self-sufficiency, if that is the underlying message, is one that has long run deep in the military soul. To get physically toughened, to endure separations from loved ones, and to see the face of horror without retreating are all billed in the military as matters of inner strength and courage. They are forms of self-reliance, ideals for military character. Yet few fighting men or women would ever advance on a front unless they trusted that they were flanked by those who would risk their lives on their behalf. Unit cohesion, camaraderie, and the brotherhood/sisterhood of arms are as much a part of a conception of military values as is self-reliance. Indeed, many who have served would argue that bonds in the military are often tighter than those between husband and wife. The very point of breaking down and rebuilding the self in boot camp is precisely to forge a new identity in which being a member of a particular group or unit or cause becomes all-important.

The cost of forging that new social identity—indeed, the cost of being a social being in general—is that self-reliance or self-sufficiency will always, in some ineliminable way, be relational. Aristotle put the point simply but profoundly when he reminded his listeners that we are *zōē politikē*, political or social creatures, and the brand of self-sufficiency we must cultivate is *kath'heteron* (in relation to one another).[8] The social and cooperative nature of military operations is obvious.

Emotionally, fighting men and women must also remember that they are social creatures. Grieving for loved ones and losses—whether it be fallen buddies or families from whom one must be separated for what can seem an eternity—is an expression of that social nature. It is an expression, too, of vulnerability—an acknowledgment that developing an attachment to others brings with it a vulnerability to their loss. The Stoics urge, in their sterner moments, that we can enjoy friendship in a way that doesn't become possessive or subject to profound and lasting grief. This Stoic ideal can resonate deeply with warriors who must continue with missions amid carnage and devastation, and who have learned, often too well, to stave off grief and its expression. In this chapter I argue that the question of how and whether one should grieve is reflected deep in the dialectic of Stoic discourse itself. Strict Stoic doctrine may call for dissociation from distress and grief. But in the more practical discourses of Seneca and Cicero the question remains, in an interesting way, open.

I begin with several objections Seneca raises to specific forms of grief as well as his own proposals for acceptable forms of grief. I then turn to Cicero's analysis and his recommendations for both the reduction of grief and its cure. Throughout, I generously draw on illustrations from the military as ways of assessing Stoic claims.

SENECA ON TEARS AND DECORUM

Seneca begins his letter to Lucilius by urging that he not grieve more than is fitting (*aequo*). "That you should not mourn at all I shall hardly dare to insist." But there is decorum even in grieving, and the limits are to be set by the limits of reasonable self-control.[9] Tears that fall, "no matter how we try to check them," are permissible; they may be genuine expressions of grief that "ease the soul." There are other "natural" tears that accompany involuntary kinds of (pre-emotional) expressions, beneath the threshold of full emotions, like "pinches of pain" or mere "stings."[10] They don't threaten tranquility, and even the sage can shed them without compromising his dignity. However, tears that are *voluntary*—feigned, "indulged in" for theatrics—are morally objectionable and an improper expression of grief:[11]

> But suppose that I forbade you to show emotion; there are certain feelings which claim their own rights. Tears fall, and by being shed they ease the soul. What, then, shall we do? Let us allow them to fall, but let us not command them do so; let us weep according as emotion floods our eyes, but not as much as mere imitation shall demand.[12]

Several claims are implicit here. First, Seneca's lesson is primarily to moral aspirants such as ourselves, who will (and morally may) cry but still need to find decorum in our tears. Second, while some amount of involuntary crying may be appropriate, keening (that is, over-the-top weeping) is indecorous. Third, we are to understand that crying has a gendered identity. Indulging in tears in general, and worse, keening, is "womanly," soft and effeminate (*molliter*). Marullus, Seneca instructs in Epistle 99, should fortify his manliness by curbing his tears.

It is hardly novel to note the connection of crying with the weakness of women. In the ancient world, perhaps the most illustrious example is Plato's portrait of Socrates's death scene, in which he urges his followers, Crito and Phaedo among others, not to cry. After all, the women were kept away from Socrates's cell precisely to avoid the histrionics; are these men now going to take their place?[13]

Still, it would be wrong to think that the wail of grief heard in the ancient world, especially during Greece's archaic period, was strictly a woman's. In the Homeric world of the *Iliad*, men cry like babies, publicly and profusely, over lost comrades, and they join the women in their wailing. Consider the moment in which Achilles learns of the death of Patroclus:

> A black cloud of grief came shrouding over Achilles.
> Both hands clawing the ground for soot and filth,
> he poured it over his head, fouled his handsome face
> and black ashes settled onto his fresh clean war-shirt.
> Overpowered in all his power, sprawled in the dust,
> Achilles lay there fallen . . .
> tearing his hair, defiling it with his own hands.
> And the women he and Patroclus carried off as captives
> caught the grief in their hearts and keened and wailed,
> out of the tents they ran to ring the great Achilles,
> all of them beat their breasts with clenched fists,
> sank to the ground, each woman's knees gave way.
> Antilochus kneeling near, weeping uncontrollably,
> clutched Achilles' hands as he wept his proud heart out—
> for fear he would slash his throat with an iron blade.
> Achilles suddenly loosed a terrible, wrenching cry . . .
> and his noble mother heard him . . .
> and she cried out in turn.[14]

At the end of the *Iliad*, Priam and Achilles, Trojan and Greek together, reunite and weep—Priam for his beloved son, Achilles for his beloved friend, slain by Priam's son. The reciprocity of their loss cuts through their enmity. Each knows the other's anguish as if it were his own. No act of simulation is needed here for empathy. The synchrony couldn't be more finely attuned:

> Priam wept freely
> for man-killing Hector, throbbing, crouching
> before Achilles' feet as Achilles wept himself,
> now for his father, now for Patroclus once again,
> and their sobbing rose and fell throughout the house.[15]

Thus, archaic warriors are permitted to grieve openly and in the bosom of their enemy. By the time of Plato's writings and continuing through the later Stoics, however, a man's public wailing has become distasteful, performance art cheapened by the fact, as Seneca says, that it can be turned on in the presence of onlookers and turned off with their departure.[16] In contrast, the unforced tear soon after a death of a beloved can be forgiven. (Indeed, he warns that he is not advising the griever to be "hard-hearted" or "to keep your countenance unmoved at the very funeral ceremony.")[17] But a tearstained face violates male ideals of dignity, gravity, and authority.[18]

Seneca's warning about excessive or feigned tears is not a recommendation to forget the dead. "To forget the beloved dead, to bury their memory along with their bodies," is the mark of a creature more lowly than man.[19] Still, he insists that grief—traditional mourning through tears—is not the best way to remember. Grief dwells on what can't be recovered rather than what still remains. We should "continue to remember, but should cease to mourn":[20]

> What resource do we find, then, in the face of these losses? Simply this—to keep in memory the things we have lost, and not to suffer the enjoyment which we have derived from them to pass away along with them. To have may be taken from us, to have had, never.[21]

The underlying issue for Seneca is once again that of reducing vulnerability. And we can achieve this if we focus not on loss but on the good of what has been, and if we conceive of the past as settled and risk-free. The "past is ours, and there is nothing more secure for us than that which has been." It is over and done, something we can look at with equanimity.[22] In essence, Seneca is saying, remember loved ones in a non-sticky, non-jealous way. Savor the memory without wishing and hoping for what could have and would have been. Be content with the good times that have passed. Don't cling to them in a way that makes you long to relive them. Seneca's tips are not without therapeutic appeal, and yet the underlying psychology is naive. First, current loss is often more raw than past loss. The challenge is to assuage the hurt, as if with the passage of time. But second, the past, no less than the present or future, is subject to our will, projections, and fantasies. We reconstruct both the content and tone of the past and alter our "official" histories as we, and others, add fresh input. We may come to peace with some bits of the past or be freshly disturbed by others. Nothing that the mind can rake over is ever fully fixed.

TEARS AND WARRIORS

Seneca's dismissal of tears as womanly and weak is entrenched within our own culture, and in a particularly deep way within the culture of the military. This bias can be dehumanizing and psychologically stunting. At a certain point a boy who cries, though still tender in years, becomes a "sissy" and violates an implicit "boy code." Tears, along with expressions of fear and sadness, are regarded as soft "girl stuff," while expressions of anger and aggression are considered acceptable boy behavior.[23] Girls can cry before one another, but boys must conceal their sorrow. Boy tears of exhaustion, desperation, or fear are weak stuff, to be dried well before they leave telltale signs. In *The Soldier's*

Return Cumbrian novelist Melvin Bragg evokes a powerful image of this. The protagonist, ex-corporal Sam Richardson, returns in 1946 from the war against the Japanese in Burma to find that his son Joe, age seven, has become a mama's boy. Too many tears and too many cuddles have softened him, or so it seems to Sam, himself hardened from years of battle, often "fought out hand to hand, ancient warfare against the fanaticism of a cruel warrior race."[24] The sound of Joe's sobbing distresses Sam. He would have to toughen the boy, cure him of being a "sissy." On an evening walk with his parents to the train station in Carlisle, Joe himself suddenly seizes upon his act of manhood, the act that would win back his father's respect. He would cross the narrow outside ledge of the bridge that spanned the train platform. It was what big boys did; he had seen them inching along like crabs, clinging with their hands to the masonry top of the bridge. His father would look on admiringly from below. But Joe's hands were small and his new sandals didn't grip the thin ledge well. He felt himself slipping just as he heard the train to Carlisle edge toward the station. He was directly over the line the train was using. He began to whimper, but his little hands kept inching across. Seconds before it reached the bridge, the train came to a hissing halt, just in time for Joe to scuttle the last few feet. Then the ordeal was over, and Joe found himself in his father's arms. "You are a little warrior! That's what you are, eh? A real little warrior."[25] Sam Richardson had heard sobs "rarely and in extremis and from gravely stricken men" caught in the hell of war. Acknowledging that these tears could be compatible with manhood was hard enough. But the sobbing of a boy, who knows no real sorrow, was inexcusable.

I remember a revealing story told to me by Betsy Holmes, a retired senior Navy captain and former psychologist at the Naval Academy. "Is it ever perceived as fitting for a commander to shed tears before the troops?" I asked. She thought, and then answered me as one woman to another: at retirement, in acknowledging the debt a commander owes to his or her spouse (typically a male referring to his wife), a commander's tears are viewed as "touching, a chivalrous gesture." "Shedding a tear of love and gratitude toward one's wife," she said, shows one's personal side in a public arena from which one is formally exiting. But then her tone changed to a guarded, critical one, and she said that a male commander is not expected to shed tears at other times, at least not in public and before others in uniform.

Jonathan Shay, a psychiatrist and author who works with Vietnam vets, is committed to breaking this image. In lectures to the Navy and Marine Corps, he argues passionately that proper decorum within the present military must allow officers to shed tears—real tears of loss and not just those that gesture at chivalry. In *Odysseus in America,* Shay's second, Homeric Vietnam narrative, he interweaves his message with the story of the homecoming of Odysseus and his struggles as a returning vet:

Odysseus' encounter with dead comrades in Hades can be seen as a metaphor for the pervasive presence of the dead in the inner worlds of some combat veterans. They are truly "haunted." I have thought long and hard about how such haunting can be prevented, and now believe that the answer lies in changing the modern American military culture on grief. After battle, once it is safe enough for everyone to sleep, it's safe enough to grieve; and the unit should do this together with the unit's direct leaders setting an example with their own tears. [26]

Shay's message is that crying in grief need not be without dignity, gravity, or authority. Nor need a leader's grief be restricted to a private moment, concealed from subordinates. Collective grieving, after the fray of battle but not long after a death, can provide the crucial moment of solidarity needed for owning grief and for beginning the process of healing. Many would argue that the human cost of indefinitely deferring grief is all too palpable among Vietnam veterans. It has left far too many broken, unable to love at home, unable to demobilize their warrior psyches.[27] In some it has exacerbated post-traumatic stress disorder.

As I write, during the second U.S. war against Iraq, collective grief work seems a more familiar notion. Thus, within a day or two of the death of fifteen soldiers when their Chinook helicopter was struck down near Al Asad, Iraq, in early November 2003, the units to which the personnel belonged held memorial services. The deaths so shocked the greater air base in Asad that three days later the commander in charge ordered a regiment-wide memorial service. The memorial service proceeded in full battle alert mode, with the regiment, some several hundred soldiers, all wearing desert fatigues and carrying rifles and sidearms. A picture on the front page of the *New York Times* shows a soldier preparing for the memorial: he meticulously plants rifles, muzzle first, into a display stand erected on a flatbed truck. A helmet is carefully balanced on top of each rifle. Dog tags dangle from the ammunition clips. The dead soldiers' boots form a line in front of the helmeted rifles. The story goes on to report that a number of soldiers pay their final respects at the flatbed truck, which has become a makeshift alter. Some "saluted or bowed," others "knelt or wept."[28] In this example, soldiers, predominantly male, do not only honor the dead—something the military has always left room for—but grieve for them. Grieving is permissible, as is weeping in grief.

Recognition of the need for soldiers to grieve is also a lesson that retired Royal Navy captain Rick Jolly brought to his troops who served in the Falklands. On Remembrance Day in November 2002, he along with some two hundred other veterans returned to the site of the battles they had fought twenty years earlier. Despite the decisive British victory, the short war had cost about 250 British and 650 Argentinean lives, with the British suffering their largest losses at sea, in the sinking of their ships. Jolly had earlier implemented one of the first Web site memorial gardens, a "virtual graveyard," as he told me, for South

Mourning at a base in Iraq.

Atlantic war veterans. Many of the veterans lacked physical graves in either Britain or Argentina. Families and war buddies yearned for public remembrance and a hallowed place. The trip to the Falklands was a continuation of the process of remembering and healing. Permission to shed tears was to be an explicit part of the remembrance. I spoke to Jolly in his home in Cornwall a few months before the trip. He was juggling phone calls, e-mails, and faxes in an effort to garner support for the fall trip:

> We'll take two hundred and thirty down. We ought to take two thousand, but there is no way to do it. And we are going to help them get better. . . . They'll go to a place like Mount Longden, climb the hill, stand at the big stainless-steel cross on the top with the names engraved on it, and just burst into tears. . . . They'll leave a poppy for each guy at the site where he was killed. And they will burst into tears and they will feel the load lifting from their shoulders, because at last they've had a chance to say goodbye.[29]

But it was one thing for Jolly to tell his British troops it was okay to cry. It was another for his soldiers to actually grant themselves permission. In a diary of the pilgrimage back to the Falklands, one entry captures Coriolanus's struggle to sweat tears of grief:

> On the day we all went to San Carlos, after the ceremony was over I stood outside the gates to the memorial just watching the huge range of emotions shown by my fellow pilgrims, I saw an ex-matelo [former sailor] struggling with his emotions. I was making my way to him to offer some comfort and support but, an ex-guardsman got there first. . . . This is how it went:

Guardsman: "You look like you need a hug"
Matelo: "But I don't know you"
Guardsman: "I won't tell if you won't"

The men embraced each other offering kind and supported words for a couple
of minutes, they shook hands and went their own way.[30]

In their own way, these soldiers reenact Seneca's worries about the decorum of male, warrior tears. Jolly invites us to recast Seneca's concerns in slightly different terms: "I always say strong men do weep. It's part of their strength. But you don't cry in front of your subordinates; you don't walk around sobbing, 'We've had a battle and I've lost eight of my men.'" But service members do cry at funerals in the field, and privately in their tents at night, and in returning to the battlefields where they fought. "No one would think anything less of the guy. . . . He is simply a human being that cares."[31] Thus in this case military decorum sets boundaries for what is seen as fitting, but not without regard for our humanity. Jolly's intuitive notion of humanity includes not just reason, as the Stoics emphasize, but our propensity for emotions as well as our need to acknowledge loss as important and as potentially affecting our happiness.[32] The last point is critical. In a follow-up study Jolly conducted after the pilgrimage to the Falklands, 76 percent of those who went reported that they felt better or much better with regard to all aspects of their life than they did before the trip. In addition, they found they were able to reduce their medicine and alcohol intake. Sixty-five percent of spouses and family members agreed that their mates' moods were markedly improved after the trip.[33]

From the point of view of the discussion so far, the overall lesson is that soldiers may weep over loss, even if there are rules of decorum. This seems to me a most important lesson for all soldiers to heed. In its emphasis on decorum, it gestures toward Stoic concerns in a liberating way.

I want now to return briefly to Seneca's more positive point—that remembrance must constitute the substantive part of grieving. Though Seneca problematically casts the past as imperturbable, his general point, that grieving involves a commitment to remember the dead, is uncontroversial. For those who have died in battle, war memorials are both historically and in our own times a part of the remembrance ritual. They etch a name in stone for present and future generations to come to know and honor. When Maya Lin conceived of the Vietnam Veterans Memorial as part of a senior-year architecture project at Yale, she had in her tactile memory four years of running her fingers over the names of Yale veterans etched into the marble walls of Wolsey Hall, which students pass through on the way to class. As her fingers traced the grooves, she felt the presence of those who bore the names. She came to believe that a geometrically simple memorial—a V descending ten feet into the ground at its vertex—bearing no symbols other than names inscribed in granite

A photograph by Lance Corporal Graham Paulsgrove
of a fellow Marine, Captain Edward Rapisarda, in Iraq:
"I . . . only snapped four frames, because I did not want to
impede his mourning."

would offer a powerful form of remembering. The memorial, like the one she
knew at Yale, would invite touching and rubbing, a direct, sensory contact
with a name.[34] But it would invite tears too.

For Shay's Boston-based veterans program, a spring trip to the Vietnam
Memorial in Washington, D.C., is the culmination of PTSD therapeutic work.
It is a time for remembrance, and also for tears. The group arrives at 3 a.m., in
the undisturbed hours of the day, when they have the wall to themselves and
can commune, in the fellowship of each other, with the dead. Shay describes
the moment:

> For many the first visits are pure grieving. Some of the veterans are physically
> very large men. A six-foot-three Marine Corps veteran weeping his heart out in
> the dark, hugged by other veterans, is a profound thing to witness. The support-
> ive presence of the trusted other veterans eliminates embarrassment. They do
> not have to go through it alone.
>
> Some veterans fear the Wall because they fear the dead will reproach them—
> for having not done enough, for having survived when the men on the Wall—"in

the Wall"—did not. The polished stone reflects the movements of the veteran along its surface giving sensory credence to the sensation that the dead are present.[35]

We can imagine Seneca reacting to the above as follows: Graves and war memorials ought to be about communion and remembrance, not about the irreversibility of loss or the guilt of being a survivor. One should psychologically be able to pry apart these reactions, remembering and keeping the dead alive, communing with them, without the futility of tears or the rage that struggles to undo loss. But these are "oughts" for later stages of grieving. Seneca himself admits that decorum in grieving is not so easy to come by. "He who writes these words to you," he confides to Lucilius, "is no other than I, who wept so excessively for my dear friend Annaeus Serenus."[36] His own tears of grief may have been indecorous, but not necessarily futile nor feigned.

In an interesting way, the kaddish, the Jewish mourners' prayer, carries a faint hint of Seneca's wish to eclipse loss from a mourner's remembrance of the dead. Although recited every day for a year following the death of a loved one, it makes no explicit mention of death or loss. Rather, it is sanctification and magnification of God's name. From the root word *kadosh,* the name of the prayer means "making holy God's name," and it implies a justification of God's judgment to end a life. Kaddish offers a ritual time to commune with the dead, but in a way reminiscent of Seneca's notion of commemorating the dead, it does not explicitly invite mourning. This has puzzled many, and in Talmudic fashion, the explanations are lengthy and enigmatic.[37] But tellingly, one Hasidic rabbi in the nineteenth century, with military matters clearly in mind, finds it necessary to insert loss back in his commentary on the kaddish:

> The saying of rabbi Bunim of Prysucha about the reason for the mourner's kaddish is well known. . . . In the ordinary world, when a small unit of a large army is lost, the loss is not felt, and it is not until an entire division is missing that the depletion must be corrected and the army must be reinforced. It is otherwise, however, in the army of God. If only a single Jew is missing, then there is already a lack in the greatness and the holiness of God. Therefore we pray that His name may be "magnified and sanctified," that is, that His blessed Name may be made complete for what it has lost with the disappearance of the deceased.[38]

The remarks pit war's faceless statistics against a mourner's faith that the death of each soldier diminishes the overall wholeness and goodness of being. In the army of God, the commander in chief knows when a single person is missing. The mourner prays that the armies of the world may know the same. We might ultimately wish Seneca to concede a similar point: that loss of a beloved—a husband or wife, or son or daughter in war—can diminish our overall good or happiness (*eudaimonia*). But to concede this would undermine a cornerstone of Stoicism.

CICERO ON THERAPIES FOR GRIEVING

In the wake of Tullia's death in the late winter of 45 BCE, Cicero retreated from public life to a country residence. He did little but read and write in an attempt at self-cure. In this letter to his dearest friend, Atticus, written roughly a month after Tullia's death, he begins to articulate ways of coping with bereavement that he will formalize in the *Tusculan Disputations:*

> It is like you to want me to recover from my grief, but you are my witness that I have not been remiss on my own behalf. Nothing has been written by an author on the alleviation of grief which I did not read in your house. But my sorrow is stronger than any consolation. . . . I write all day long, not that I do myself any real good, but just for the time being it distracts me. . . . And I try all I know to bring my face if not my heart back to composure, if I can. While I do this I sometimes feel I am committing a sin, at others that I should be sinning if I failed to do it.[39]

Immersion in consolation literature—the self-help books of the time—is Cicero's first step toward self-cure. If nothing else, he reasons, it's a distraction. He also tries posturing, hoping pretense will turn into sincerity. But it's not easy to be a poseur, he confides, when the loss is as profound as his. It's a sin not to try to put on a good face, but it is also a sin to misrepresent his heart. Still, he concludes, some Stoic feigning is necessary for his public persona, and for his sanity. His absence from Rome, ten years after the fall of the Republic and Caesar's rise, was already cause for suspicion. Only one month after Tullia's death, he needed a formal note of excuse to explain his absence at a function in Rome. He feigned physical illness.[40] A week or so later he wrote to Atticus, "I seek the lonely places; though if anything happens to bring me back to Rome I shall do my utmost, if it lies in my power (and it will), to make my grief imperceptible to everyone but you." But it's still just posing: through consolation literature "I reduced the outward show of grief; grief itself I could not reduce, and would not if I could."[41]

Cicero points here to a limited cognitive and behavioral therapy that he will endorse more robustly later, when his own grief subsides. As he will put it (redacting the teaching of Chrysippus, the third of the ancient Greek Stoic patriarchs, after Zeno and Cleanthes), even if one cannot (or chooses not to) change underlying beliefs about the importance of one's loss, how one *reacts* to those beliefs may be changed. Indeed, in the *Tusculan Disputations,* Cicero will endorse a mild form of Stoic therapy directed at outer comportment. But here, when Cicero's grief is at his rawest, even this is medicine too hard to swallow.

With this as a preface, we can turn to the *Tusculan Disputations* and the therapeutic strategies it reviews.[42] Though Cicero's own grieving is for a daughter who died in childbirth, his remarks have wide application, whether the loss is on the battlefield or at home. In the third book, Cicero considers five therapeutic techniques for preventing and alleviating grief. The techniques are eclectic, drawing on different ancient schools, but ultimately Cicero will champion the Chrysippean method, which focuses on control of outer comportment.

(1) Some hold that the comforter has only one responsibility: to teach the sufferer that what happened is not an evil at all. This is the view of Cleanthes. Others, including the Peripatetics [i.e., the followers of Aristotle], would teach that it is not a great evil. (2) Still others, for instance, Epicurus, would draw attention away from evils and toward good things, (3) and there are yet others who think it sufficient to show that nothing has happened contrary to expectation. And the list goes on. (4) Chrysippus, for his part, holds that the key to consolation is to get rid of the person's belief that mourning is something he ought to do, something just and appropriate. . . .

But with sicknesses of the mind, no less than with those of the body, it is important to choose the right moment for treatment.[43]

To this list, Cicero adds a final technique:

(5) Remember, "that you are not the only one to have this happen."[44] Many before you have loved and lost. And they have endured in their suffering.

A twenty-first-century psychotherapist would find the list a motley assortment of the helpful and harmful. Cicero seems to share that view. He begins his list with the orthodox Stoic intervention of trying to persuade the sufferer that "what happened is not an evil," or, in the related Peripatetic move, that it is not a *great* evil. For those who have suffered fresh losses, Cicero protests that this is clearly not "the right moment for [such] treatment." Indeed, it would be peculiar consolation to try to persuade Cicero a month after his daughter died that her death is an indifferent that ought not affect his happiness. Not only would the timing be off—medicine administered when the patient's mind was too "swollen," as he puts it—but the therapy is overly intellectualized and assumes that the ordinary patient, or even a Cicero, is on the verge of Stoic enlightenment about values.[45] So Cicero comments, his own case clearly in mind, "I pass over the method of Cleanthes, since that is directed at the wise person, who does not need consoling. For if you manage to persuade the bereaved person that nothing is bad but shameful [i.e., vicious] conduct, then you have taken away not his grief, but his unwisdom. And this is not the right moment for such a lesson."[46]

The second technique listed is the Epicurean method of distraction, of diverting attention away from evils to pleasures one has enjoyed in the past or will enjoy in the future. The method doesn't try to change values, but rather simply redirects focus, so that the patient comes to dwell on the good rather than the bad. The technique has its practical merits. We do try to help those bereaving to take their mind off grief, sometimes simply by offering our company. But deep losses aren't easy to put aside, and even if they vacate conscious thought, they can return with a vengeance in sleep. Moreover, Cicero argues, once the Epicurean concedes that pain not only feels bad but is the greatest evil, the game is up and the patient loses all motivation to resist:[47] "It is not within our power to forget or gloss over circumstances which we believe to be evil, at the very moment they are piercing us. They tear at us, buffet us, goad us, scorch us, stifle us—and you tell us to forget about them?"[48]

The third technique is a preventive method: we are to anticipate or prerehearse evil, "show that nothing has happened contrary to expectation." The method is practiced by several ancient schools. Seneca returns to it regularly, as does the Stoic Epictetus; here Cicero invokes its Cyreniac or early Epicurean roots. The core claim is that anticipation of future evils can minimize the sense of helplessness that overcomes us when unforeseen calamities strike. In this connection, Cicero repeats the famous response of the pre-Socratic Anaxagoras upon learning of the death of his son: "I knew my child was mortal." Epictetus spells out the drill: through daily prerehearsal, we are to remind ourselves of the mortality of loved ones, kissing them each morning as if it might be the last time. Prerehearsal, Cicero explains, becomes a way of exploiting, in prospect, time's natural healing power.[49]

Immunization techniques of this sort have some appeal. Contemporary trauma specialists urge, as I noted in the last chapter, that combatants should know in advance the kinds of psychological reactions that tend to come with trauma (e.g., panic attacks, combat-alert states of readiness, flashbacks, etc.) in order to alleviate some of the anxiety they are likely to feel should they start to enact them. But awareness of this kind is one thing, and routinely premeditating one's morbidity is another. Some might argue that that sort of preparedness is more a recipe for depression than equanimity. Cicero's own response is that prerehearsal may work, but if it does, it requires embracing Stoic views of what is in fact evil.[50] As with healing that comes with time, it is not the passage of time itself that heals, but the kind of change of views that time makes possible. And not everyone is sufficiently "enlightened" to have those changed views.

The fourth view, which Cicero ultimately defends, is the Chrysippean view of monitoring and changing one's outer response to a felt emotion. The change requires revising a judgment of appropriate comportment. I shall say more about this momentarily, but first I need to say a few words about the fifth and final Stoic intervention. Here the therapist urges us to remember that "we are not alone" and to find inspiration in "wise sufferers [who] have endured" with dignity before us.[51] Taken in a positive light, the intervention might be seen as a kind of rallying gesture, a way of offering support from a community of fellow sufferers. But this is not how most of us would, in fact, experience the remark. Rather, we'd feel it deflationary and lacking in any genuine empathy. In moments of despair, few of us are comforted by the thought that others suffer worse than we do. Like children, what we want instead is some acknowledgment of our feelings—some "mirroring," to use therapy talk. Cicero is not unaware of the point. The good therapist, he insists, must be a skillful artist who knows "the needs of the moment," the "nature of the case," "the persons involved," and "what sort of cure each hearer is able to accept."[52] Present-day psychotherapists would find little to criticize in this piece of advice.

But let's return now to the fourth Stoic method—the one that Cicero favors and employs repeatedly in his own bereavement. In the background is the Stoic conception of emotions as two-tiered opinions. In the case of grief, there is the opinion/belief that a bad thing has taken place, as well as a further opinion/belief about how it is appropriate to respond in light of that judgment of evil. Here, in an intriguing way, Cicero is returning to the notion of decorum, discussed in Chapter 3, and ultimately giving a more theoretical account of how it is that we can take control of aspects of our comportment:

> But when our belief in the seriousness of our misfortune is combined with the further belief that it is right, and an appropriate and proper thing, to be upset by what has happened, then, and not before there comes about that deep emotion which is grief. It is this latter belief that gives rise to all those despicable forms of mourning such as smearing oneself with dirt, scratching at one's cheeks like a woman, and striking oneself on the chest, head, and thighs.[53]

Full-blown Stoicism requires that we deny the first belief (that a serious misfortune has taken place). Cicero objects, pointing to the impracticality of the method—it would require being a sage and getting rid of all of our unwisdom. A milder and more pragmatic Stoicism works on only the second belief, about what constitutes appropriate comportment. This thinner therapy would be open to those, including Cicero himself, who maintain that the loss of a beloved *is* in fact a bad that can undo happiness but who nonetheless want to act in a way that shows more composure than the person in the throes of grieving typically does. In principle, the intervention is a form of Stoic cognitive empowerment. The task is to make the mourner aware that many of her responses to grief are voluntary and based on implicit assent. If, through reflection, she can undo an assent to what she comes to view as inappropriate behavior, then she may be in a position to assent rationally to other judgments about what she regards as more fitting. Cicero's own prejudices (whether Stoic or simply Roman) enter—that one will rationally reject traditional lamentation rituals and assume a quieter kind of "male" dignity. But the actual principle is neutral as to content. The key point for the griever to realize is that *experiencing* an emotion such as grief and *acting* on or *expressing* it can be conceptually decoupled. To change *how* one grieves doesn't require denouncing one's grief. In some cases, as we have suggested in earlier chapters, to enact what is fitting may involve role playing—putting on a good face, "posing."

But we may think that the Stoics simply go too far here. Surely not all of the ways we manifest our emotions are voluntary or could be voluntary. Indeed, we cannot control everything about facial expressions. Blushing and pallor may come upon us without assent, and trembling and teeth chattering also.[54] While we may sometimes make our teeth chatter, it is harder to turn ourselves white as a ghost. And some of us have eyes and mouths that naturally take on certain looks, despite our best efforts at tweaking expression. Moreover, even when we can control our faces, we still may not bluff the gifted reader of faces who can discriminate the sincere agent from the poseur.[55] In short, changing the outer component of emotion, especially when it comes to facial expression, may be quite different from changing other aspects of comportment that have to do more properly with intentional, voluntary behavior—for example, hugging out of affection, or saluting out of respect.

As we have seen, the Stoics tend to relegate expressions of emotions that are involuntary to preemotional phenomena. As such, they fall below the threshold of proper emotion and its expression. But the line between preemotional phenomena and full-blown ordinary emotions is fairly arbitrary, and the Stoics can be criticized for shifting the line to suit their needs. Trembling that doesn't impugn a sage's equanimity is preemotional. It is residue that shows up now and again; it is a benign "bite," they like to say, like a twitch or a tickle.[56] But an expansive or contracted spirit, the sort of mood that *we* may think of as involuntary, they are prepared to gloss as voluntary and intentional, the result of a belief that one thinks "it is right" to swell the mind, or "to lower and contract it," as in the case of grief.[57] In this sense, the Stoics may overstate the control we have over our emotional reactions and, in a question-begging way, disqualify phenomena as not properly emotional when they cannot easily be reined in.

Still, we should not lose sight of what is central to Cicero's therapeutic claim. A Stoic therapist can urge her patient to make behavioral changes without necessarily insisting on *radical* underlying value change. In the case of grief over a friend, a patient need not give up the profound sense of loss even when imposing on herself an outer look of decorum and control.

The view has implications for the military. One may accept the appropriateness of being Stoic in one's bearing without accepting deeper Stoic doctrines about elimination of ordinary emotions or reduction of vulnerability. And like Captain Jolly, one may hold that certain occasions require Stoic decorum more than others. Of course, even this thin Stoic doctrine may demand too much control of us. Our behavior may flow spontaneously from our felt emotions in ways we cannot always check. But Cicero's claim is that we are more likely to be able to fake calm decorum than experience it authentically from changed views. And, I would add, it may be far healthier, in the case of loss of loved ones, to be a Stoic only in this thin sense.

Of course, the orthodox Stoic will not be satisfied, for on the orthodox view, loss itself must come to be viewed as no longer a genuine evil. However, Cicero challenges a part of this doctrine by suggesting that even if loss of a friend is not, on strict Stoic grounds, a real evil for which to feel grief, ought not moral failing be an evil that *does* warrant legitimate grief? Cicero reminds his readers of a scene from the *Symposium* in which Alcibiades weeps before Socrates in shame over his moral imperfections. Won't such grief, Cicero asks, be directed toward just the kind of deficit—namely, the absence of virtue—that is, for an orthodox Stoic, the only genuine evil? But despite the philosophical challenge, Cicero's real purpose in raising the point is not to take a theoretical stance, but to push the Stoic into a pragmatic posture, like the one he embraces above. True, in principle, the Stoic purist should allow grieving over one's own vice. But even if one does, the key point is in the choice of behavior by which one responds to loss. Crying over one's character will do little to change it; a greater commitment and effort at virtue will.

But Cicero seems too ready to join the Stoic view that tears are futile and pointless. In the *Poetics*, Aristotle famously puts forth the rejoinder that the expression of certain emotions can be cathartic and a medium for enlightenment and purification. He has in mind an audience's response to tragedy and the learning that takes place through the mimetic responses of fear and pity. In a parallel way, however, grief as a response to failure and tragedy in our own life can itself stimulate cathartic tears, not unlike those an audience sheds in learning of more remote losses. Tears may signal an occasion to reflect more deeply about what the tears represent. They may offer an opportunity to acknowledge a loss or sorrow, which in the absence of that external sign we may try to deny or forget. I am reminded of a CNN interview with a Marine who served in Vietnam. He sought his own defense from war's hurt by limiting his war friendships to two. "Two," he repeated to the interviewers. That way he would have fewer to grieve for.[58]

We have seen in this chapter how Seneca and Cicero struggle with the Stoic renunciation of grieving. Seneca's response is to find ways of grieving with decorum. But in recasting memory as a sanitized form of mourning, he fails to appreciate memory's own power to disturb and uproot. Cicero makes the more formal point that we can seek to be Stoic on the outside without having to be Stoic within. Again, the central point is about Stoic decorum. The military leader may embrace these points, upholding the importance of a calm exterior amid war's horrors. But the cost of denying or deferring grief's natural expression must never be underestimated. It is one thing to find the right time to grieve openly and authentically. It is another to defer that grief indefinitely. The latter course denies both the dead and the living their due.

And still the memory of the Company haunts me and wrings my heart and I hear them saying, "When's the Captain coming back?"

—Siegfried Sassoon,
The Memoirs of George Sherston

It wasn't until the newcomer mentioned that he wished he were back in Iraq that anybody else chimed in. "I miss it, too," another soldier said. . . . "I wish I was in Iraq because my buddies are there."

—Sara Corbett, "Coming Home:
The Permanent Scars of Iraq,"
New York Times Magazine,
February 15, 2004

Bottom line, we will follow our conscience and do what is morally right.

—Major General Antonio M. Taguba before the
Senate Armed Services Committee,
recalling his orders to his subordinates
commissioned to investigate the abuses
in the Abu Ghraib prison in Iraq

7

The Downsized Self

AN "ARMY OF ONE"?

As we have seen, central to Stoicism in almost all its forms are the notions of self-command and self-reliance, autonomy and an "in-control" agent.[1] The ideal of a "Stoic warrior," in this view, becomes one who has the inner resources necessary for coping in the most dire straits. This may fall short of vanquishing an enemy single-handedly or surviving the most violent blows. But it does suggest that psychological resilience is largely a matter of inner strength and of limiting dependence on and vulnerability to others. Epictetus fastens on this notion of self-reliance as a facet of the virtue of steadfastness: "If you want anything good, get it from yourself."[2] Some seventeen centuries later, Ralph Waldo Emerson echoes this Stoic sentiment in his celebrated essay on self-reliance. Those who have the virtue of self-reliance know that the "secret of fortune is joy in our own hands."[3]

Yet it is easy to see that the virtue of self-reliance, if taken to the extreme, is a flawed ideal that constricts our social and emotional natures. We live and flourish in communities. Some of these communities are "found" communities, like the families we are birthed or reared in; others are communities by choice, as marriage and the military are for some. It is in the context of these social structures that we frame our ends and achieve them. As Aristotle put it pointedly, making clear our distinct status from the gods, we are social and political animals, and our brand of self-sufficiency is always relational (*kath'heteron*).[4] The point is a truism within the military. Aviators, sailors, Marines, and soldiers serve within hierarchically nested groups of units. They serve alongside some, and above and below others: they are horizontally and vertically bound. The motivation to fight hangs in no small part on solidarity, and ideally on a respect that travels upward to the commander in chief and downward to the lowliest grunt. Moreover, successful military operations are

characteristically collaborative matters that rely on concerted effort and a complex choreography of skills.[5] Anyone who has witnessed the split-second timing with which planes catapult off and tailhook onto an aircraft carrier knows
well the precision and grace that choreography can have, and the price of mistake. There is no "army of one," despite the U.S. Army's Madison Avenue logo.
To be in the military requires a self-sufficiency that is social to the core.

But can Stoicism, with its stress on self-command and autonomy, adequately
address this deep social fact about military character? Are there elements in its
teaching that help us understand the camaraderie, respect, and empathy that
motivate military men and women and give them a source of strength in the
hell of war and its aftermath? Readers who have come this far will not be sur-
prised to learn that the report is mixed. Stoicism's anxious concern to armor
the individual against the vulnerabilities of externals can be self-defeating if,
as we should expect, a good part of our strength and resilience comes precisely
from connectedness to others, who, on Stoic views, must be counted among
those externals. On appreciating the role of friendship and the contribution of
attachment emotions to psychological and moral sustenance, Aristotle and
his followers simply do better.[6] And yet the Stoics, in their own way, do not
turn their backs on community. They try to accommodate it formally in a
manner that preserves individual autonomy within a larger community. More
precisely, they claim that as persons with reason, we are fellow citizens in a
global or cosmopolitan community. Piggybacking on a Cynic notion, they create a cosmopolitanism that is meant to include but reach beyond natural affection and mutual acquaintance to the kind of respect that strangers, even
enemies, can have. The ideal is the seed for enlightenment theories, such as
Kant's, and for natural law theory before that. I cannot tell those stories here.
But what I should like to indicate in this last chapter is how a lesson in Stoic
cosmopolitanism might have helped to avert the U.S. Army's Abu Ghraib prison
abuse scandal that unfolded as I was writing in the late spring of 2004.

I turn to that case at the end of this chapter. Before doing so I discuss nearer
forms of community that are at the heart of military service and which any
military leader ignores at her own peril. In particular, I look at camaraderie as
a critical element in combat courage and resilience, and as essential to psychological recovery in the aftermath of war. Though at times I borrow from clinical and research psychology, I bring the issue back to Stoicism and argue that
Stoic notions of self-reliance and self-mastery can be only partial elements of
a healthy sense of resilience and humanity. Emotions of love, friendship, and
attachment must be included in a more complete account. That more complete account must also include ways of relating to and respecting those who
are more distant and different from us, whether because of national borders,
religion, or ethnicity—or, worse, because of a demonization process that can
be part of war's portrayal of the enemy. Here Stoicism is extremely illuminating, with clear lessons about the roles of respect and empathy necessary for

building a sense of humanity and global community. I begin by presenting three cases—three *exempla*, as Seneca would put it—that underscore the role of camaraderie in self-sufficiency and, ultimately, human well-being.

TWINS AND COMRADES IN ARMS

The Case of Milt and Murray Friend

On June 6, 1944, an auspicious day in world history, Milton Friend, a twenty-two-year-old second lieutenant in the Army Air Corps, was on the second mission of his first European tour with the 15th Air Force.[7] The twelve-plane formation was to bomb the Ploesti oil fields in Romania. It was common knowledge that the target was the most dangerous that could be assigned to the 15th— one year earlier, 80 percent of American planes venturing into the area had been destroyed. Even on the night of his flight, Milt noted that the sky was so blackened by flak that he momentarily wondered how planes could survive in the sky. But fear was not something you could harbor and still fly, so as Milt put it, the thought evacuated his mind as quickly as it had entered.

Just as the bombers were over the target and about to release their bombs, another American squadron came right under them. Milt, as navigator, had to find a heading for an alternative target. All was going well, and just as they were coming off the new target, Milt announced to his crew that in half an hour they'd be "back at the Red Cross base drinking coffee and eating doughnuts." Seven minutes later, his B-24-H, the lead plane in the squadron, was attacked by German Me-109 fighters and caught fire.

The pilot immediately gave the order to bail out. Milt was behind the nose gunner turret in the navigator's compartment. He waited for the gunner to evacuate, but the gunner's heavy sheepskin-lined boots (notorious for the clumsiness they imposed on their wearer in a tight plane) had caught on the turret control pedals, and he had trouble breaking free. Finally, the gunner broke loose and gave Milt the okay to exit. He jumped, but his chest chute caught on the bay door, and he began swinging in the slipstream. (In World War II, members of the military didn't make practice jumps. So all his training came in a rush to his mind, not to his muscle memory.) It was fifteen seconds of swinging in the wind. But then, after what seemed an eternity, the wind did him the favor of loosening him from his mooring. With the parachute still attached to him and intact, Milt at last pulled the rip cord. Two German fighters buzzed near him, and though they had been known to shoot parachutists, they didn't shoot him. He finally landed, his parachute caught again, this time on tree branches, in a town 120 miles southwest of Belgrade. Milt's story of survival is in part due to the care of Chetnik forces under General Dragoljub-Draza Mihailovich, who played a role in one of the largest air evacuations of Allied airmen, an operations that came to be known as the "Halyard mission."

Milt told me this story on a beach in Florida some sixty years later. He munched on a Krispy Kreme doughnut as he began his story (perhaps the doughnut was an echo of the one he never got to have at the Red Cross base sixty years earlier).

Milt's tale is one of courage and adventure. To this day, he doesn't quite understand why he wasn't paralyzed with fear. But as I pressed him, he insisted on two points to help explain his resilience.

The first is this: when Milt's chute finally opened, his thoughts briefly went toward the memory of a beloved grandfather, an Orthodox Jewish immigrant from Russia, whom he and his twin brother, Murray, had adored. The boys would often ask for their grandfather's help when they were in trouble; he was their spiritual guardian. Milt reckoned that he had helped, spiritually, this time too. The grandfather had died a few months before Milt had gone into the service; he had, in fact, died in Milt's arms. The attachment to this beloved grandfather was Milt's lifeline. He was with Milt as he dangled in the air.

The second has already emerged: Milt is an identical twin. His brother, Murray, was also an aviator during World War II, though at the time of the shoot-down, Milt had no idea where he was stationed. Throughout their childhood in Passaic, New Jersey, they were very, very close, and enlisted and went to aviator school together. Shortly after Milt was shot down, Murray got word that someone had seen a parachute come out of the nose of Milt's plane, and Murray assumed his brother, if alive, was in a POW camp. Still, he remained hopeful, and had a portentous dream one night in which Milt walked into his bunk. The dream was so vivid that he shared it with his mother in a letter. One week after the dream and some two months after D-Day, Murray, then stationed in Foggia, Italy, received orders to greet a visitor. The visitor was Milton, just as it had been in his dream.

The twins went on to serve in the Air Force for some twenty-eight years, each rising to the rank of

Milton and Murray Friend.

lieutenant colonel. Their careers included extended tours of duty in Korea. Milt describes that tour: "I'd leave the barracks from seven to twelve p.m. for a flight, and Murray would do the ten-to-three-a.m. run. Like clockwork, every night at 3 a.m. I would automatically wake up to see if Murray was back in bed. Though each of us flew fifty-five flights in Korea, it was really more like doing a hundred and ten."

Why do I linger on this twinship? Because buddies in war simulate something like it. They live intertwined lives, dependent for survival on each other's skills and strength, ready to sacrifice for each other, guilty if one makes it when the other doesn't. They feel responsible for each other in the way that close family members do. They turn to each other for solidarity both in war and in making sense of their lives after. As one father put it after learning of the death of his son, Chief Warrant Officer Second Class Bruce E. Price, in Afghanistan in May of 2004, "He basically had two families. He has his natural family, and he has his Army family. Everyone's going to miss him."[8]

Stoicism does not deny this sort of friendship or family connection. Stoic writers follow Aristotle's basic lead that we are social by nature. Seneca conceives of this sociability as a kind of "natural law" rooted in our biological natures.[9] Cicero elaborates that the ancient Stoic writers viewed our biological natures as following a social orientation process—a "social coming home," we might say (a social *oikeiōsis*)—that explains the developmental emergence of affiliation and attachment:

> Now the Stoics consider it important to realize that parents' love for their children arises naturally. From this starting-point we trace the development of all human society.... Thus our impulse to love what we have generated is given by nature herself as manifestly as our aversion to pain.
>
> This is also the source of the mutual and natural sympathy between humans, so that the very fact of being human requires that no human be considered a stranger to any other.... We are fitted by nature to form associations, assemblies and states.[10]

The passage is ennobling, but it raises as many questions as it answers. For example, why should it be that an instinct toward sociality is first manifested only in adulthood, as we care for our own progeny? And how do we extend outward from a concern for what is part of ourselves (our offspring) toward others with whom we have no previous attachment or relation? We shall see shortly that Hierocles, a Stoic of the time of Hadrian (117–138 CE), helps to answer the latter question. But still, the Stoic "natural" account of attachment as emerging at the moment of becoming a parent yields a notion of sociality with an oddly delayed onset. What happens on the child's side of the relationship? And what of those who never become parents? Are they socially handicapped for life? Moreover, the attachment of parent to child as prototype for an *emotional* bond is itself strained, given Stoic teachings on detachment. Sociality may be a kind of natural law, but there is also a "law of mortality," and it requires that we prepare, in our hearts and demeanor, for an investment that minimizes vulnerability and loss. The Stoics' repeated appeal to Anaxagoras's words upon learning of his son's death—"I always knew that my child was a mortal"—is a brute lesson in the law of mortality and a clue about how we are to love and lose as a good Stoic. However attached we are by nature to our progeny, we must ultimately come to appreciate, as the sage does, that reason (perfected in virtue and wisdom) is the only unconditional good in our lives. To value it and our virtuous efforts above all else is the way to become fully consistent with our true natures.

The view is a response to the Aristotelian claim that our happiness is itself marred when we lose our dearest family members and friends. As Aristotle explains, "By self-sufficient we do not mean what is sufficient for a man by himself, for one who lives a solitary life, but also for parents, children, wife, and in general for his friends and fellow citizens."[11] Our highest good (or happiness and flourishing) is necessarily framed in terms of a life with others:[12]

> Yet evidently, as we said, it [happiness] needs the external goods as well; for it is impossible, or not easy, to do noble acts without the proper equipment. In many actions we use friends and riches and political power as instruments; and there are some things the lack of which takes the luster from happiness, as good birth, satisfactory children, beauty; for the man who is very ugly in appearance or ill-born or solitary and childless is hardly happy, and perhaps a man would be still less so if he had thoroughly bad children or friends or had lost good children or friends by death.[13]

We might be a bit uneasy with Aristotle's requirement of beauty for the good life (and, too, the military's often prejudicial notion of looking good in a uniform), but we are likely to have little dispute with him on the view that friendship is a crucial means to and essential part of the good life. More strongly, Aristotle suggests that friendship structures our very form of flourishing as a human: "no one would choose to have all good things on condition of living alone."[14] Aristotle lists friendships among external goods. But they are not as external to us as, say, power or money. Friendships are expressions of our character and efforts, and the finest friendships, Aristotle himself says, are themselves exemplifications of virtuous activity.[15] In profound and pervasive ways, friendships structure a life that is active and morally fine, full of pleasure and zest and self-reflection. A passage from the *Magna Moralia* captures this last point:

> We are investigating the self-sufficiency not of a god, but of what is human, and whether the self-sufficient person will need friendship. Now if a person looks upon his friend and sees what he is and what sort of character he has, such a

friend will seem to him to be another self, just as it is said, "This is my second Hercules, a friend is another self." Now to know oneself is very difficult, as even some philosophers have said, and most pleasant (for knowledge of self is pleasant). Moreover, direct study of ourselves is impossible (this is shown by the fact the very things that we censure others for, we don't notice ourselves doing, and this comes about through partiality or passion, which in many of us blind our judgment of what is right). And so, just as when we want to see our own faces, we see them by looking in a mirror, similarly when we wish to know our own characters, we can know them by looking at a friend. For a friend, as we say, is another self.[16]

It is tempting to read a less-than-attractive narcissism into Aristotle's twin-ship metaphor of a friend as a second self. But a mutual admiration club is not what Aristotle has in mind. The force of his remarks, here and elsewhere, is that intimate friendship is a privileged arena for genuine self-knowledge and self-growth. Friends notice our irritating sides in a way we are blind to; they offer a looking glass that doesn't just mirror back what we can see on our own.[17] A good friend is not just honest but empathic—capable not only of sharing grief but, as Aristotle puts it more metaphorically, of being of "one mind" with us when we are in need of emotional solidarity and support.[18] Moreover, in a healthy friendship, we appreciate a friend as "another" but a separate self, sufficiently different so that our shared voyage expands horizons for mutual growth. In the best friendship, there is the kind of modeling we see in spades in the parent-child relationship: "The friendship of good persons is good, being augmented by their companionship; and they are thought to become better too by their activities and by improving each other; for from each other they take the mould of characteristics they approve."[19]

Can the Stoics endorse the notion of friendship as structuring our very well-being and self-sufficiency? I do not believe so. It is not that they want to dismiss friendship or family or the social glue and fellowship that come with doing kindnesses and showing sympathy. (I have addressed some of these issues in Chapter 3.) It is that, in principle, they must necessarily be wary of the emotions they involve, for they are forms of attachment to externals that lie beyond our full control. They make us vulnerable to loss, upheaval, and distress. What the Stoics underplay is the fortifying power of love, even as it opens us to those risks. Too, they vastly underplay the vulnerability of virtue itself, in the absence of nurturing conditions of friendship and solidarity.

The Case of Siegfried Sassoon

The role of war buddies in shaping one's adult identity and helping to repair it at war's end is a repeated theme in war literature. It emerges forcefully in the memoirs of the World War I poet Siegfried Sassoon. We met Sassoon briefly in a previous chapter, in the context of Pat Barker's trilogy of World War I novels.

Now we meet him again, in an account drawn from his first of two trilogies of war memoirs, a fictionalized autobiography, *The Memoirs of George Sherston*.[20]

But first some brief background. Sassoon's prewar years were spent in bucolic Kent, living the dual life (as he was later to portray in his memoirs) of fox-hunting and horse-riding "heartie" and aspirant poet-aesthete.[21] War interrupted that pastoral idyll, and at age twenty-eight Sassoon enlisted as a cavalry trooper, becoming later commissioned in the Royal Welsh Fusiliers. During a second tour of duty in France, a wounded right shoulder and a mix of shell shock and pacifism took him off the battlefield and returned him to Britain for convalescence in the spring of 1917. Though declared fit to be returned to duty in July, he defied orders on pacifist grounds. His view, like that of Bertrand Russell (with whom he had met the year before), "was that the war was being unnecessarily prolonged by the refusal of the Allies to publish their war aims."[22] Glorifying phrases such as "the supreme sacrifice" papered over the harrowing losses of the common infantry man. Through the intervention of his good friend and fellow war poet Robert Graves, Sassoon escaped court-martial and was sent to Craiglockhart War Hospital, a mental hospital outside Edinburgh. There he received Freudian-inspired psychotherapy from the eminent physiologist and anthropologist Captain W. H. R. Rivers.

What emerges as salient in Sassoon's story is that despite his principled, public protest of the war, once at Craiglockhart he begged to be returned to France on the grounds that he belonged with his company. A combination of love for and guilt about those left behind in the trenches, plus a sense of futility at his war protest, made the separation at once an abandonment and a banishment. To return to the front line might well be a kind of "death," he writes in his memoirs, but it is also "my only chance of peace."[23]

> I am banished from the patient men who fight.
> They smote my heart to pity, built my pride.
> Shoulder to aching shoulder, side by side,
> They trudged away from life's broad wealds of light.
> Their wrongs were mine; and ever in my sight
> They went arrayed in honour. But they died—
> Not one by one: and mutinous I cried
> To those who sent them out into the night.
> The darkness tells how vainly I have striven
> To free them from the pit where they must dwell
> In outcast gloom convulsed and jagged and riven
> By grappling guns. Love drove me to rebel.
> Love drives me back to grope with them through hell;
> And in their tortured eyes I stand forgiven.[24]

Another poem, "Sick Leave," concludes with the battalion whispering softly to Sassoon, "When are you going out to them again? Are they not still your brothers through our blood?"[25]

Augustus Saint-Gaudens, Memorial to Robert Gould Shaw and the
Massachusetts Fifty-fourth Regiment of the Civil War.

By February 1918 Sassoon did return to the war front, having persuaded
Rivers that he was once again battle-ready. *The Memoirs of George Sherston*
concludes with the protagonist writing one last time, in the summer of 1918,
from the safety of a clean white London hospital bed, after having been
wounded in the head by friendly fire. It is an absurd way to be knocked off the
battlefield, the author muses. But satirical whimsy never fully vanquishes his
guilt for being a survivor. The memory of the company continues to haunt
him: "When's the Captain coming back?" The captain is left, with the help of
his beloved Dr. Rivers, to broker an uneasy peace between his cravings to keep
his newfound safety and his "tantrum of self-disparagement" that he has abandoned his beloved mates.[26]

Sassoon's story is a testament to military motivation fueled not by some
abstract ideal of patriotism or belief in the war's just cause but by the love of
one soldier for another.[27] Phaedrus, in Plato's *Symposium*, voices a similar sentiment when it is his turn to give an encomium to love. "An army made of
lovers," he asserts, is the bravest kind of unit. It is easy to focus exclusively on

the homoeroticism of the sentiment, given what we know of Plato's social milieu (and of Sassoon's). But sexual attraction is not Phaedrus's principal point, nor Sassoon's. Their point is about *philia*—the friendship of brothers and sisters in arms as a source of strength in battle and, Sassoon will add, recovery after. Sassoon returns to his war buddies, over and over, in writing and rewriting six volumes of memoirs over a period of twenty years. Images of his friends intrude upon his consciousness, in the way traumatic flashbacks do, but he also invokes their memory as a way of paying tribute and of reconfiguring his own life in their presence. Along with Rivers, they will constitute a privileged audience to help him remember, and not just compulsively repeat, his war memories. They are second selves, mirrors, Aristotle would say—and witnesses, we can add, critical for his self-restoration: "We were the survivors; few among us would ever tell the truth to our friends and relations in England. We were carrying something in our heads which belonged to us alone, and to those we had left behind us in the battle."[28]

It is generally agreed that Sassoon suffered symptoms that would today fall under the category of PTSD. His treatment, though still in the earliest years of humane treatment of "war nerves," illustrates some of the general lines researchers now believe to be critical for recovery. Judith Herman, whose pioneering *Trauma and Recovery* remains a landmark in the treatment of trauma, argues that "the core experiences of psychological trauma are disempowerment and disconnection from others" and that recovery, as a result, depends upon empowering the agent and creating new social connections.[29] The therapeutic context must itself be a trusted relationship within which three characteristic stages of recovery can begin to unfold: first, the establishment of safety; second, the ability to remember and mourn; and third, a robust reconnection with social life. As Herman herself warns, the three-stage model imposes an artificial simplicity on the actual progress of any given recovery. Traumatic syndromes are complex disorders that affect biological, social, and psychological functioning; there is no simple treatment or trajectory for healing. Even so, she suggests compelling evidence that something like the progression she outlines can be found across a wide spectrum of traumatic syndromes.[30]

Sassoon's recovery bears some of this out. The hero of the memoirs is without a doubt Rivers, who acts as friend, therapist, and senior military cohort. Craiglockhart is a safe haven, even though its very safety is cause for wrenching guilt. Moreover, the narrative process is Sassoon's way of rejoining his company and mourning in their presence. And it is a way of remembering and reliving, complete with the affects of terror, guilt, and helplessness, as they felt then.[31] His social reconnection is at the heart of his satirical sketches of an imaginary parade of hospital visitors. To the "Charming Sister of Brother Officer," he is "jocular, talkative, debonair, diffidently heroic," "wishful to be wearing all possible medal-ribbons on pyjama jacket." To "some Senior Officer under whom I'd served," he's politely subordinate, ready "to jump out of bed and salute," and so on.[32] This reads as quintessential English stuff—a parody of class and manners by an acute social observer. But there is a subtext here. Sassoon is reconnecting with others while keeping them at arm's distance from the truth: there is the hell of war—"the one-legged man" and the "woeful crimson of men slain" (themselves only metaphors for that hell)—and then there are the niceties of polite conduct and conversation about it.[33] In a diary dated March 1921, Sassoon suggests as a tentative title for his memoirs "The Man Who Loved the World." The title would change, but the architectonic he finally settles on preserves its theme: he would elegize his young friends killed in the war. He would reconnect with them and with his own prewar English idyll, destroyed by the traumatic nightmare of war.

In significant ways, the goals of trauma recovery that Herman outlines, and Sassoon illustrates, are more Aristotelian in spirit than Stoic, for they hang on the idea that sufficiently positive social and physical and political environments are critical to our recovery and crucial to ongoing well-being. They are important not just in the sense that we would rather have safety and friendship than their opposites (that is, we would select them as "preferred indifferents"). Rather, they are necessary conditions for our sustained empowerment; they are necessary for our forms of dignity and strength, and for becoming the kinds of agents who can experience the world with some measure of calm. To be able to feel secure from violent assault or threats of assault and to be able to find companionship in others and to trust them in our worlds in part define, in most basic ways, our form of doing well and our capabilities to do well.[34] Events that are experienced as traumatic strain those capabilities. "Traumatic events are extraordinary, not because they occur rarely, but because they overwhelm the ordinary human adaptations to life."[35]

A Stoic turn of mind tends to throw the burden of those "adaptations" onto will and attitude. But empowerment, or a sense of being able to control one's destiny, is not just a matter of tapping into reserves of inner strength. Fortitude plays a role, but so too do supportive political and social institutions, adequate medical and mental health care, security from retraumatizing circumstances, and, as I have emphasized, emotional attachments to people and things outside ourselves that we view as important in our lives. Having these goods makes us less vulnerable agents. Family and friends, in particular, refortify and refuel us, even if they can ultimately be taken from us.[36] But then again, virtue itself is not a permanent holding, except in some ideal world in which not even sages dwell. It may have more permanence than external goods, as Aristotle claims (as do the Stoics in an extreme way). But for most of us it is not incorruptible or fully sustainable in conditions of extreme deprivation, humiliation, or psychological and physical coercion.[37] It is subject, even in the case of the sage, to the mental deficits that come with age and with physical and mental deterioration.

What we have seen, then, is that in their move inward, the Stoics constrict agency far too narrowly. They underestimate the strength and restorative power that come from trusting and being emotionally connected to others. And they undervalue the shared journey that commits someone such as Sassoon to battle and which enables him to survive the psychic hell afterward. But the Stoics will have something of a reply to this charge. They will claim that reason within each person can be the basis of a more far-flung community than Aristotle envisions. To anticipate, they will argue that rational agents can build community simply by recognition of the fact of each other's share in rationality. In other words, they can build community with a cement that doesn't need to rely on sticky emotions or attachments. The fact of reason (that is, reason that is common to all) is sufficient. I shall come to this shortly, and to its assessment. But first I offer one more World War I story to help locate the role of social connection in recovery from war trauma. The vignette is fictional, drawn from Virginia Woolf's *Mrs. Dalloway*.

The Case of Septimus Warren Smith

Septimus Warren Smith was decorated for his bravery in World War I. But Septimus, at age thirty, returned to England a changed man. He was a man who could no longer feel. He was numb, and he had become numb when his soul mate and war buddy, Evans, was killed. Through the war, they had become so close that it was a

> case of two dogs playing on a hearth-rug . . . they had to be together, share with each other, fight with each other, quarrel with each other. But when . . . Evans was killed, just before the Armistice, in Italy, Septimus, far from showing any emotion or recognizing that here was the end of a friendship, congratulated himself upon feeling very little and very reasonably. The War had taught him. It was sublime. He had gone through the whole show, friendship, European War, death, had won promotion, was still under thirty and was bound to survive. He was right there. The last shells missed him. He watched them explode with in-difference . . . he could not feel. . . . The truce [was] signed, and the dead buried. . . . He could not feel.[38]

The remarks may, for a brief moment, bring to mind Milton and Murray Friend. Septimus and Evans are kindred spirits, twins of sorts. They are attached; affection and shared life in the trenches have fused them. But in Woolf's story, Evans is killed and Septimus snaps. In Septimus, Woolf paints a classic portrait of the shell-shocked veteran: he alternates between numbness and bouts of terror, he suffers flashbacks and hallucinations, at some moments he feels paralyzed and at others as if moving in slow motion, he has lost his sense of time and his taste for sweets and beauty. Beauty, for Septimus, "was behind a pane of glass."[39] But Woolf also paints a telling portrait of the man before the war.[40] The young Septimus is a socially inept man. He is a loner who runs away from home to become a poet in London. He is "one of those half-educated, self-educated men whose education is all learnt from books borrowed from public libraries, read in the evening after the day's work, on the advice of well-known authors consulted by letter." He is "shy, and stammering," and "anxious to improve himself." He has fallen in love, puppy love at a distance, with Miss Isabel Pole, who lectures on Shakespeare at the Waterloo Road. As she lectures on *Antony and Cleopatra*, Septimus lives out a romance with her in his mind. Other than the ethereal Miss Pole, Septimus has no friends, lives by himself in a bed-sit off London's Euston Road, clerks in an auction house by day, and escapes to his fantasy world by night. Evans, we are to imagine, is his first real friend.

Woolf's description sets up the thought in the reader that Septimus's uneasy sociability may have contributed to the effect of war's stresses.[41] Herman points to research that lends some support to the conjecture:

> The impact of traumatic events also depends to some degree on the resilience of the affected person. While studies of combat veterans in the Second World War have shown that every man had his "breaking point," some "broke" more easily than others. Only a small minority of exceptional people appear to be relatively invulnerable in extreme situations. Studies of diverse populations have reached similar conclusions: stress-resistant individuals appear to be those with high sociability, a thoughtful and active coping style, and a strong perception of their ability to control their destiny. For example, when a large group of children were followed from birth until adulthood, roughly one child in ten showed an unusual capacity to withstand an adverse early environment. These children were characterized by an alert, active temperament, unusual sociability and skill in communicating with others, and a strong sense of being able to affect their destiny, which psychologists call "internal locus of control."[42]

These studies suggest that the factors that influence resilience are not only the coping skills we associate with a sense of self-reliance or independent autonomy, but the coping skills that face outward—an ability to communicate well with others and to be engaged and effective in a social environment. In this regard, Septimus's early social deficits are only compounded after the war. In a moment of panic and isolation, he marries a Milanese innkeeper's young daughter. They return to London, but still, five years later, Septimus cannot feel. Lucrezia prattles to fill the emptiness: "The English are so silent," she says. And Septimus mutters to himself, "Communication is health; communication is happiness." But how can he share with her the grotesqueries that hijack his mind?

With what, no doubt, is firsthand experience of the Harley Street doctors of the time, Woolf parodies the psychiatric help Septimus receives. We meet the rich doctor Sir William Bradshaw, who ushers his patient into a "home" where they will teach him "to rest," and where communication, confession, and any chance of a bond are quickly cut off because the doctor must run to his motorcar waiting outside. "Trust everything to me," Sir William says as he dismisses them. But they were abandoned: "Sir William Bradshaw was not a nice man!" Lucrezia pouts in her child bride's voice. No analogue of the therapeutic bond between Rivers and Sassoon is part of this story. "I ... I ...," Septimus stammers to Sir William as he tries to confess the crime of outliving Evans and the worse crime of killing humanity, but the doctor must run, the hour is growing late. And Septimus never recovers; in his mind, suicide is his only chance of putting to rest "remorseless" human nature.[43]

DISSOCIATION AND DETACHMENT

What is relevant for our purposes in this literary portrait is Septimus's profound social isolation. He is isolated in his illness, and he was isolated before. His therapy makes a mockery of empathy and respect. Whatever social connection is needed for recovery, Septimus cannot find it. His palpable disconnection from others is matched by his dissociation from his own feelings and mental states. He is anaesthetized, in permanent escape mode from the stress of war. Generally speaking, the dissociative symptoms of PTSD are part of nature's adaptive mechanism for facing catastrophic stress. They offer a mental escape when no physical escape is possible.[44] But in Septimus's case, as with many PTSD sufferers, acute dissociation outlives its usefulness.

One way of construing the Stoic view of the sage is as an idealization of some form of dissociation (i.e., splitting or compartmentalization). As we have seen, Stoic language sometimes pushes us in this direction. Seneca, in On Anger, speaks of handling unwanted emotions as a matter of keeping the enemy at the gates. We are to hold them at bay, fight them off: "the enemy must be stopped at the very frontier" before they storm the city.[45] In a parallel vein, Epictetus bids us to learn to no longer hold as important the objects and persons that can destabilize our happiness. One is to persuade oneself "that these things are nothing to me, not at all."[46] Remarks such as these suggest a conscious training in dissociation whereby we will ourselves to detach from the emotional weight of certain experiences and connections to persons. But, as we have seen throughout the course of this book, *permanent* dissociating or splitting from psychological states of attachment and loss is no way to thrive. And conceiving of self-sufficiency as a radical, emotional independence from others is itself a mistaken view of human well-being and human resilience.[47]

But we need to tread very carefully here. Some contemporary psychologists would argue that certain forms of dissociation have a place in the healthy life. They can be adaptive without necessarily creating hardened, impenetrable walls.[48] Mundane examples come to mind: While sitting in a department meeting, I suddenly become in my mind's eye a freshly hatched junior professor, articulating a point before colleagues very senior to me. My comportment and psychological orientation take me back to that place for a transient moment: I flush and sweat; I am no longer confident in my speech. I catch myself, but still I notice the drift. Or consider another scene: One of my son's friends, a bearded young man of twenty-one, muses at dinner, "I often picture myself as a fifth grader with some of my friends' younger siblings, frozen as second graders. When those second graders answer the phone with the deep voice of a sixteen-year-old, I'm caught off guard!" So it is with much of our psychological lives. We slip back and forth into different selves, sometimes replete with different sensory capacities and ranges of affect and thought. We are less unified than Plato's great notion of the harmonized soul would lead us to believe. As psychoanalytic writer Philip Bromberg puts it, psychic health "is the ability to stand in the spaces between realities without losing any of them—the capacity to feel like one self while being many." "Standing in the spaces" is shorthand, in his view, for being able to make room for bits of subjective reality that a person doesn't readily experience as "me" at that moment.[49] The crucial point is that we are multiple selves, multiply faceted, able to move fluidly, often undetected by others, from and to very different representations of the self in relation to others.

Researchers writing from the perspective of evolutionary biology point to a similar notion:

> Multiple versions of the self exist within an overarching, synthetic structure of identity. . . . [T]he idea of an individual "identity" or a cohesive "self" serves as an extremely valuable metaphor for the vital experience of relative wholeness, continuity, and cohesion in self-experience. Yet, as has often been noted, when we look within the psyche of well-put-together individuals, we actually see a "multiplicity of selves" or versions of the self coexisting within certain contours and patterns that, in sum, produce a sense of individuality, "I-ness" or "me-ness." . . . The cost of our human strategy for structuring the self in a provisional fashion—around a sometimes precarious confederation of alternative self/other schemas—lies in the ever-present risk of states of relative disintegration, fragmentation, or identity diffusion.[50]

The terror of annihilation, the threat of physical or sexual violence, and the witnessing of grotesque death are all factors that can undo this "precarious confederation." These are the kinds of experiences that can provoke extreme, and at times, pathological dissociation. A combat veteran of the Second World War reports his experience of fragmentation: "Like most of the 4th, I was numb, in a state of virtual dissociation. There is a condition . . . which we called the two-thousand-year-stare. This was the anesthetized look, the wide, hollow eyes of a man who no longer cares. I wasn't to that state yet, but the numbness was total. I felt almost as if I hadn't actually been in battle."[51] A victim of repeated sexual abuse as a child speaks of a similar feeling of self-detachment. She related the following story to me some forty years after her abuse had stopped: She was driving on an icy Vermont road when her van flipped over. After being taken to a local emergency room, she repeatedly told a doctor that she felt no pain at all. But X-rays revealed she had suffered complicated head and leg injuries that characteristically cause severe pain. After years of enduring violent abuse from her father, she had come to experience physical injuries as outside her own body. She learned how to make herself numb.[52]

Now, I am not suggesting that Stoicism has clinical insights into this hypnoidal type of dissociation. But one way we can imagine the detached calm the sage feels is by analogy with concrete forms of dissociation. In some ways this is to follow the Stoics' own lead. After all, they ask us to think of perfectionist virtue and invulnerability to externals in an *embodied* form. They don't simply tell us to minimize our dependence on highly vulnerable goods and strengthen our independence. Rather, they tell us to look to the sage, who can do it all—to get our inspiration from that model, however rare it may be in history.[53] This invites us to create a portrait for ourselves that has some psychological credibility. And one way of doing that is by thinking of models that involve processes of dissociation.

In one model, we can imagine the sage as someone who knows firsthand both the experience of messy engagement in the world and the state of serene detachment from those vicissitudes. But her primary identity—her "me" self, if you will—is in that world of detachment. She watches her life of births, family, and death (and in the case of a combatant, casualties, loss, and brutality) from that detached self, in whom the hurt or grief of the world of action is dulled—felt like a scar, as the Stoics put it.

However, the concern this portrait raises is whether one can really still know what the messy world of engagement is like when one is no longer fully vulnerable to its effects.[54] And we may wonder, too, just how this reduced state of vulnerability is substantively different from the numbness of traumatic dissociation. The path to its arrival is, of course, markedly different. A sage's detachment, according to Stoic theory, is an achievement of philosophical therapy. It is a conscious and studied realignment of values. It is not an involuntary disintegration caused by profound psychological stress. But interestingly, in function it serves a somewhat similar goal: to arm us against the fragility and worst tragedies of life so that we can endure them, as if from the outside. Yet security often comes at a price. The price in this case may be a kind of distance that is simply too costly.

This worry invites us to consider a second model. Imagine the sage this time as one who can still step into the messy world, not just look on at it with detachment. Rather, to use Bromberg's metaphor, she has room for experiences that are "not me." In this regard, she is not so different from us at our healthiest moments: as we've said, we consciously and unconsciously float back and forth to different periods of our life, representing ourselves in different self-other relationships; we are porous to "not me" moments that can have potent psychological reality. Consider again the example of battle. In moments of intimate killing and the horrors of war up close, this sage-warrior may feel profound anguish and the most severe pain (full-fledged feelings, not just preemotional arousals that mimic them). But then, with agility and control, she can transition from those perturbed states to a calmer state of consciousness. That is, she can find equipoise readily: she can experience the highs and lows of life, but then rebalance.

This is a more appealing model than the first. The second sage seems a real participant in this world, not like the first one, who keeps his cool by sitting safely perched on its rim. But for some of us, this sage may not seem sagelike enough; after all, she still feels the ordinary sorrow and joy in the world, even if she doesn't primarily identify with that part of her self. For others, the model may feel too sagelike, still have a superhuman feel—at least in certain circumstances. Few of us can imagine finding equanimity if we are threatened with extreme torture, or watch our children suffer that fate. In the news, as I write, photographs of the parents of two civilian contractors who were beheaded in Iraq in the late spring and early summer of 2004 (the American Nick Berg and the Korean Kim Sun-II) have been published. Berg's father is cradled by a surviving son. Kim's parents embrace each other, with eyes redder than crimson.[55] There is only anguish in their faces and bodies, the anguish of a Priam who learns just how Hector's body has been defiled by the wrath of Achilles. Surely, anguish of this sort does not recede quickly, if ever, no matter how emotionally sturdy we might be before. Still, these are extreme examples. In less extreme circumstances, we might find both inspiring and plausible a brand of wisdom that allows us to partake both of our world and of a world of quiescence.

Strictly speaking, however, it is not clear that we are entitled to think of the sage of most Stoic texts in this way. For the sage doesn't really go back into the messy world in the way Plato's philosopher-king, by definition, must.[56] Rather, Stoic enlightenment is a definitive move to a new way of seeing and feeling the world. The sage no longer experiences emotions in the old and ordinary way. He has sloughed off the old skin. He has a new emotional palette and a new vision of what is genuinely good and evil. These radically alter what the old world is like and how it is experienced.

These thought experiments give us some sense of the challenge we face in figuring out the complex psychology of highly idealized models that are also to be practical and inspirational. Contemporary studies of wisdom religions, such as Buddhism, might help us understand further possibilities.[57] But one thing seems clear: however stoic we might like our resilience to be, we are unlikely to find it if we minimize the importance of attachments and friendship in our lives. Nor are we likely to find recovery from the devastating psychological effects of war in the absence of renewed social connections and therapeutic and emotional bonds with trusted others. This is a crucial lesson for those going into war and for those returning from it.

It is a lesson of critical importance when we consider the likelihood of mental health risks faced by those who have been in combat in Iraq.[58] One survey, conducted at the Walter Reed Army Institute of Research in June 2004 and based on interviews of two thousand soldiers and Marines fighting in the beginning of the war, puts the overall rate of mental health concerns, including depression, anxiety, and post-traumatic stress disorder, at around 17 percent. (The soldiers were assessed three to four months after returning from combat.) Matthew Friedman, executive director of the National Center for Post-Traumatic Stress Disorder, thinks the numbers are likely to rise (in Vietnam, about twice as many, 30 percent, dealt with the symptoms of post-traumatic stress disorder) because of the war's increasing unpopularity at home and in Iraq and because of its shift to guerilla-style warfare. In a guerilla war "you don't know what's going to happen; whether you are combatant or driving a truck in a convoy, it doesn't make any difference in terms of how safe you might be."[59] These are the kinds of experiences, according to Friedman, that tend to precipitate PTSD or related symptoms. They are the kinds of symptoms that need to be recognized, he has urged, without stigma or shame. And such symptoms often require treatment.

Combat veterans of past wars may be the best suited to make the argument. At airports in recent times, it is not uncommon to see them greeting young soldiers and Marines as they return from their deployments in Afghanistan and Iraq. "Look, maybe now's not the time that you want to talk about it, but war—I've been there and this is what you can expect. And here's my card and you can call me. And no matter what's going on in your world, you and I can talk because I've served and I know what's going on."[60] Social outreach of this sort, by an "army of veterans," may be the first step in the process of reconnection and recovery.[61]

STOIC COSMOPOLITANISM

I have criticized the Stoics for undervaluing the emotional bonds of social connection. Still, the Stoic story does not end here. Significantly, the Stoics will argue that they have not abandoned the ideal of community, nor the attitudes that build and maintain it. They point to the possibility of a new kind of community—a community of rational agents, a *universal* ethical commonwealth—that will replace in moral importance narrower bonds of personal, ethnic, tribal, religious, or national affiliation. And they point to attitudes of respect and empathy critical for maintaining this community. In this view, we need to respect allies and enemies alike, friends and fellow citizens, good persons as well as those who are evil or who have done evil. Enlightenment theorists will run with these notions. Kant himself, in making respect the cement of that ethical commonwealth, will argue at length (not ultimately convincingly, to my mind) that respect is a sui generis emotion that will not be subject to the upheavals or partialities that plague ordinary emotions. This, however, is a story for another time and place.[62]

We might say the Stoics begin where Aristotle leaves off. Aristotle emphasizes face-to-face friendships and civic friendships within the city-state (*polis*); those outside civic borders are barbarians, due little in terms of respect or goodwill. The Stoics emphasize the community that extends beyond political and familial boundaries; they establish a community that extends to all of humanity in virtue of shared reason. The notion is captured in Diogenes the Cynic's maxim that each of us is a world (universal) citizen (*kosmopolitēs*), or as the Roman Stoics, Marcus Aurelius and Epictetus, prefer to say, a *politēs tou kosmou*, literally, a citizen of the cosmos or universe.[63] Cicero, explicating Stoic views, gives our duties to general human fellowship pride of place: "Let the following, then, be regarded as settled: when choosing between duties, the chief place is accorded to the class of duties grounded in human fellowship."[64]

We can begin with Marcus Aurelius's view of this community. His conception can be understood against the general Stoic doctrine that as rational beings we are to live in agreement or consistency with nature. It is not at all obvious what this means or why it is good to live according to nature, but on one plausible reading, living in agreement with nature is living in accordance with the orderliness and coherence of a universe (*kosmos*) that is governed by reason. We have an interest in living in accordance with cosmic reason because it provides the best rational order.[65] But for the Stoics, cosmic reason is not something outside ourselves. We each partake of that most perfect or divine reason; we are parts of the cosmic whole. As we mature, we come to realize that adherence to the rational arrangements of that whole provides proper standards for individual conduct. If we cut ourselves off from that whole, we lose the integrity of our own rational (and moral) agency. The imagery is graphic:

> If you have ever seen a dismembered hand or foot or head cut off, lying somewhere apart from the rest of the trunk, you have an image of what a man makes of himself, so far as in him lies, when he refuses to associate his will with what happens and cuts himself off and does some unneighbourly act. You have somewhat made yourself an outcast from the unity which is according to Nature; for you came into the world as a part and you have cut yourself off.[66]

And so we are always to recall our membership: "Whenever you feel something hard to bear, you have forgotten . . . the great kinship of man with all mankind, for the bond of kind is not blood nor the seed of life, but mind. You have forgotten that every individual's mind is of God and has flowed from that other world."[67] These are abstract lessons, but it is worth bearing in mind that the *Meditations* was written in 172 CE in the fleeting moments of quiet Marcus must have found while commanding his troops on the battlefront along the shores of the Danube. He writes to himself, not to young disciples or moral aspirants. He writes against a backdrop of imperial and martial rule, even if there are few signs of connecting the concrete details of political realities with the improved world polity he envisions.

But if Marcus is vague in his political theory, he is less vague in his moral psychology. We build community and renew our sense of shared humanity by remembering and renewing our membership in that community. If we commit injustices, as he has just told us, it may be that that community was not vivid enough before our minds. We may have "forgotten" that we are bound by its supreme laws.[68] We should refresh our memory, he adds,

Marcus Aurelius.

through exercises in imagination and empathy: one must "enter into the governing self of every man and allow every other to enter into your own."[69] In essence, Marcus suggests that respect becomes concrete through empathy. And he implies that empathy requires a process of imagination or role reversal: we enter each other's minds.[70] In the next section, we consider other Stoic texts that make this point even more strongly. In critical ways, they offer practical lessons in how to instill cosmopolitan ideals that are sorely lacking in the mindset of those who carried out and abetted the torture in Abu Ghraib.

RESPECT AND EMPATHY

For the early seeds of a notion of respect, Seneca's Epistle 41 is key. Here we are told that our divine capacity for reason—the "god within us," to use his metaphor—inspires a feeling of reverence. Our reason is what is most peculiarly our own. Like a wild lion whose spirit is unbroken, this is what we "marvel" at, this is what we "glory" in, this is what inspires a special feeling of "reverence" and "fear."[71] In a passage from *On Duties* that I have already commented on, Cicero reports similar Stoic views. In light of our shared humanity, we owe a duty of respect to all humans, good or otherwise. "We must exercise a respectfulness towards men, both towards the best of them and also towards the rest."[72] And he adds to this later, in the context of duties to the young and old alike, citizens and foreigners, in both their private and public capacities, "In short, . . . we ought to revere, to guard and to preserve the common affection and fellowship of the whole of humankind."[73]

The language of respect is potent. In virtue of one's rational nature, one is worthy of a kind of divine reverence. And one's regard for others—all others, whether they are good or evil persons, whether they are friends and acquaintances or outside one's immediate community and nation-state, whether they are allies or enemies—must incorporate an attitude of respect. Respect becomes the cement of the cosmopolitan community. In a sense, it replaces sentiments of kinship and mutual affection and attachment, so ubiquitous in Aristotelian ethics.

But exactly how do we galvanize this attitude of respect, especially toward those of whom we have little understanding or who are our sworn enemies? It is one thing to preach respect as an abstract emotion that ties together the citizens of the universe. It is quite another to realize that attitude. Marcus, as we have seen, suggests exercises in imagination and memory: we are to remember the bond of humanity and practice reversing roles.

Hierocles, a Stoic writing a little earlier than Marcus, during the time of Hadrian (117–38 CE), is more detailed in his instructions for empathy training. In an adaptation of a well-known Stoic motif, he urges that we think of ourselves as standing in a series of concentric circles. Our task is to imagine those in the farthest orbits of our lives as connected to us in ways that make them more like those closest to the center, namely ourselves, and family, and friends.

> The outermost and largest circle, which encompasses all the rest, is that of the whole human race. Once these have all been surveyed, it is the task of a well-tempered man, in his proper treatment of each group, to draw the circles those from the enclosing circles in the enclosed ones. . . . It is incumbent on us to respect people from the third circle as if they were those from the second, and again to respect our other relatives as if they were those from the third circle. For although the greater distance in blood will remove some affection, we must still try hard to assimilate them. The right point will be reached if, through our own initiative, we reduce the distance of the relationship with each person.[74]

Hierocles's (and Marcus's) point is that the capacity for respect is enlivened through acts of imagination. That is, we need to actively empathize with people, to try to become attuned to their habits and ways and needs, so that however foreign or different they may be, we come to see them as persons in their own right, worthy of dignitary respect. Adam Smith, writing in Glasgow in the eighteenth century, put it forcefully when he said that "sympathy" (his term for what in the nineteenth century came to be dubbed "empathy") is an epistemic capacity that allows us to "trade places in fancy," "to beat time" with others' hearts, to bring the case home "to one's bosom."[75] His contemporary in Edinburgh, David Hume, put the emphasis less on imagination than on vicarious arousal or affective contagion. To feel sympathy (again, read "empathy"), in Hume's view, is to feel oneself attached to others by a cord: a vibration at one end of the cord causes a vibration at the other.[76]

However we construct a conception of empathy—in terms of imaginative acts or vicarious arousal—some such notion undergirds our capacity to respect persons. Not surprisingly, Marcus and Hierocles, as Stoics, favor a cognitive route for identifying with others. Hierocles's comments are incisive: when we imagine others as part of our own inner circle, we respect them, honor their rights and concerns, and make them a part of a community that takes their humanity seriously. Respect on its own is too abstract a notion to do much of the work for which we employ it. We need to add to it concrete visualization—a face, a set of circumstances, a story, photojournalistic coverage, insight into other cultures, and so on. It is not just that we need to ask ourselves whether in those circumstances we would find such treatment demeaning, humiliating, or an assault on dignity. We need to ask whether *they* would find it so. And this most likely requires some sort of active process of trading places in imagination.

The implications of this are profound in beginning to understand our duties as citizens of the universe. The Stoics are surely wrong in thinking that we can become rock-ribbed and resilient if only we protect ourselves against the vulnerability love and friendship invite. They are right, however, to suggest that those attachments cannot be the limits of our moral regard. We need to conceive of a community whose bonds go beyond the partialities of love and affection and religious or tribal kinship. But we cannot build that community simply by reciting mantras of respect and dignity for fellow humans. As Hierocles insists, we need to do the hard work of positioning ourselves to make that respect available in the hardest cases.

With this as preface, I reflect on the prison abuse scandal in Abu Ghraib, disclosed to the world in the late spring of 2004. What happens to respect for persons, in particular enemy POWs, in the political climate of war against terror?

THE CASE OF ABU GHRAIB AND GENERAL TAGUBA

Constraints on the treatment of enemy POWs, like constraints that fall under *jus in bello* (just conduct in war), have to do with recognition of human dignity in situations that themselves seem to be suspensions of it. That is, war is hell, but that hell, as Michael Walzer eloquently writes in his classic work *Just and Unjust Wars*, is still a "rule-governed activity, a world of permissions and prohibitions."[77] And it is a rule-governed activity of *equals*, of victims, who despite their individual national or tribal allegiances, have the same human standing.[78] In this regard, they are cosmopolitans, fellow citizens of the universe, subject to universal, moral laws. Traditionally, in *jus in bello*, those prohibitions amount to noncombatant immunity (however conventional the line may seem between combatant and noncombatant) and some form of proportionality, that is, a commitment to limit collateral damage in meeting military goals.[79] In this sense, there are moral rules to mutual slaughter, rules that replace the decorum of a bygone age of chivalrous warriors. The treatment of wounded soldiers or those who surrender and are held in enemy captivity (i.e., POWs) is also regulated by war conventions' "permissions and prohibitions." These formally fall under the Geneva accords pursuant to World War II.

Terror, however, as we have seen in the post-9/11 world, plays havoc with the rules of war. It is not just that terrorists exempt themselves from those rules. It is that they challenge their victims to do the same. In all war, war conventions, in a sense, stand in the way of victory—they slow down a peace, put off the end of aggression. But when war is waged against terrorists (alleged or real), the moral cost of observing war conventions can seem even greater. To fight clean can seem like fighting with one arm tied behind one's back.[80]

And yet moral outrage was the predominant response in Senate hearings and national public media to the disclosure of the Abu Ghraib prison abuses in the spring of 2004. In that atmosphere of outcry, the infamous "torture memo" of August 1, 2002, written for the Bush administration by Jay S. Bybee from the Justice Department's Office of Legal Counsel and claiming that torture was permissible so long as it did not cause "organ failure," was publicly repudiated in favor of a less permissive notion of interrogation techniques. As I prepare this book for publication in January 2005, senators participating in confirmation hearings are grilling Alberto R. Gonzales, President Bush's pick for attorney general. Among Gonzales's more attention-catching claims is the statement that a war on terrorism renders "obsolete" the Geneva Convention accords on the interrogation of enemy prisoners. Gonzales was believed to have been present at meetings that encouraged as permissible interrogation techniques open-handed slapping, the threat of being buried alive, and the use of "waterboarding" (a procedure in which detainees are strapped to a board, with feet raised above the head, and the head dipped in water to give a sensation of drowning). The administration's views on torture were further reviewed by the Defense Department's Schlesinger Report, which claimed that the president's torture policy played a key role in creating the climate of interrogation policies at Abu Ghraib.[81] As of this writing, Army Specialist Charles A. Graner Jr., the alleged ringleader of the abuse at Abu Ghraib, has been convicted and sentenced to ten years for his involvement. While the court-martial rejected his defense that he was merely following a superior's orders, many have argued that the rejection does not mean that senior officers will not be called to stand trial.

Amid the continuing disclosures of torture in Iraq and at the American detention center at Guantánamo Bay, Cuba, I limit my focus here to one of the earliest investigative reports on the abuses at Abu Ghraib: the Taguba Report, written for the U.S. Army by General Antonio Taguba and widely publicized in May 2004. That report cites "egregious" "sadistic abuses" and "grave breaches of international law."[82] The abuses were viewed neither as morally justified because expedient for interrogation, nor as morally wrong but a practically necessary "lesser evil" in the war against terror.[83] Rather, there was a sense of the categorical wrongness of the violations.

It is instructive to recall some of the details and background of the Taguba report. While at the time of this writing, the legal issues have been widely discussed, what to my mind has not been adequately analyzed are the moral and psychological dimensions and their implications for military leadership. As I take up these issues, the connection to Stoic themes will become apparent.

In early May 2004, Seymour Hersh, the Pulitzer Prize–winning journalist who exposed the massacres of My Lai to the world some thirty years earlier, wrote about Major General Antonio Taguba's investigation on prison abuse in the Baghdad Central Confinement Facility (known as Abu Ghraib prison). Taguba's report followed on allegations of detainee abuse from both an internal source, a military police guard within the 800th Military Police Brigade (Army Specialist Joseph M. Darby), and the International Committee of the Red Cross.

In the report followed up by now all too familiar photograph and video images, Taguba cites numerous incidents of "sadistic, blatant, and wanton criminal abuses . . . intentionally perpetrated" by members of several of the military police companies in the 800th Military Police Brigade. The incidents include principally physical threats and physical abuse—punching, slapping, kicking, slamming detainees against a wall and jumping on their naked feet, pouring cold water and liquid chemicals on them, using dogs to intimidate detainees (and in one case bite and seriously injure a detainee), putting a naked detainee on a box with his head hooded and wires attached to his fingers, toes, and penis in a simulation of electric torture. They also included sexual humiliation and sexual abuse—forced nudity for days at a time, forced masturbation while being videotaped, threatened male rapes, sodomizing of a male detainee with a chemical-light stick and broomstick, and stacking naked males on top of each other with the penis of one touching the buttocks of another. "Abuse with sexual themes occurred and was witnessed, condoned [and] photographed, but never reported," wrote Colonel Henry Nelson, the Air Force psychiatrist who served on the investigative team.[84]

The acts were, in general, condoned as part of the "softening-up" process to enable interrogation by the military intelligence. As Taguba reports, "Military intelligence . . . and other interrogators actively requested that MP [military police] guards set physical and mental conditions for favorable interrogation of witnesses."[85] While the 800th Military Police Brigade and its commanders had never been explicitly directed to "enable" interrogations, the tasking was done at lower levels of the military with complicit acceptance at the top.[86] The practice, as has now been widely documented, was imported from the detention facility at Guantánamo Bay and given encouragement by General Miller, in charge of that center and eager to expedite intelligence gathering in the Iraqi theater.

The centerpiece of Taguba's report is that treatment of detainees is in blatant violation of the third Geneva Convention. Article 17 of that convention is clear: "no physical or mental torture, nor any other form of coercion, may be inflicted on prisoners of war to secure from them information of any kind whatever. Prisoners of war who refuse to answer may not be threatened, insulted, or exposed to unpleasant or disadvantageous treatment of any kind."[87] Article 13 more generally prohibits physical mutilation and requires that enemy POWs be protected at all times against "acts of violence or intimidation and against insults and public curiosity." Taguba's repeated recommendation is that soldiers at all levels involved in the abuse, from the brigadier general who was the commander of the brigade, Janis Karpinski, to platoon sergeants, are in dereliction of duties for "failing to ensure that soldiers in their units "knew, understood, and adhered to the protections afforded to detainees" under the Geneva Conventions.[88] (Other reports have suggested that higher-up brass, as well as the secretary of defense, Donald Rumsfeld, and President George W. Bush, are in part responsible for establishing a culture in which the Geneva accords were viewed as obsolescent in these circumstances.)

Taguba's recommendation is striking in several ways. In his eyes, the Geneva Conventions on POW treatment are not at all quaint texts, but thoroughly accessible and relevant documents that all soldiers and sailors, whether members of reserve or permanent units, must understand and be held accountable for. They are to be displayed prominently in detention centers in English and the language of the detainees. He is unequivocal that they are applicable to the war with Iraq and part of what a soldier swears to when she takes an oath to uphold the Constitution (and the treaties and conventions to which it is signatory) as her highest loyalty. (He makes these claims acknowledging the complexity of circumstances at Abu Ghraib: chains of command were unclear; messages from the commander in chief on down were at best ambivalent about the applicability of the Geneva Conventions; discipline and supervision were absent; working conditions were poor and overcrowding was a problem; and civilian contractors or "corporate warriors," who were exempt from punishment under the Uniform Code of Military Justice and who did not have clear lines of command, worked alongside uniformed soldiers and sailors as reserve units. In addition, the 800th was called up quickly, without adequate training or clear delineation of its role.)[89]

It is worth noting that Taguba makes his recommendations not as a lawyer or military ethicist but as one who knows about POW camps up close, from a time when there were no Geneva accords: his father, Tomas Taguba, a Philippine Scout fighting alongside U.S. troops, survived a Japanese POW camp and escaped during the Bataan Death March.[90] However twisted the legal definition of torture in the Office of Legal Counsel's advisory memo to the Bush administration just six months before Taguba's report, Taguba is clear that sexual abuse, threats to and humiliation of detainees, stomping on their fingers and hands, intimidation by guard dogs, and simulated torture are unequivocal dignitary violations.[91] They fail, in the plain words of the Geneva Conventions, to give what POWs, as equals in war, are entitled to—"respect for their persons."[92] Taguba argues as a soldier taking orders not just from his superiors but ultimately from his conscience and from a commitment to constitutional values. "Bottom line," he instructed his investigative staff, "we will follow our conscience and do what is morally right."[93]

As we have said, the seed notion of the Geneva accords—indeed, of international law and respect for peoples beyond one's national border—is as old as the Stoics.[94] With the breakdown of the Greek *polis*, or city-state, and the expansion of Roman rule across foreign continents, the ideal of Stoic cosmopolitanism took practical and legal shape in the Roman concept of the law of peoples—*jus gentium*. The law of peoples "was meant to incorporate," in the words of philosopher Jerome Schneewind, "commonly accepted ideas of honesty and fair dealing that might be accepted by civilized people everywhere," and it was to be "simple enough so that everyone could understand and use it."[95] This is precisely Taguba's conviction about the Geneva Conventions. And, in a sense, it is a conviction that is Stoic at its core.

But there are two aspects of the Stoic legacy that are especially important in understanding the dynamics of Abu Ghraib and that fall outside the discussion of international law and its roots. These are points of moral psychology that build on our earlier discussion. The first is Hierocles's notion of making respect concrete through empathy. The second, and the most profound from the vantage point of this book, is Seneca's warning that anger and abusive rage wreak havoc on the lives of not just the violated but the violators as well. The points, as we will see, are inextricably linked, and they have profound bearing on military leadership.

If Hierocles were one of our talking heads today, he might well argue that understanding the Geneva Conventions and their prohibitions on detainee torture and abuse is itself inadequate for instilling the sort of respect they demand. By nature, we are selective in our respect; respect is neither automatic nor ubiquitous. Even if, in a generous spirit of moral universalism, we believe that respect reaches out to the dignity of all persons, to whom we show that respect is a matter of cultivated habit as well as calculated decision. It may be that respect, unlike love, is *due* to all. But as a practical attitude dispensed by combatants or civilians, the circles are always drawn more or less narrowly. Hierocles would argue that the good military leader knows how to draw those circles wider. One way to do this, as I have elaborated, is through exercises in imagination: to heighten empathy by becoming others for a moment, to trade places and become the victim of racism and cultural ignorance, to make the corrective adjustments needed to break down ethnic or religious or cultural barriers. Empathy may be a natural propensity, evident in the earliest motor and vocal mimicries of a three-day-old infant. But untutored, it can do no moral work. Military leaders, bound by the humanitarian laws of the Geneva Conventions, have a moral mandate to try to make it serviceable. Indeed, all soldiers, in swearing to uphold the Geneva Conventions, have indirect moral duties to cultivate the imaginative skills that underlie a capacity for the empathy necessary for dignitary respect. In Abu Ghraib, a familiarity with the Geneva accords and leadership that unequivocally reinforced its importance (all the way up to the commander in chief) would have been steps in the right direction.

This is one Stoic teaching. But it is opposed by the sober reality that Seneca paints for us in detail, and which I have examined in previous chapters. We are creatures with propensities for unbridled anger and rage. In positions of power, whether as Roman household masters or American soldiers and prison guards, we can turn abusive. When mixed with vengeance and punitive hatred, our wrath can become ugly fast. Philip Zimbardo, in his famous Stanford "prison guard" experiments in the early 1970s, showed just how fast legitimate authority can devolve into sadistic and psychopathic abuse. Twenty-four students were divided into two groups, "prisoners" and "prison guards." None had a criminal record. None showed signs of sadism. They knew it was a matter of chance whether they would be a prisoner or a guard. In the basement of the Stanford University Psychology Department, they simulated detention life. What ensued? Zimbardo had to stop the experiment after six days, a week short of its scheduled run, because of the escalating brutality of the guards. A consensus and conformity emerged not around the behavior of the "good guards" but around that of the "bad guards." Guards subjected prisoners to sleep and food deprivation. They made them live with their own excrement. They took away blankets and companions. They put in solitary confinement those who protested their incarceration through hunger strikes.[96] As Zimbardo explains, "I called off the experiment not because of the horror I saw out there in the prison yard, but because of the horror of realizing *I* could have easily traded places with the most brutal guard or become the weakest prisoner full of hatred at being so powerless."[97]

Zimbardo reminds us of the psychological degradation and shame that can come with victimization. The title of Primo Levi's account of Auschwitz speaks volumes here: *If This Is a Man*.[98] But we are often less attuned to the damage to the victimizer. It is on this subject that Seneca is often his most forceful, and his words have application to all torturers, whether in ancient Rome or modern day Iraq. Let us remember again how Seneca begins *On Anger*:

> Raving with a desire that is utterly inhuman for instruments of pain and reparations in blood, careless of itself so long as it harms the other, it [anger] rushes onto the very spear points, greedy for vengeance that draws down the avenger with it.[99]

Wrath unleashes "the hideous horrifying face of swollen self-degradation."[100] When it escalates into sustained forms of sadistic and cruel pleasure, "it casts out all sense of human solidarity from the mind."[101] It becomes "hardened" into hatred."[102] Capacities for empathy and respect are suppressed, as are capacities for self-empathy and self-respect. This is the ravaged soul that the torturer must live with.

The push to equanimity that we have puzzled over so often in this book is a move to release oneself from these forms of all-consuming, violent passion. The Stoic point, at its most congenial, is not to eradicate all emotions and turn persons into machines, but to eradicate the emotions of sadistic hatred and wild revenge that can tyrannize a soul. True, Seneca himself, in the hyperbolic *Of Anger*, fails to make adequate discriminations—most conspicuously, as we have said before, between wild rage and the righteous indignation that is a proper part of moral sensibility.[103] Still, his principal psychological insight remains an indispensable lesson for warriors: vengeful violence is self-abuse as well as abuse of others. It undoes a sense of humanity, in ourselves and in others. Again, this is a lesson for ancient warriors and modern warriors alike.

But one might still worry that *killing* in war, even in a just war that is justly prosecuted, can do the same. The psychological hell of war doesn't observe neat moral boundaries. This may be true. Yet if we are to fight wars with some sense of honor, courage, and commitment, then we must be committed to being morally scrupulous, from commander in chief down to foot soldier, about the boundaries between legitimate and illegitimate forms of violence. And this is especially so in the climate of war against terror, where the terrorists' gambit is precisely to wreak havoc on our sense of shared humanity.

In this chapter, we have seen that self-reliance and self-mastery are only partial components of a viable conception of resilience and self-sufficiency. In addition, we need to include the fortification and renewal that comes from human fellowship. We have looked at many expressions of human fellowship central to the military, from the camaraderie and twinship of war buddies to the therapeutic bond between shell shock patient and psychiatrist to notions of ourselves as citizens of the world who share in reason. The last idea gives rise to the ideal of a cosmopolitan community. As a loose legal and economic entity, it remains an ideal toward which the international community is only slowly making progress. And yet each of us, civilian or soldier, as citizen of the world, must do his or her own part to realize the ideal. This, our Stoic authors say, requires drawing the outermost circles of our world inward. In short, it requires cultivating humanity through empathetic identification and respect. "Let us cultivate humanity," Seneca exhorts in his famous final injunction in *On Anger*.[104] The words should be a part of any warrior's honor code.

Notes

Preface and Acknowledgments

1. Scott Shane, "Military Plans a Delayed Test for Mental Issues," *New York Times,* January 30, 2005.
2. *On Anger,* in *Moral and Political Essays,* 3.41–43.
3. McMahan 2004.

Chapter 1

1. Stockdale 1994.
2. The chair was established through the generous gifts of William Brehm and Ernst Vogenau.
3. *Handbook of Epictetus* 1 (White trans.).
4. See Long 2002 for an account of Epictetus along these lines.
5. Epictetus himself accepts the general notion of "preferred" and "dispreferred" indifferents, though he does not himself use the terminology. Thus, see his endorsement of Chrysippus's view on the propriety of selecting natural advantages over disadvantages (e.g., health over disease) at *Discourses* 2.6.9–10 (using Hard trans. in Gill's edition [1995] unless otherwise noted). For further discussion, see Long 2002, 184, cf. 201–2.
6. These remarks, and those that follow, are based on an interview with James Stockdale in October 2001. Stockdale answered my questions during the interview, as well as read aloud from a prepared essay (Stockdale 2001). Stockdale was Ross Perot's running mate in the 1992 presidential election.
7. Stockdale 2001.
8. Ibid., and interview in October 2001.
9. Stockdale 2001.
10. I interviewed Ward Carroll in August 2001.
11. See *Discourses* 1.1.7; 1.3.4; 1.12.34; 1.20.15 for a sampling. For more on this cardinal principle of good living, see Long 2002, 85.

12. *On Mercy* 2.5.2, in *Moral and Political Essays*.
13. *Discourses* 3.25.1–5.
14. I use the following sources for these biographical sketches: Annas 1993, Colish 1990, Long 1974 and 2002, Rist 1969; also Griffin and Atkins's introduction to Cicero's *On Duties* (1991); King's introduction to Cicero's *Tusculan Disputations* (1989); Staniforth's introduction to Marcus Aurelius's *Meditations* (1964); Cooper and Procopé's introduction to Seneca's *Moral and Political Essays* (1995); Gill's introduction to Epictetus's *Discourses* (1995); Oldfather's introduction to Epictetus's *Discourses* (1989).
15. *On Mercy* 2.5.2 (using Cooper and Procopé in their edition of Seneca's *Moral and Political Essays* [1995]).
16. *On Mercy* 1.11.4.
17. Long 2002.
18. *Meditations* 1.17 (Farquharson trans.).
19. *Meditations* 8.61.

Chapter 2

1. See Ricks 1997; Feaver and Kohn 2001.
2. As I write in the fall of 2004, 154 members of the 108th Congress have had some military service, some 14 fewer than in the 107th Congress. The House has 118 veterans; in the Senate, 35 members are veterans. The steady decline in numbers can be attributed, in part, to the end of the draft in 1973. See www.senate.gov/reference/resources/pdf/RS21379.pdf, accessed September 30, 2004.
3. *Discourses* 1.18.21 (using Hard trans. in Gill's edition [1995] unless otherwise noted).
4. Ibid., 1.24.1–2, and see 3.10.7.
5. According to statistics from the National Institutes of Health (based on the National Health and Nutrition Examination Survey) in 1994, 22.3 percent of Americans were obese, compared to 13.4 percent in 1960. By 2000, that figure had gone up to 30.5 percent, making almost one-third of U.S. adults obese. Add to that the 34 percent of Americans who are overweight but not yet obese, and nearly two-thirds of U.S. adults are overweight. Statistics on obesity are determined through the Body Mass Index (BMI). The algorithm is this: multiply an individual's weight (in pounds) by 700, divide by height (in inches), and then divide this again by height (in inches). Individuals are considered overweight if their BMI exceeds 25. They are considered obese if that number exceeds 30.
6. Pope, Philips, and Olivardia 2002, 10–11.
7. Ibid., 7.
8. Ibid., 9.

9. Fussell 1991, 24.

10. Ibid., 25.

11. Indeed, authors of *The Adonis Complex* argue that pathological preoccupation with muscle size could not have reached its present proportions without anabolic steroids. As medical researchers and clinicians, they argue that the dangers of anabolic steroid use ought not be underestimated. Medical hazards include increased risk of heart failure, stroke, and prostate cancer; psychiatric risks include irritability, depression, aggressive and violent behavior ("roid rage"), and dependence on other addictive and performance enhancing drugs. The present concern is not that actors or elite athletes may use anabolic steroids (they have been using them since the sixties and seventies), but that ordinary boys and men not in the limelight but keen to achieve the same Herculean image will turn to them. In 1988 the *Journal of the American Medical Association* reported the results of a survey of 3,403 twelfth-grade boys in forty-six public and private high schools. According to the study, 6.6 percent of boys reported that they were using or had used steroids. In 1993, an independent study conducted in Georgia and published in the *New England Journal of Medicine* reported almost identical findings. While anabolic steroids were banned at the Naval Academy during my time there, creatine, a supplement that increases lean body mass, was not. It was sold over the counter—towers of white creatine jars were regularly on display at the midshipmen's store. Academy officials were concerned about its widespread use, but it was not on the banned list and coaches found it hard to keep athletes away from it.

12. Fussell 1991, 138.

13. Ibid., 19; italics added.

14. From Arnold Schwarzenegger's *Posedown!*, as quoted in Fussell 1991, 73.

15. For the Platonic legacy of this point, see *Meno* 87c–88a and *Euthydemus* 280e; cf. Diogenes Laertius 7.94, 7.103; *Discourses* 3.20.4.

16. *Discourses* 4.1.66.

17. Ibid., 2.2.10.

18. Ibid., 1.1.9.

19. Ibid., 3.22.40–41.

20. Ibid., 4.1.79–80.

21. See note 15 above.

22. *Discourses* 3.20.4.

23. *On Moral Ends* 4.36 (using Woolf trans. in Annas's edition [2001] throughout). Interestingly, from a metaphysical point of view, the Stoics were physicalists in their conception of what mind actually is; it is *pneuma*, or breath, an animating, fine material.

24. *On Moral Ends* 3.43.

25. For a very helpful discussion on the notion of "what is appropriate" in Epictetus and its distinction from notions of "what is good," see Long 2002, 115–16, and especially 126–27. For more on Epictetus's usage of the field of "what is appropriate" and its nuanced differences from early Stoic usage, see Inwood 1985, 115–26.

26. *Discourses* 3.24.27.

27. Ibid., 3.2.4, but note that the specific context here is things that are appropriate with respect to social relations. Again see Long 2002, 115–16.

28. *Discourses* 2.22.5.

29. Ibid., 3.22.86.

30. Ibid., 4.11.19.

31. Ibid., 3.12.16; see also 4.11.5–9.

32. I have been reminded of this by conversations with Joe Lang, former director of athletics at Georgetown, with whom I worked closely for several years on a university-wide athletics review. He encourages young people to go into sports, not simply so that they can become athletes, but so that they can become individuals who have internalized the rigors of discipline and focus. The point was not missed on Jim Stockdale in his years as a POW. Even in leg irons, with a broken leg, and in solitary, he forced himself to do more than a hundred sit-ups each morning. Controlling his own body, in the face of relentless torture and deprivation, was his way of reinforcing the rigors of self-discipline and mental alertness.

33. *Discourses* 4.11.13–14.

34. Ibid., 4.11.15–16; see also 4.11.32–33. The overall tone of the passage brings to mind Joel Feinberg's classic (and humorous) work on offensiveness (1984).

35. *Discourses* 3.23.27.

36. Ibid., 3.22.86–87; 4.11.23–24.

37. Ibid., 4.11.18.

38. Ibid., 4.11.28–29.

39. *Symposium* 211ff., in *Complete Works*. The progression, as Socrates reports through the mouthpiece of Diotema, is a gradual one: From love of individual bodies one moves to love of bodies in general; from love of bodies in general one moves to love of the inner beauty of a soul and then to souls, as a whole, and their intellectual products. From here one is ready to grasp the idealization of beauty in a Platonic Form, that is, beauty in its fullest perfection.

40. *Discourses* 3.12.16–17.

41. *Epistles* 14.1; see also 71.33.

42. Contrast Aristotle at *Nicomachean Ethics* 1.10 1100b25–27. (For Aristotle references, I am using Jonathan Barnes' [1984] edition throughout except where otherwise noted.)

43. *On Moral Ends* 3.45.
44. See Irwin 1986 on this.
45. *On Moral Ends* 3.22.
46. For the classes of indifferents as in accord and not in accord with nature, see Diogenes Laertius 7.102; also Cicero, *Tusculan Disputations* 5.29.
47. This view might still accommodate the Stoic notion that our natural attractions and repulsions toward the indifferents are part of a developmental story of acquiring virtue. On this view, expounded well by Glen Lesses (1989), preferred and dispreferred indifferents are "nature's starting points" (*On Moral Ends* 3.22). We select them in acting on our earliest instincts toward self-preservation (ibid., 3.20–23; also Diogenes Laertius 7.104–9), e.g., in the case of bodily qualities, selecting life, health, strength, good condition and soundness of bodily organs, beauty, and so on, and rejecting death, disease, weakness, unfitness, mutilation, ugliness, and so on. (Contrast this, say the texts, with truly indifferent or neutral states of affairs, e.g., whether we pick up a twig or hold a pen or a scraper. Here we have no natural attractions or repulsions to guide us.) With the development of reason (characteristic of a sage), we come to recognize these goods for what they are—mere starting points that lead us to what is *truly* valuable and "in accord with nature," namely, reason itself and its exercise in deliberating about indifferents and virtue (*On Moral Ends* 3.21). As Cicero analogizes, it is as if one person introduces you to another to whom you then become closer and value more. But even if we go with this developmental story, we might still want to hold that our starting points may retain some value (however conditional) within our mature conception of happiness.
48. I defend this view in Sherman 1989, though one might argue that Aristotle is not explicit enough about the hierarchical structure of the components of happiness.
49. *Nicomachean Ethics* 1.10.1101a8.
50. Ibid., 1.10.1100b32–1101a7, substituting "person" for "man."
51. Ibid., 1.5.1095b26.
52. I am grateful to Tony Long's exposition (2002, 195–96). I use his translation here.
53. *Discourses* 3.215.1–5.
54. For major texts, see Von Armin 1924, 3.757–68.
55. For a helpful discussion of the Stoic view of suicide and careful reading of the texts, see Englert 1996 with Nussbaum's comments; also Griffin 1994 on Romans and suicide. It is worth recalling here the suicide of Zeno, the founder of Stoicism: "As he was leaving the school, he tripped and fell breaking a toe. Striking the ground with his fist, he quoted the *Niobe*, 'I come, I come, why do you call for me?' and died on the spot

through holding his breath" (Diogenes Laertius 7.28, replacing "dost" and "thou" with "do" and "you").

56. "But while I am employed in your service, what would you have me be? An official or a private man, a senator or a common man, a soldier or a general, a teacher or the master of a household? Whatever post or rank you assign me, as Socrates said, I will die a thousand times rather than desert it. Where would you have me be? At Rome or at Athens, at Thebes or at Gyara? Only remember me there. If you send me to a place where men cannot live in accordance with nature, I shall depart this life, not out of disobedience to you, but in the belief that you are sounding the signal for my retreat" (*Discourses* 3.24.99–101). For further discussion of Epictetus on suicide, see Long 2002, 203–4, 206, 264.

Note that Epictetus has often been interpreted as putting forth a mono-theistic view of God. I concur, however, with Long (2002) that the mono-theism of Judaism, Christianity, and Islam is not a Stoic doctrine. Just what the points of comparison are with our own modern religious per-spectives is a complex matter. And Long rightly warns that we are likely to fall victim "to either over-assimilation or excessive differentiation" (143). But a few points can be noted here briefly: when Epictetus speaks of God or Zeus or Nature or the gods, he has in mind a providentially organized view of the world and a pantheism in which we, humans, par-take of divine or cosmic reason. For more, see Long 2002, 143–206.

57. Ibid., 196. Note that while Aristotle does not think of *eudaimonia* (i.e., happiness) as primarily a feeling of contentment, he does think that it is a life blessed with some prosperity or lucky charm (*daimōn*) and that true virtue, the major component of happiness, yields a derivative kind of pleasure.

58. "I went crazy when they first told me I couldn't see. . . . I'd trade both arms and both legs for my eyesight. That's how much it means to me." These are the words of Private Sam Ross, a paratrooper blinded by a bomblet in Iraq, May 2003. See Dean Reynolds, "High Costs of War," ABCNews.com, March 8, 2004, accessed July 16, 2004 (http://abcnews.go.com/sections/WNT/US/war_wounded_04308.html).

59. For testimony here, see the accounts in Barstow 2000.

60. The title for this section comes from Patrick O'Driscoll, "Amputee Still 'Fit for Duty' in Iraq," HonoluluAdvertiser.com, May 10, 2004, accessed July 16, 2004 (http://the.honoluluadvertiser.com/article/2004/May/10/mn/mn02a.html).

61. William Shakespeare, *Coriolanus*, Act 5, Scene 3.

62. For Rozelle's story, see O'Driscoll, "Amputee Still 'Fit for Duty' in Iraq."

63. Ibid., 185.

64. Ibid.

65. Ashby 2002, 162.
66. Ibid., 251–56.
67. Ibid., 255.

Chapter 3

1. I adapt a Kantian phrase here (see the *Doctrine of Virtue*, 406), though I do not mean to imply, as Kant sometimes does, that the aesthetic of virtue is mere optional trim on virtue. By the "aesthetic of character" I mean how we appear to others as conveyed through formal manners and decorum, as well as manner in the wider sense of personal bearing and outward attitude.
2. See Walzer's interesting remarks here (2004), 3–22.
3. Buss 1999.
4. I owe thanks to Chris Gill for helping me sharpen this point.
5. Although in battlefield conditions, as one military author notes, "saluting, shiny boots, and social distance" quickly disappear. See Stewart 1991, 125.
6. See Schofield 1991, 14.
7. For a lively book on "faking it," see Miller 2003.
8. Goffman 1967a, 60.
9. Ibid., 58.
10. *Anthropology from a Pragmatic Point of View* (hereafter: Anth.), 151.
11. Cf. Kant's *Groundwork of the Metaphysic of Morals*. See Paton's 1956 edition, 398.
12. On posed and spontaneous facial expressions that correspond to specific emotions and social manners, see Ekman 1982, esp. Part II.
13. So Pascal's advice to the skeptic: practice as if you believe and you will find yourself believing. On this, see De Sousa's (1988) discussion of examples of bootstrapping that do not shade into deceptions.
14. For a lively review of his work, which I draw on here, see Gladwell 2002.
15. Strack, Martin, and Stepper 1988.
16. See Ekman 1982 for a review of the literature.
17. Moved by these sort of arguments, Bill Clinton urged school uniforms in two of his State of the Union addresses. Though federal and state agencies don't track statistics on this subject, a study conducted in 2000 by the Centers for Disease Control and Prevention found that uniforms were required in 20 percent of public and Roman Catholic elementary and middle schools and 10 percent of high schools. See *New York Times*, Sept. 13, 2002.
18. From conversation with Mary King, August 2002.

19. See Driver 1992. Driver's views draw from Kant's—see *Lectures on Ethics*, esp. 111. As Driver points out, Kant uses other arguments to underscore the moral importance of semblance and resemblance. One such argument comes from the treatment of animals: we ought not to practice cruelty against animals not because of animals' inherent dignity, but because the practice of treating them inhumanely can through resemblance reinforce cruelty toward humans. See *Lectures*, 239, in the Infield edition (Hackett).

20. "Tailhook" refers to the way naval aviators must land their planes by hooking the tail of the planes on a taut wire on the flight deck of carriers. Aviators annually meet at a Tailhook convention, widely known for its bawdiness and sexual promiscuity. In 1992, Lt. Paula Coughlin, one of the women aviators who was sexually assaulted at the 1991 convention, went public with her complaint. The charge shook the U.S. Navy, leading to a series of resignations from the secretary of the Navy down. It led to massive policy review within the Navy of the treatment of women.

21. See Driver 1992.

22. *On Duties* 1.95 (using Griffin and Atkins's edition [1991] throughout).

23. Ibid., 1.5; see 1.96.

24. From Griffin and Atkins's notes to ibid., 1.95; also see 1.126–28 on the themes of shame, public decency, and the "approval of eyes and ears." Specifically on decorum as that aspect of virtue that "will shine forth"— *ex quo elucebit omnis constantia omnisque moderatio,* see 1.102; on the appropriate fit of a house for "public gaze," see 1.138.

25. Ibid., 1.98.

26. Ibid., 1.99, 105.

27. Ibid., 1.103–6.

28. Ibid., 1.103–4.

29. Not that it always does. Date rape continues to be a serious concern on this campus (just as it is on civilian campuses), though the incidents, unlike those at the Air Force Academy in recent years, have not drawn the same congressional and public attention.

30. See Gill's (1988) illuminating article on this.

31. See *On Duties* 1.107, 115, 117.

32. *Handbook of Epictetus* 17.

33. *On Duties* 1.74.

34. Ibid., 1.114.

35. Ibid., 1.120, 110, 116.

36. Ibid., 1.117.

37. Ibid., 1.118.

38. Ibid., 1.114.

39. Ibid., 1.109. The roster of examples is culled from 1.109–13.

40. I am indebted to Capt. Mark Clemente for clarification here.
41. *On Duties* 1.111.
42. Ibid., 1.99. I have altered the Griffin and Atkins translation of *homines* from "men" to "humans" to try to capture the inclusive and cosmopolitan sentiment of the passage.
43. From a case prepared by her attorney Eugene R. Fidell in June 2000.
44. *On Duties* 1.126, 128, 131, 146; on issues of body care that amplify the discussion in Chapter 2, see 1.130.
45. Ibid., 1.102.
46. Diogenes Laertius 7.173.
47. *On Duties* 1.136–37.
48. Ibid., 1.133–37.
49. For further reflection here, see Sherman 1989, 1997a.
50. For a fuller treatment of the themes in this section, see Sherman 2004a, 2005a.
51. Anth. 282.
52. For more on this theme, see Sherman 1997a, ch. 4, esp. 141–64.
53. *Moral and Political Essays* (Cooper and Procopé trans.), 183. Also, see Miriam Griffin, "The Paedagogic Strategy of *De Beneficiis*" (unpublished ms.) as charting the course of Liberalis's moral progress and the shifts in pedagogical method that match that progress. So, she argues, the early books show a preoccupation with *praecepta* (rules and admonitions), while the latter books, 4–7, examine the *decreta* (tenets) of Stoic theory. See Inwood 1995a on two levels of discourse in Seneca's essay—that of commonsense morality and that of strict Stoic theory, with its paradoxes and redescriptions.
54. See my discussion of this as it relates to Aristotelian magnanimity in Sherman 1988.
55. For further reading, see Long and Sedley 1987a, especially sections 58 and 65. Also, Inwood 1985, 127–81, and Algra et al. 1991, esp. B. Inwood and P. Donini's chapter on "Stoic Ethics," 675–738.
56. Epictetus, *Discourses* 4.12.19 (using Hard trans. in Gill's edition [1995] unless otherwise noted).
57. See, e.g., *On Favours* 2.18.4 (using Cooper and Procopé trans. in *Moral and Political Essays* [1995]).
58. See Branham and Goulet-Caze 1996 and Dudley 1937. The Cynic criticism of convention is important background to Seneca's work, though Seneca is far too much a subscriber of Roman convention to share the Cynic attitude. On Roman culture, see Rawson 1985 and 1991; on the practice of Hellenistic "euergetism," see Veyne 1990. For a fascinating study of second-century manners of self-presentation and male deportment, see Gleason 1995.

59. See the classification at *On Favours* 1.11.1.
60. Ibid., 1.12.3.
61. Ibid., 1.11.6.
62. Ibid.
63. Ibid., 1.12.1–2—*extet, haereat amico meo, convivat.*
64. Ibid., 1.6.2.
65. Ibid., 1.5.3.
66. Ibid., 1.5.2. See also 15.4; on the Stoic theme of making do in strained circumstances, see 4.21.
67. Ibid., 1.5.6.
68. On this, see the insightful analogy of gift giving and gratitude with playing a game of catch. In both types of reciprocal exchanges, timing and attunement to a recipient are critical (ibid., 2.17.3–7 and 2.32).
69. Ibid., 2.9.1.
70. Too, given the realities of patronage and hierarchy in Roman society, he is keen to liberate the recipients of favors—often those considerably less well off than benefactors—from hefty burdens of *quid pro quo.* See ibid., 1.1.3. On this, see Inwood 1995a, 263.
71. *Pace* Inwood, "true benefits are" *not* "purely intelligible intentions" (ibid., 256). In correspondence, Inwood has replied that his interpretive emphasis on the intelligible (on the *animus* as the action of giving a *beneficium*) is a consequence of Seneca's conception of Stoic theory of action, that "action is fundamentally the mental event which causes the physical movement." This said, he agrees with me that the care and thought given to the choice of action and benefit are vital to determining what the action is.
72. For a similar tension, see Epictetus, *Discourses* 2.5.6: "Externals must be used with care, because their usage is not an indifferent matter, yet at the same time, with composure and tranquility, because the material being used is indifferent." I would argue that what matters is not just "usage," but a particular embodied usage, in this or that expression or vehicle. Material may be indifferent, but not the specific way it is worked up, or invested by intention.
73. *On Favours* 1.2.4; italics added.
74. Ibid., 2.1.1; italics added.
75. Ibid., 2.2.2.
76. Ibid., 1.1.4.
77. Ibid., 1.1.7, 1.7.3, 2.11.6, 2.3.1, 2.6.2, 2.7.1; see also 2.4.1.
78. Ibid., 2.3.1.
79. Ibid., 2.33.1. On this, see Inwood's (1995a) helpful discussion, 259–61.
80. *On Favours* 2.22.1; see 2.25.3, 23.2.
81. See Darwin reprinted in Calhoun and Solomon 1984; Izard 1971; Tomkins 1962; Ekman 1982, 1984, 1992, and 1993.

Chapter 4

1. *On Anger* 1.9 (using Cooper and Procopé's translation in *Moral and Political Essays* [1995]; for the Latin text, see the Loeb Classical Library edition of *Moral Essays* (1989).
2. Ibid., 2.35.1.
3. See Shay 2002 for an insightful analysis of the emotions that figure in battle, and post-traumatic stress disorder (PTSD).
4. From an interview conducted in February 2003.
5. See, for example, Kindlon and Thompson 1999, who discuss anger in the context of a boy's emotional development, and Pollack 1998 for the notion of a "boy" code of honor.
6. See Vistica 2001.
7. For more on Buddhism, see Thurman 1995; Guenther 1991; Thera and Bodhi 1986; Garfield and Samten, forthcoming.
8. See *The Republic*, 375 ff. and 439ff.
9. Ibid., 440c.
10. *Iliad* 1.170.
11. Ibid., 1.138–40.
12. More specifically, they held that Boorda did not stand behind the nomination of Adm. Stanley Arthur for CINCPAC (commander in chief of the U.S. Pacific Command). His nomination was held up in the Senate because a female junior officer charged that she had been routed out of helicopter flight school after complaining about sexual harassment. Arthur acknowledged that there had been sexual harassment but refused to reinstate her, on grounds of poor performance. See Philpott 1995 for further details.
13. I have been told that the commandant of the Marines, Mike Hagee, removed three medals before being sworn in, because he lacked properly documented citations. In this regard, several officers have told me that medals are often awarded in haste without proper documentation. Consider also the accusations now in the air, as I write, about Senator John Kerry's medals earned in Vietnam.
14. *Iliad* 1.217–21.
15. Ibid., 1.343–47.
16. Ibid., 9.782–85.
17. Ibid., 18.128.
18. On this, see Harris 2001, 77.
19. *Iliad* 18.105; 94–96.
20. Ibid., 9.857–61; 65.
21. Ibid., 22.398–405; 24.64–65.
22. From an interview, October 2001.

23. For a modern treatment of just-war theory, see Walzer 1977. For a radical revision of just-war theory, and the claim that the resort to war (*jus ad bellum*) and the conduct of war (*jus in bello*) should not be decoupled, see McMahan 2004.
24. *Iliad* 22.398–405.
25. From conversation with Lt. Col. Ted Westhusing, January 2003.
26. For a more thorough review of Aristotle on the emotions, see Sherman 1989 and 1997a.
27. Lazarus 1984, Scherer 1993, Frijda 1986, Oatley 1992. See Zajonc 1984 for an important criticism. Among philosophers, see Solomon 1973, Stocker 1996, De Sousa 1987, Goldie 2000, and Nussbaum 2002 for a sampling.
28. Schachter and Singer 1962; Cannon 1927.
29. *Rhetoric* 1378a30–32, my trans. (For other Aristotle references, I use Barnes' translation of the *Complete Works* [1984].)
30. *Nicomachean Ethics* 1102b26–32.
31. Ibid., 1102b31–32.
32. Ibid., 1125b32–33.
33. See Shay 2002.
34. *Nicomachean Ethics* 1126a2–8.
35. Ibid., 1149a25ff.
36. Plutarch's *Moralia: On the Control of Anger* 464c–d; 453d. For abstaining from anger on the AA model, see also Seneca, *On Anger* 2.12.3.
37. See Cooper and Procopé 1995, introduction.
38. I thank Rebecca Kukla for making this distinction.
39. From an interview conducted by the author, December 2002.
40. See Velleman 1999.
41. Seneca, *On Anger* 1.6.1, 2.11; 2.14; 2.17; see Cicero, *Tusculan Disputations* 4.55 (using Graver's translation [2002] throughout).
42. To make a slightly different point, the sergeant's anger is mock in the sense that it is not so much a "readout" of what he is feeling as a social signal designed to communicate the real costs of failure and whining. On psychology literature that distinguishes between the read out and social communication roles of emotion, see Jakobs, Manstead, and Fischer 1999.
43. I am grateful to Alisa Carse for help in formulating this point.
44. I am grateful to Brad Inwood for pressing me on this question.
45. Others who have gone through the same training, such as Ted Westhusing, have suggested to me that the challenges are far from trivial. This is especially so when doing mass tactical jumps at night, with over a thousand soldiers (twelve aircrafts with one hundred paratroopers each) all parachuting at the same time. There the fear of colliding into another's "chute" seems real and reasonable.

46. See Griffin 1992, 319 n. 5, 84 n. 5; also Cooper and Procopé in *Seneca, Moral and Political Essays,* 1995, 15–16.

47. *On Anger* 1.1.4.

48. Ibid., 2.36.1.

49. Ibid., 2.11.2.

50. For a lively piece on Paul Ekman's studies of the facial expression of emotion and its implications for law enforcement, see Gladwell 2002.

51. *On Anger* 1.2.1–3.

52. Ibid., 3.43.5; See Plutarch, *On the Control of Anger* 464d, in *Moralia,* for an anger-free soul as a humane (*philanthropon*) soul. Also, see Nussbaum 1994 for an important discussion of this.

53. *On Anger* 3.1.5.

54. *Tou logou diastrophas,* Von Armin 1924 (SVF I 208).

55. *Accurate* judgments of good and evil are components of *eupatheiai,* "good emotions," (sometimes translated as "equable" or "fine" emotions). I discuss this later in the text.

56. Although the Stoics take emotions to be fully cognitive, this does not entail, on their view, that emotions are flat or affectless. Emotions are accompanied by a kind of mental tension or arousal—"shrinkings" and "swellings," "stretchings" "contractions," and "tearings." In Zeno's novel metaphor, emotion is a "flutter." Thus, locating emotion in a unitary, rational soul need not detract from emotion's characteristic feel. Zeno underscores the point by adding that the belief must be fresh (*prosphatos*), again, a striking metaphor meant to call up in the Greek listener associations with freshly cut meat or corpses that still, in a sense, have some life. Cicero gives a temporal gloss to the term, translating with the Latin *recens.* But, of course, emotions such as anger can linger and "bite" (*Tusculan Disputations* 3.83) long after a perceived offense. So *recens* cannot be restricted to a temporal meaning. Cicero himself adds that a judgment remains fresh "as long as it retains some force, some liveliness or, as it were, greenness" (*viriditatem*) (ibid., 3.75). For insightful discussion, see White 1995, 230.

57. *On Anger* 2.1.3–4.

58. On the twofold evaluation view, see ibid., 2.1.3. Also, *Tusculan Disputations* 3.24, 4.14, and Graver's commentary. For further discussion, see Sorabji 2000, 29; Brennan 1998, 335; White 1995, 230–32.

59. For a contemporary version of this, see Solomon 1973.

60. See Sherman 2002b, 2000a, and 1999b.

61. *Arius Didymus* 2.90, 19–91, 9 in Stobaeus 1884 (Long 1987a, 65E).

62. We may think it better classified as a kind of distress at present evil, and close cousins with some emotions that fall under that genus. (The list includes malice, envy, jealousy, pity, grief, worry, sorrow, annoyance,

mental pain, and vexation.) But note that in the conversion of ordinary emotions to more rational ones (*eupatheiai*), nothing corresponding to distress will survive—for the sage enjoys a stress-free life of equanimity. In contrast, emotions corresponding to appetites do survive as rational wishes (*bouleseis*).

63. *On Anger* 1.7.4; 3.1.4; also 3.16.2.
64. Galen, *On Hippocrates' and Plato's Doctrines* in De Lacy 1984, 4.2.10–18 (Long 1987a, 65J); also the latter's comments, 420. See also *On Anger* 2.35.2, 1.7.4.
65. *On Anger* 1.17.5–7.
66. Peters and Mace 1962.
67. See my important qualification of this in Sherman 1997a and 1997b.
68. *Tusculan Disputations* 3.83.
69. *On Anger* 2.2.6.
70. Freud, "Inhibitions, Symptoms and Anxiety" (1925–26), in Freud 1955.
71. Chused 1991; also Sherman 2004c.
72. *On Anger* 2.5.
73. Ibid., 3.3.
74. Ibid., 2.7.1.
75. Ibid., 2.8.2.
76. *Nicomachean Ethics* 4.5.
77. See Bishop Butler's *Fifteen Sermons* (1964) for insightful remarks on resentment and forgiveness.
78. See Govier 1999, Blumenfeld 2002, Hughes 1995.
79. For this example and for a popular and insightful discussion of revenge, see Jacoby 1983.
80. See Simon Wiesenthal's (1997) moving, autobiographical account of such an encounter and the follow-up symposium.
81. For a discussion of women as victims of war crimes, see Barstow 2000.
82. See Strawson 2003. Also Murphy and Hampton 1988 on this.
83. My remarks are limited to a discussion of *On Anger*. For a fuller consideration of Seneca's views on punishment and forgiveness, see his essay *On Mercy*.
84. Kant, *Doctrine of Virtue* (Gregor trans.), 460.
85. *On Anger* 2.5.3.
86. As Bishop Butler puts it in his sermon, "Upon Resentment," "Resentment against vice and wickedness: it is one of the common bonds, by which society is held together." Butler 1964, 126.
87. See *On Anger* 3.38.1–2.
88. See Seneca's recounting of the atrocities committed by King Cambyses and Harpagus's king at 3.14 and 15. See Nussbaum 1994 for a moving discussion of these examples.
89. *On Anger* 3.14.1–3.

90. Ibid., 3.14.3.
91. Ibid., 2.10.7. For a valuable discussion of this, see Nussbaum 1994.
92. Ibid., 2.10.8.
93. See Hampton in Murphy and Hampton 1988.
94. Morris 1995; Murphy, ed., 1995.
95. *Tusculan Disputations* 3.6.
96. *On Anger* 2.14.4.
97. Ibid., 3.16.1.
98. Ibid., 3.27 and 26.
99. Ibid., 2.34.1.
100. Bilton and Sim 1992, 98–99.
101. See Moore in Murphy, ed., 1995; Butler 1964.
102. Exodus 10.1–2 (in *JPS Hebrew-English Tanakh* trans. [Philadelphia: Jewish Publication Society, 1999]). See also 9.12 and 7.3.
103. God's resentment toward Pharaoh may also betray a trace of self-doubt in his own authority and envy of Pharaoh's power; see Hampton for envy resentment, in Murphy and Hampton 1988, ch. 2.
104. See Murphy 1995b and Jacoby 1983.
105. Klein 1975, ch. 6: "Some Theoretical Conclusions Regarding the Emotional Life of the Infant."
106. The following is based on an interview conducted in December 2002.
107. *Nicomachean Ethics* 1117b10–15, Barnes translation slightly modified.
108. I am indebted to Mardy Rawls for confirming the details.
109. From an interview conducted in December 2002.
110. See, for example, the Ten Commandments of the Code of Chivalry outlining the Church's attempt to have knights fight in compliance with some notion of just conduct, Gautier 1965.
111. From a talk given at the Carnegie Council on Ethics and International Affairs, New York, January 29, 2002. For a compelling study of the use of children in war, see Singer 2005.
112. The term is from Maass 2002.
113. See Power 2002, 388–89.
114. I relate the following narrative in some detail both as a record of events and as a way to track emotions. I draw on my own conversations and interviews with Hugh Thompson in spring 1998, spring 1999, and February 2002; Bilton and Sim 1992; and a CBS *60 Minutes* broadcast on Thompson.
115. Bilton and Sim 1992, 13.
116. *On Anger* 3.12.4; 3.32.2.
117. Ibid., 3.13.1–2.
118. Ibid., 3.12.3.
119. Ibid., 3.36–37.
120. Ibid., for example, 1.7 and 3.3.

121. Ibid., for example, 1.8.
122. Ibid., 1.8.3.
123. Frankfurt 1988, 174. I am indebted to David Velleman's discussion of Frankfurt in Velleman 2002.
124. Frankfurt 1988, 170.
125. This Freudian reading of Frankfurt is due to Velleman.
126. Freud, "Notes upon a Case of Obsessional Neurosis" (1909), in Freud 1955, 158.
127. Ibid., 177. Velleman nicely puts it this way in critiquing Frankfurt.
128. Ibid., 180–81.
129. Ibid., 238.
130. See *On Anger* 3.13 for suggestions of something like repression.
131. Frankfurt 1988, 1701–3.
132. I borrow here from Jamison 1995, 214, who uses similar language to describe coping with manic depression.
133. *On Anger* 3.13.

Chapter 5

1. *Discourses* 3.24.116 (using Hard trans. in Gill's edition [1995] unless otherwise noted).
2. *Tusculan Disputations* 5.40–41, as quoted in Long and Sedley 1987a, 63L.
3. *Epistles* 113.27.
4. Quoted in Shephard 2001.
5. Here I follow John Cooper's general line in his very illuminating unpublished 2004 manuscript, "The Emotional Life of the Wise."
6. Spiller 1988, 63.
7. *The New York Times,* May 26, 2003: "Black Granite Roll Call Is Now 58, 235."
8. See Long 2002, 24 for comments on Epictetus along these lines.
9. *Discourses* 4.7.37–41.
10. I am indebted to Martha Nussbaum for this point in her response to a seminar I presented at the University of Chicago, April 2003, on material in Chapter 4.
11. *On Anger* 3.15.
12. Ibid., 3.14.
13. *Discourses* 4.7.15–24.
14. Ibid., 4.7.1.
15. Ibid., 4.7.5.
16. Ibid., 3.84.
17. See Diogenes Laertius 7.107; Sedley 1999. See also *Discourses* 4.12.19.
18. Powell 1995, 46; see also 323.

19. See Julia Annas's comments in her brief remarks on Stoic emotions in Solomon 2003.
20. This move brings to mind Kant's pathological emotions and their "practical" counterparts in the person of virtue.
21. Cicero, *Tusculan Disputations* 4.12 and 13 (using Graver's trans. [2002] throughout); Diogenes Laertius 1972, 7.116.
22. *Tusculan Disputations* 3.77.
23. Ibid., 4.12–14.
24. My remarks in this paragraph are a response to conversations with Margaret Graver. My position owes much to John Cooper's unpublished 2004 manuscript. See also Brennan 1998 and Nussbaum 1994, 398–401. For earlier formulations of my view, see Sherman and White 2003.
25. See *Tusculan Disputations* 4.12–14. I thank Margaret Graver for helping me to clarify this example.
26. This worry parallels the "moral purity" objection often raised against Kantian ethics.
27. In this sense, it is a bit like Freud's notion of signal anxiety—a warning to defend oneself against a possible conflict or temptation.
28. So Cicero claims in objecting to the overly narrow limits of Stoic "good emotions." See his discussion of Alcibiades' shame at his lack of moral progress (as Plato depicts it at the end of the *Symposium*). *Tusculan Disputations* 3.77.
29. Neither does joy, but that, at least, doesn't presuppose one's own vice.
30. *On Anger* 2.3.3.
31. Gellius, vol. 3, 19.1.
32. *Epistles* 57.4–5.
33. *Epistles* 71.30.
34. Ibid., 71.27.
35. Ibid., 57.5.
36. See Herman 1992, 34.
37. See LeDoux 1996 and his notion of fear as a "low-road emotion" that bypasses higher-order cortical circuitry. While the quick response is an adaptive advantage for survival, the cost of the thinner cognitive circuitry is that we sometimes hold on to our fears irrationally, despite more reflective evaluations that tell us we are not, in fact, in danger.
38. *Nicomachean Ethics* 3.6–9; see especially 1115a11–12.
39. Ibid., 1115b7–8 (using here Rowe's translation [2002], though I add "sense" to help translate "*noun*").
40. Ibid., 1117a30–b21.
41. In this regard, see John Huston's documentary *Let There Be Light,* which follows seventy-five war veterans over an eight-week period at a psychiatric war hospital, Mason General Hospital. For a discussion of the documentary, see Shephard 2001, 271–78.

42. *Nicomachean Ethics* 1115a29–b5; 1116b4–10. Current research concurs with this point. See Garber and Seligman 1980; Peterson, Maier, and Seligman 1993.
43. I interviewed Rick Jolly in July 2002.
44. See Moran 1945.
45. *Epistles* 5.4, Gummere's Loeb translation slightly altered.
46. See a story on Jolly in *Soldier,* January 2001, "Honors Even for the Doc," by Ray Routledge.
47. *Epistles* 57.4–5.
48. See Keegan and Holmes 1986, discussing Alfred de Vigny (as quoted in Grossman 1995, 86).
49. *Iliad* 22.398–405.
50. Swofford 2003, 172–74.
51. Stewart 1991, 76.
52. Ibid.
53. See *Epistles* 13.4.
54. Ibid., 13.10–12.
55. Crane 1969, 202.
56. Shephard 2001, 284.
57. Bremner and Charney 1994.
58. Friedman 1995.
59. Herman 1992, 89.
60. *Epistles* 14.3–6.
61. Herman 1992, 33.
62. Marshall 1978, 182.
63. Note recent reports of detainees attempting suicide at the American naval base at Guantánamo Bay, Cuba. See "23 Detainees Attempted Suicide in Protest at Base, Military Says," *New York Times,* Jan. 25, 2005.
64. *Epistles* 82.15.
65. Ibid., 82.23; see 82.8–9, 24.
66. Ibid., 83.20–21.
67. Ibid., 82.8–9; 82.20.
68. Ibid., 82.21.
69. I follow Cooper's general line here in his unpublished 2004 manuscript.
70. Ibid., 76.33–35.
71. See Cicero for similar remarks, *Tusculan Disputations* 4.57.
72. Swofford 2003, 195.
73. Ibid., 242.
74. See discussion in Walzer 1977, 138–43, of remarks by Robert Graves, Wilfred Owen, and George Orwell, among others.
75. See Exodus 30.11–16; Numbers 31.50.
76. From an interview, September 2002.
77. See Spiller 1988; Grossman 1995.

78. Grossman 1995, citing Lord 1976.
79. Crane 1969, 252.
80. On flight and fear responses, see Cannon 1929, and on posturing in intraspecies aggression, see Lorenz 1966. Also see Grossman 1995.
81. *On Duties* 1.107–15.
82. Ibid., 1.107.
83. See Walzer 1999, 35–41. For an important critique of this, see McMahan 2004. McMahan's view is that soldiers who fight without a just cause are "unjust combatants" and that this status undermines any presumption of moral equality on the battlefield. Thus he challenges the claim "that unjust combatants do not do wrong merely by fighting in an unjust war."
84. Barker 1992, 102–3. I also draw on the other novels in the trilogy, Barker 1993 and 1995.
85. For an insightful discussion of the symptoms of war neurosis by the historical Rivers, see Rivers 1918.
86. From conversations with Matthew Friedman, executive director of the National Center for Post-Traumatic Stress Disorder, June and July 2003. For extensive information and publications on PTSD, see the organization's Web site: www.ncptsd.org.
87. See Friedman 2003a.
88. On this see Herman 1992. Also, I am indebted to Arthur Blank for his helpful discussion with me about the early history of PTSD and the treatment of Vietnam veterans. See Sonnenberg, Blank, and Talbott 1985; also Blank's three articles in the volume.
89. Kukla et al. 1990.
90. Friedman 2003b.
91. See Hoge et al. 2004. For comments on the study, see Friedman 2004.
92. See the "National Comorbidity Survey Report" in Kessler et al. 1995, and Friedman 2003b.
93. See Friedman 2003a. One might wonder, though, why more psychiatric illnesses do not have external events as part of their etiology.
94. An interpretation of Seneca as acknowledging fear in the face of threats of tragic loss might put him outside the traditional Stoic view here.
95. American Psychiatric Association 1994, 427–28.
96. See Carlson and Dalenberg 2000.
97. Ibid.
98. *Tusculan Disputations* 3.52, adding numbers to Gravers's translation.
99. From a conversation with Matthew Friedman, July 2003.
100. Here, consider the master/slave dialectic of the nineteenth-century German Idealist Georg Wilhelm Friedrich Hegel. Hegel's insight was that a slave could become a freeman through the attitude with which he took on his labor; in turn, the master would devolve into a slave by his utter dependency on someone else's will.

101. Carlson and Dalenberg 2000.
102. It is worth noting in discussing resilience that some studies suggest that those who successfully make it through stressful military training have a substance in their urine that those who don't make it lack—namely, a hippocampal protein, neuropeptide Y. The substance may exert an anti-depressant response, critical in facing stress. From conversation with Matthew Friedman, June 2003.
103. Pharmacology also has a place, with SSRI drugs such as Prozac and Zoloft having shown to be effective in treatment (from conversations with Matthew Friedman). Also, clinical reports indicate that immediate stress debriefing (within 24–72 hours) may prevent the encoding of traumatic memories. See Friedman, Charney, and Deutch 1995.
104. See Follete, Ruzek, and Abueg 2001; Foa and Rothbaum 1998.
105. See Jaycox, Zoellner, and Foa 2002.
106. See Seneca, *Epistles* 94.
107. Crane 1969, 222.
108. *Meditations* 8.32.

Chapter 6

1. From an interview with Seymour Sherman, fall 2003.
2. Seneca, *Epistles* 63.6.
3. *Tusculan Disputations* 4.58; see 3.5–6 (using Graver's translation [2002] throughout, unless otherwise noted).
4. Ibid., 4.9, 3.25.
5. *Epistles* 27.1–2.
6. Ibid., 63.14. See Marcus Wilson's essay (1997) on Seneca's *Epistles*.
7. See Griffin 1992, 42.
8. *Nicomachean Ethics* 1.7.1097b8–11; *Eudemian Ethics* 1245b18–19 (using Barnes 1984 for Aristotle references throughout).
9. *Epistles* 63.1; see also 99.16.
10. Ibid., 99.15, 14.
11. Ibid., 99.18–21.
12. Ibid., 99.16; see 74.31 and 99.15.
13. *Phaedo* 117c–e. Some ancients would argue that "natural" deficits—including lacking rational authority or control, as Aristotle might put it—help explain women's penchant for tearfulness. But there is no short-age of conventions in the ancient world that reinforce the association of women with grieving. Vase paintings from ancient Greece attest to the fact that women were often assigned the role of lamenters, surrounding a corpse, cradling the dead body's head, tearing their hair out, wailing and singing dirges (see Ashenburg 2002). Kinswomen joined professional

women keeners, "hire[d] . . . foreign choruses," as Plato quips in the *Laws* (800e1–3), to lament the dead (in *Complete Works*). Some texts suggest that the professional singers sang a proper dirge, the kinswomen merely wailed. However, by the time of Solon in the sixth century, legislation officially banned the use of hired hands for wailing, in an attempt to curtail the excesses of public funerary ritual and the arousal of what was viewed as dangerous, and often violent, sentiments. For more on ancient Greek mourning rituals, see Alexiou 1974.

14. *Iliad* 18.23–42.
15. Ibid., 24.595–600.
16. *Epistles* 99.17.
17. Ibid., 99.15; see 99.21.
18. Ibid., 63.13. His remarks echo the general division of social labor during antiquity—of lamentation as a woman's job and the more dignified, funeral oration, a man's: Alexiou 1974, 108.
19. *Epistles* 99.24.
20. Ibid., 99.24.
21. Ibid., 98.11.
22. Ibid., 99.5.
23. See Pollack 1999; Kindlon and Thompson 1999. For a humorous twist on the gendered phenomenon, see "Boys Crying and Girls Playing Dumb" in Miller 2003.
24. Bragg 1999, 7.
25. Ibid., 215–19.
26. Shay 2002, 81.
27. See Sonnenberg, Blank, and Talbott 1985; also Matsakis 1988. For one of the most moving depictions of returning vets, see Erich Maria Remarque's second novel, *The Road Back* (1931).
28. Joel Brinkley, "At a Base in Iraq, American Troops Honor Victims of Copter Attack," *New York Times*, November 7, 2003, A8.
29. From an interview, July 2002.
30. From the Web site www.SAMA82.org.uk ("SAMA" stands for "South Atlantic Medal Association").
31. From an interview, July 2002.
32. In this sense it is thicker than Cicero's notion of humanity, discussed in Chapter 3, as the fundamental persona we take up insofar as we share reason.
33. From a phone conversation with Rick Jolly on October 26, 2004.
34. See "The Reluctant Memorialist," by Louis Menand, *New Yorker*, July 8, 2002, 55–65; Mayo 1988.
35. Shay 2002, 170.
36. *Epistles* 63.14.

37. For a reflective and scholarly memoir on the kaddish, see Wieseltier 1998.
38. Ibid., 24. I quote here from Wieseltier, who in turn quotes from the writing of his relative who cites this Hasidic teacher. Wieseltier suggests that this writing is the source for a prayer composed by the Israeli writer S. Y. Agnon, delivered at military funerals (22–24).
39. *Letters to Atticus* 12.14 (using Shackleton-Bailey's translation [1999]); on Tullia's death, see also Cicero, *Letters to Friends* 248, 249 (Shackleton-Bailey's trans. [2001]).
40. *Letters to Atticus* 12.13.
41. Ibid., 12.23, 12.28.
42. For an excellent discussion of this subject, to which I am indebted, see White 1995.
43. *Tusculan Disputations* 3.75–76; numbers added to Graver's translation.
44. Ibid., 3.77, 79.
45. Ibid., 3.76.
46. Ibid., 3.77; see 4.60 and 63.
47. I am grateful to Stephen White (1995, 237) for pointing this out.
48. *Tusculan Disputations* 3.35.
49. Ibid., 3.58.
50. Ibid., 3.31.
51. Ibid., 3.77, 79; 4.63.
52. Ibid., 3.79.
53. Ibid., 3.62; changing Graver's "distress" to "grief."
54. On blushing and contemporary medical research, see Gawande 2001.
55. See Gladwell 2002 for a fascinating discussion of research on face reading, and the skills of such researchers as Sylvan Tomkins, Erving Goffmann, and Paul Ekman.
56. See *Tusculan Disputations* 4.19.
57. Ibid., 4.14.
58. From a CNN documentary, *The Ghosts of War*, aired October 26, 2003.

Chapter 7

1. The term is from Care 1996; see especially the chapter "Problematic Agency," 69–97.
2. *Discourses* 1.29.4 (using throughout Hard trans. in Gill's edition [1995]).
3. Emerson, "Self-Reliance," *Essays*, 77.
4. *Eudemian Ethics* 1245b18–19; see *Nicomachean Ethics* 1097b9–11; *Magna Moralia* 1218a8. (For Aristotle references, I am using throughout Barnes's translation [1984] unless otherwise specified.)
5. This is to allow that some units may require less teamwork than others and in these, there may be a limited argument for individual rather than

group replacements. For an extended criticism of individual replacement policies, see Vandergriff 2002; Shay 1994, 2002.

6. I have discussed the Aristotelian conception of friendship at length in Sherman 1989, ch. 4, and 1997a, ch. 5.

7. My remarks are based on interviews with Milton Friend conducted in May 2003 and January 2004, and from Michael Ruane, "Brothers in Arms," *Washington Post,* Jan. 24, 2001. Also, see Lt. Cmdr. Richard Kelly, "Halyard Mission," *Blue Book Magazine* 83, 4 (1946): 52–62.

8. *Washington Post,* May 19, 2004, A19.

9. See Inwood and Miller's helpful discussion in "Law in Roman Philosophy," forthcoming.

10. Cicero, *On Moral Ends* 3.62–64 (using throughout Woolf's translation in Annas 2001).

11. *Nicomachean Ethics* 1097b8–12.

12. Friendship is the primary theme of two of the ten books of the *Nicomachean Ethics* and occupies an equally central role in the other ethical treatises.

13. *Nicomachean Ethics* 1099a31–b6.

14. Ibid., 1169b17ff.

15. Ibid., 1155a9, 1159a28–31.

16. *Magna Moralia* 1213b8–24; see the parallel though more obscure passage in *Nicomachean Ethics* 9.9. For discussion of this see Cooper 1999b.

17. See Aristotle's *Rhetoric* 1381b29–32; cf. 1381a31–32.

18. *Eudemian Ethics* 1240b2, 1240b9–10; see also 1240a36–39. For further discussion, see Sherman 1989, 128–36.

19. *Nicomachean Ethics* 1172a10–14.

20. I use Paul Fussell's edition (Sassoon 1983). For a trilogy of novels based on Sassoon's life (and discussed in Chapter 5), see Pat Barker 1992, 1993, and 1995.

21. *Sherston's Progress* would focus on the first half of that identity; his second trilogy, a nonfictionalized autobiography, would focus on Sassoon as aesthete.

22. Fussell 1983, 131.

23. Ibid., 138.

24. Ibid., 140. The poem is entitled "Banishment."

25. Ibid., 141.

26. Ibid., 170–73.

27. Ibid., 22.

28. Ibid., 120; see also 122. For this sentiment in spades, see Erich Maria Remarque's celebrated World War I novel, *The Road Back* (1931).

29. Herman 1992, 133, 197.

30. Ibid., 155–236.

31. Ibid., 177. Herman reminds us of Freud and Breuer's words a century earlier: "Recollection without affect almost invariably produces no result." See Breuer and Freud, "Studies on Hysteria" (1893–95), in Freud 1955, 6.
32. Sassoon 1983, 122–23.
33. Ibid., 132, 158.
34. On an Aristotelian notion of central human capabilities, see Nussbaum 2000, 79–110, and esp., 78–80.
35. Herman 1992, 33.
36. Consider here Herman's discussion (ibid., 135) of the therapeutic goals of autonomy and empowerment set by Evan Stark and Anne Flitcraft in their work in battered women's shelters. "Empowerment," in their view, is "the convergence of mutual support with individual autonomy." A "strong survivor" in a shelter environment is one whose "experience is validated and her strengths are recognized and encouraged."
37. Survivors' accounts of life in the Nazi death camps make this all too clear. Their suicides, as in the case of Primo Levi, are even more painful reminders. See Levi 1996; Kluger 2001. For a moving biography of Levi, see Angier 2002.
38. Woolf 1981, 86.
39. Ibid., 87–88, 65–71.
40. Ibid., esp. 84–85.
41. Obviously, no single factor is sufficient, and the case is fictive. Additionally, to read nonfiction accounts of Holocaust survivors is to appreciate that whatever factors enter into survival and resilience, luck of all sorts is no insignificant player. On this, see Primo Levi's interview with Philip Roth (Levi 1986). Also, for a complex account of surviving the trauma of a near fatal rape, see Brison 2002.
42. Herman 1992, 58. Relevant also is the work of Seligman et al. on learned helplessness in Peterson, Maier, and Seligman 1993.
43. Woolf 1981, 98.
44. "These alterations of consciousness are at the heart of constriction or numbing, the third cardinal symptom of post-traumatic stress disorder [the other two being hyperarousal and intrusion]. Sometimes situations of inescapable danger may evoke not only terror and rage but also, paradoxically, a state of detached calm, in which terror, rage, and pain dissolve. Events continue to register in awareness, but it is as though these events have been disconnected from their ordinary meanings. Perceptions may be numbed or distorted, with partial anesthesia or the loss of particular sensations. Time sense may be altered, often with a sense of slow motion, and the experience may lose its quality of ordinary reality. The person may feel as though the event is not happening to her, as though

she is observing from outside her body, or as though the whole experience is a bad dream from which she will shortly awaken. The perceptual changes combine with a feeling of indifference, emotional detachment, and profound passivity in which the person relinquishes all initiative and struggle. This altered state of consciousness might be regarded as one of nature's small mercies, a protection against unbearable pain" (Herman 1992, 43).

45. *On Anger;* see 1.8 especially, in Cooper and Procopé's translation of *Moral and Political Essays,* 1995.
46. *Discourses* 1.29.7.
47. Even autonomy is misconceived when glossed, as it often is, as independent and enabling free choice. Good choosing often depends upon a division of epistemic labor that allows for deference to experts who have specialized skills and access to the relevant data. On this in the area of patient autonomy and deference to medical experts, I am grateful to Rebecca Kukla in a seminar presented at Georgetown University Philosophy Department, May 2004.
48. In particular, see the important work of Philip Bromberg (1998).
49. Ibid., 274.
50. Slavin and Kriegman 1992 as quoted by Bromberg 1998, 274.
51. Herman 1992, 33, quoting Frankel and Smith 1978, 89.
52. From conversations with Wynona Ward in February 2004. For a glimpse into her life story and law practice, which advocates on behalf of victims of domestic violence in rural Vermont, see http://www.havejustice willtravel.org.
53. As Seneca poetically puts it, a sage "springs into existence, like the phoenix, only once in five hundred years" (*Epistles* 42.1).
54. I qualify here because in previous chapters I have spoken of the sage as emotionally vulnerable in at least two limited ways: he can suffer the involuntary arousals of preemotions but then quickly catch himself and recover control. And he is susceptible to "good emotions" (*eupatheiai*)— the enlightened emotions that come with a recalibration of values: external goods pursued or avoided, without the ordinary desire and pleasure of possession or ordinary fear and pain of loss.
55. The parents of Kim Sun-II are pictured in the *Washington Post,* June 23, 2004, "S. Korean Is Beheaded in Iraq." Michael Berg collapses into his son David's arms in a picture in the *Washington Post,* May 12, 2004, "American Beheaded in Web Video."
56. This is not to underestimate comparable problems in understanding the notion of a philosopher-king or the application of ideal Forms to experience in this world.
57. Here, I am grateful to conversations with Tenzeng Sharcock and Geshe N. Samten.

58. The following two paragraphs are based on the transcript of a National Public Radio story, "Analysis: New Study on the Mental Health of Troops in Iraq," aired on *All Things Considered,* June 30, 2004.

59. Matthew Friedman in comments aired in the NPR story cited in the previous note.

60. These are the words of Steve Robinson, who runs the National Gulf War Resource Center. He was interviewed in the NPR story mentioned in note 58.

61. The term is Robinson's.

62. For more on this, see Sherman 1998a, 1998c, and 1997a, 175–81.

63. Diogenes Laertius, 6.63; see also *Discourses* 2.10.3, 1.9.2–6.

64. Cicero, *On Duties* 1.153–60 (using the Griffin and Atkins translation [1991] throughout). Note that Kant will famously echo this thought in his notion of a Kingdom (or Realm) of Ends in which all persons, in virtue of their reason, are due respect. The notion of the Categorical Imperative fills out the idea in so far as it gives a formula of how persons in that realm legislate moral law. Kant's debt to Stoicism is clear, but he parts ways in insisting that moral law is an autonomous construction of rational humans, not a divine given (or natural) feature of an ethical commonwealth. For further discussion, see Sherman 1997a.

65. Striker 1991, 10–13.

66. *Meditations* 8.34; see also 11.8 and 9.23.

67. Ibid., 12.26.

68. Ibid.

69. Ibid., 8.61.

70. For more on empathy and respect, see Sherman 1998a, 1998b; on empathy specifically, see Sherman 1998c and 2004b.

71. Seneca, *Epistles* 41.4–7.

72. Cicero, *On Duties* 1.99.

73. Ibid., 1.149. In Kant's hands, the notion of respect (*Achtung*) becomes a complex rational emotion that preserves both poles of reverence and fear: On the one hand, we are awestruck at the majesty of our autonomous rational natures; on the other, we fear the authority of its moral law and are burdened by the yoke of its constraints. Kant's Stoic legacy here is clear.

74. Long and Sedley 1987a, 57 G (Hierocles, *Stobaeus* 4.671, 7–673 11).

75. *The Theory of Moral Sentiments,* 140–42, 146, 167. See Sherman 1998c.

76. *A Treatise of Human Nature,* 317–427 (1968 edition).

77. Walzer 1977, 36.

78. At least, where justice in prosecuting war (*jus in bello*) is decoupled from justice in going to war (*jus ad bellum*). For a persuasive argument against decoupling the notions, see McMahan 2004.

79. Proportionality is, notoriously, a morally weak rule, for it doesn't set the relative values of military goals against other moral costs. As such, it can become an open-ended argument for expediency and "military necessity." See Walzer 1977, 129–30, 119–20 for further discussion of this.

80. "We do not live in Benelux [Belgium, Netherlands, Luxembourg]," an Israeli government official said recently in defense of Israeli interrogation policies toward detainees. The implication is that the needs of security need to be balanced against those of liberty. But *balance* is a slippery term, and the concerns of a nation's security can quickly cause others' rights to disappear; on this, see Luban 2002. In "ticking bomb" cases, security might rightly get the upper hand. But not all cases of detainee interrogation are ticking bomb cases, and it is all too easy for interrogation to be portrayed as if it were.

81. R. Jeffrey Smith and Dan Eggen, "Gonzales Helped Set the Course for Detainees," *Washington Post*, January 5, 2005.

82. All citations are from the Executive Summary of "Article 15-6 Investigation of the 800th Military Police Brigade" (henceforth "Taguba Report"), prepared by Major General Antonio M. Taguba. Posted on MSNBC.com on May 4, 2004, accessed on June 25, 2004 (http://www.msnbc.msn.com/id/4894001/).

83. See Ignatieff 2004.

84. R. Jeffrey Smith, "Soldiers Vented Frustrations, Doctor Says," *Washington Post*, May 24, 2004.

85. Taguba Report, 18.

86. Ibid., 12, 20.

87. Convention III relative to the Treatment of Prisoners of War, August 12, 1949. Accessed at Information Clearing House.info on June 1, 2004 (http://informationclearinghouse.info/article5019.htm).

88. At the time of this writing, three soldiers have been court-martialed.

89. See R. Jeffrey Smith, "Soldiers Vented Frustration, Doctor Says," *Washington Post*, May 24, 2004.

90. Ellen Nakashima, "Taguba Has Filipinos Lauding the Rise of Their Native Son," *Washington Post*, May 17, 2004.

91. The now infamous Bybee "torture memo" was released by the *Washington Post* on WashingtonPost.com on June 13, 2004, accessed July 1, 2004 (http://www.washingtonpost.com/wp-srv/nation/documents/dojinterrogationmemo20020801.pdf).

92. Article 14, Geneva Convention III.

93. *Washington Post*, May 12, 2004.

94. This paragraph owes a debt to the discussion in Schneewind 1988, 17–18.

95. Schneewind 1998, 17.

96. As discussed in Sabini 1992.

97. Zimbardo 1972. For a related study in sobering detail of the climate of violence in prisons and among prisoners themselves, see Gilligan 1996. He is particularly astute in analyzing the connection of violence with profound feelings of shame and humiliation.

98. Levi's *If This Is a Man* is also known under the title *Survival in Auschwitz*.

99. *On Anger* 1.1.1.

100. Ibid., 1.1.4.

101. Ibid., 2.5.3.

102. Ibid., 3.41.3.

103. See Boxill 1976 for a moving discussion of the moral importance of the emotion of indignation.

104. *On Anger* 3.41–43. For an eloquent discussion of this injunction and the problems it raises in Seneca's *On Anger*, see Nussbaum 1994, ch. 11.

Bibliography

Ackerman, Felicia. "A Man by Nothing Is So Well Betrayed as by His Manners? Politeness as a Virtue." *Midwest Studies in Philosophy* 13 (1988): 250–58.

Adams, Robert Merrihew. "Involuntary Sins." *The Philosophical Review* 44, 1 (1985): 3–31.

Alexiou, Margaret. *The Ritual Lament in Greek Tradition*. New York: Cambridge University Press, 1974.

Algra, Keimpe, Jonathan Barnes, Jaap Mansfeld, and Malcolm Schofield, eds. *The Cambridge History of Hellenistic Philosophy*. New York: Cambridge University Press, 1999.

Allason-Jones, Lindsay. "Women and the Roman Army in Britain." *Journal of Roman Archaeology*, supp. series 34 (1999): 41–51.

Alperovitz, Gar. "Navy Leaders." In *The Decision to Use the Atomic Bomb*. New York: Random House, 1995.

Alter, Jonathan. "Beneath the Waves." *Newsweek*, May 27, 1996, 30–31.

Amichai, Yehuda. *The Selected Poetry of Yehuda Amichai*, rev. edition. Translated by Chana Bloch and Stephen Mitchell. Berkeley: University of California Press, 1996.

Anderson, Elijah. *Code of the Street: Decency, Violence, and the Moral Life of the Inner City*. New York: Norton, 1999.

Angers, Trent. *The Forgotten Hero of My Lai: The Hugh Thompson Story*. Lafayette, LA: Acadian House Publishing, 1999.

Angier, Carole. *The Double Bond: Primo Levi*. New York: Farrar, Straus, Giroux, 2002.

Annas, Julia. "Marcus Aurelius: Ethics and Its Background." *Rhizai: Journal for Ancient Philosophy and Science* 2 (2004).

———. *Hellenistic Philosophy of Mind*. Berkeley: University of California Press, 1992.

———. "The Hellenistic Version of Aristotle's Ethics." *Monist* 73, 1 (1990): 80–96.

Aphrodisias, Alexander of. *Alexander of Aphrodisias on Fate*. Translated by R. W. Sharples. London: Duckworth, 1983.

Aristotle. *The Complete Works of Aristotle.* Edited by Jonathan Barnes. 2 vols. Princeton, NJ: Princeton University Press, 1984.

———. *Nicomachean Ethics.* Translated by Christopher Rowe. Oxford: Oxford University Press, 2002.

Arnim, Joannes von. *Stoicorum Veterum Fragmenta.* 4 vols. Dubuque, IA: William Brown, 1905.

Ashby, Phil. *Unscathed: Escape from Sierra Leone.* London: Pan Macmillan, 2002.

Ashenburg, Katherine. *The Mourner's Dance: What We Do When People Die.* New York: North Point Press, 2002.

Asmis, Elizabeth. "The Stoicism of Marcus Aurelius." In *Aufstieg Und Niedergang Der Romischen Welt (Rise and Decline of the Roman World),* edited by Wolfgang Haase, 2228–52. New York: Walter de Gruyter, 1989.

Atherton, Catherine. *The Stoics on Ambiguity.* Cambridge: Cambridge University Press, 1993.

Atkins, E. M. "'*Domina et Regina Virtutum*': Justice and Societas in *De Officiis*." *Phronesis* 35, 3 (1990): 258–89.

Aurelius, Marcus. *Meditations.* Translated by A. S. L. Farquharson. Oxford: Oxford University Press, 1989.

Averill, James. *Anger and Aggression: An Essay on Emotion.* New York: Springer-Verlag, 1982.

Axinn, Sidney. *A Moral Military.* Philadelphia, PA: Temple University Press, 1989.

Barker, Pat. *The Ghost Road.* New York: Plume, 1995.

———. *The Eye in the Door.* New York: Plume, 1993.

———. *Regeneration.* New York: Penguin, 1992.

Barnes, Jonathan. "Roman Aristotle." In *Philosophia Togata II: Plato and Aristotle at Rome,* edited by Jonathan Barnes and Miriam Griffin, 1–69. New York: Oxford University Press, 1997.

Barnes, Jonathan, and Miriam Griffin, eds. *Philosophia Togata I.* New York: Oxford University Press, 1989.

———. *Philosophia Togata II.* New York: Oxford University Press, 1997.

Baron-Cohen, Simon. *Mindblindness: An Essay on Autism and Theory of Mind.* Cambridge, MA: MIT Press, 1999.

Barstow, Anne Llewellyn, ed. *War's Dirty Secret: Rape, Prostitution, and Other Crimes Against Women.* Cleveland, OH: Pilgrim Press, 2000.

Bartky, Sandra Lee. *Femininity and Domination: Studies in the Phenomenology of Oppression.* New York: Routledge, 1990.

Barton, Carlin A. *The Sorrows of the Ancient Romans: The Gladiator and the Monster.* Princeton, NJ: Princeton University Press, 1993.

Beardsley, Elizabeth Lane. "Moral Disapproval and Moral Indignation." *Philosophy and Phenomenological Research* 31, 4 (1970): 161–76.

Becker, Lawrence C. *A New Stoicism.* Princeton, NJ: Princeton University Press, 1998.

Benson, Paul. "Free Agency and Self-Worth." *The Journal of Philosophy* 91, 12 (1994): 650–68.

Beston, Paul. "Hellenistic Military Leadership." In *War and Violence in Ancient Greece*, edited by Hans Van Wees, 315–36. London: Duckworth/Classical Press of Wales, 2000.

Bett, Richard. "Carneades' Distinction Between Assent and Approval." *Monist* 73, 1 (1990): 3–20.

Bilton, Michael, and Kevin Sim. *Four Hours in My Lai*. New York: Penguin, 1992.

Birley, Anthony. *Marcus Aurelius*. Boston: Little and Brown, 1966.

Blank, Arthur S., Jr. "Irrational Reactions to Post-Traumatic Stress Disorder and Viet Nam Veterans," "The Unconscious Flashback to the War in Viet Nam Veterans: Clinical Mystery, Legal Defense, and Community Problem," and "The Veteran's Administration's Viet Nam Veterans Outreach and Counseling Centers." In *The Trauma of War: Stress and Recovery in Viet Nam Veterans*, edited by Stephen M. Sonnenberg, Arthur S. Blank Jr., and John A. Talbott. Washington, DC: American Psychiatric Press, 1985.

Blumenfeld, Laura. "The Apology." *The New Yorker*, March 4, 2002, 37–40.

Bobzien, Susanne. *Determinism and Freedom in Stoic Philosophy*. Oxford: Clarendon Press, 1998.

———. "Stoic Conceptions of Freedom and Their Relations to Ethics." In *Aristotle and After*, edited by Richard Sorabji, 71–89. London: Institute for Classical Studies, 1997.

Bok, Sissela. *Mayhem: Violence as Public Entertainment*. Reading, MA: Addison-Wesley, 1998.

Bonhoffer, Adolf Friedrich. *The Ethics of the Stoic Epictetus*. Translated by William Stephens. New York: Peter Lang, 1996.

Bordo, Susan. *The Male Body: A New Look at Men in Public and Private*. New York: Farrar, Strauss and Giroux, 1999 (1999a).

———. *Twilight Zones: The Hidden Life of Cultural Images from Plato to O. J.* Berkeley, CA: University of California Press, 1999 (1999b).

Bourke, Joanna. *An Intimate History of Killing*. New York: Basic Books, 1999.

Boxill, Bernard. "Self-Respect and Protest." *Philosophy and Public Affairs* 6 (1976).

Bragg, Melvyn. *The Soldier's Return*. London: Hodder Headline, 1999.

Branham, R. Bracht, and Marie-Odile Goulet-Caze, eds. *The Cynics*. Berkeley: University of California Press, 1996.

Braund, Susanna Morton, and Christopher Gill. *The Passions in Roman Thought and Literature*. Cambridge: Cambridge University Press, 1997.

Brazelton, T. Berry, and Michael W. Yogman, eds. *Affective Development in Infancy*. Norwood, NJ: Ablex Publishing Corporation, 1986.

Bremner, J. Douglas, and Dennis Charney. "Neurobiology of Posttraumatic Stress Disorder." In *Current Therapeutic Approaches to Panic and Other Anxiety Disorders*, edited by G. Darcourt, 171–86. Basel/Karger: International Academy for Biomedical Drug Research, 1994.

Brennan, Tad. "The Old Stoic Theory of Emotions." In *The Emotions in Hellenistic Philosophy*, edited by Juha Sihvola and Troels Engberg-Pederson, 21–70. Dordrecht, Netherlands: Kluwer, 1998.

———. "Reasonable Impressions in Stoicism." *Phronesis* 41, 3 (1996): 318–34.

Breuer, Josef, and Sigmund Freud. "Studies on Hysteria" (1893–95). In *Standard Edition of the Complete Psychological Works of Sigmund Freud*. London: Hogarth Press, 1955.

Brison, Susan J. *Aftermath: Violence and the Remaking of the Self*. Princeton, NJ: Princeton University Press, 2002.

Bromberg, Philip M. *Standing in the Spaces: Essays on Clinical Process, Trauma, and Dissociation*. Hillsdale, NJ: The Analytic Press, 1998.

Brunschwig, Jacques. *Papers in Hellenistic Philosophy*. Translated by Janet Lloyd. Cambridge: Cambridge University Press, 1994.

Brunschwig, Jacques, and Martha C. Nussbaum, eds. *Passions and Perceptions*. New York: Cambridge University Press, 1993.

Brunt, P. A. "Stoicism and the Principate." *Papers of the British School at Rome* 43 (1975): 7–35.

———. "Marcus Aurelius in His *Meditations*." *Journal of Roman Studies* 64 (1974): 1–20.

———. "Aspects of the Social Thought of Dio Chrysostom and of the Stoics." *Proceedings of the Cambridge Philological Society* 19 (1973): 9–34.

Burnett, John. "Sexual Assault in the U.S. Military." Report on *All Things Considered*, National Public Radio, 2004.

Buss, Sarah. "Appearing Respectful: The Moral Significance of Manners." *Ethics* 109 (1999): 795–826.

Butler, Joseph. *Fifteen Sermons*. London: G. Bell and Sons, 1964.

Caesar, Adrian. *Taking It Like a Man: Suffering, Sexuality and the War Poets*. Manchester, England: Manchester University Press, 1993.

Calhoun, Cheshire. "Standing for Something." *The Journal of Philosophy* 92, 5 (1995): 235–60.

Calhoun, Cheshire, and Robert Solomon, eds. *What Is an Emotion?: Classic Readings in Philosophical Psychology*. New York: Oxford University Press, 1984.

Calvin, John. *Calvin's Commentary on Seneca's De Clementia*. Translated by Ford Lewis Battles and Andre Malan Hugo. Leiden: E. J. Brill, 1969.

Cannon, Walter. *Bodily Changes in Pain, Hunger, Fear, and Rage*. New York: Harper and Row, 1929.

———. "The James-Lange Theory of Emotions: A Critical Examination and an Alternative Theory." *American Journal of Psychology* 39 (1927): 106–24.

Care, Norman. "Problematic Agency." In *Living with One's Past*, 69–97. New York: Rowman and Littlefield, 1996.

Carlson, Eve, and Constance Dalenberg. "A Conceptual Framework for the Impact of Traumatic Experiences." *Trauma, Violence and Abuse* 1, 1 (2000): 4–28.

Carlyle, Thomas. *On Heroes: Hero-Worship and the Heroic in History*. London: Oxford University Press, 1968.

Carr, Caleb. *The Lessons of Terror*. New York: Random House, 2002.

Carroll, Andrew, ed. *War Letters: Extraordinary Correspondence from American Wars*. New York: Scribner, 2001.

Carroll, Ward. *Punk's War*. Annapolis, MD: Naval Institute Press, 2001.

Caruth, Cathy, ed. *Trauma: Explorations in Memory*. Baltimore, MD: Johns Hopkins University Press, 1995.

Chang, Iris. *The Rape of Nanking: The Forgotten Holocaust of World War II*. New York: Penguin Books, 1997.

Christman, John, ed. *The Inner Citadel: Essays on Individual Autonomy*. New York: Oxford University Press, 1989.

Chused, Judith Finger. "The Evocative Power of Enactments." *Journal of the American Psychoanalytic Association* 29 (1991): 615–39.

Cicero. *Cicero on the Emotions: Tusculan Disputations 3 and 4*. Translated by Margaret Graver. Chicago: University of Chicago Press, 2002.

———. *De Finibus*. Translated by H. Rackham, *Loeb Classical Library*. Cambridge, MA: Harvard University Press, 1971.

———. *De Natura Deorum Academica*. Translated by H. Rackham, *Loeb Classical Library*. Cambridge, MA: Harvard University Press, 1933.

———. *De Officiis*. Translated by Walter Miller, *Loeb Classical Library*. Cambridge, MA: Harvard University Press, 1913.

———. *De Oratore*. Translated by E. W. Sutton. 2 vols. Loeb Classical Library. Cambridge, MA: Harvard University Press, 1967.

———. *Epistulae ad Quintum Fratrem et M. Brutum*. Edited by D. R. Shackleton Bailey. Cambridge: Cambridge University Press, 1980.

———. *Letters to Atticus*. Translated by D. R. Shackleton Bailey. 4 vols. Loeb Classical Library. Cambridge, MA: Harvard University Press, 1999.

———. *Letters to Friends*. Translated by D. R. Shackleton Bailey. 2 vols. Loeb Classical Library. Cambridge, MA: Harvard University Press, 1999.

———. *On Duties*. Translated by M. T. Griffin and E. M. Atkins. New York: Cambridge University Press, 1991.

———. *On Moral Ends*. Translated by Raphael Woolf. Edited by Julia Annas. New York: Cambridge University Press, 2001.

———. *Tusculan Disputations*. Translated by J. E. King. *Loeb Classical Library*. Cambridge, MA: Harvard University Press, 1989.

Coke, Jay S., C. Daniel Batson, and Katherine McDavis. "Empathic Mediation of Helping: A Two-Stage Model." *Journal of Personality and Social Psychology* 36, 7 (1978): 752–66.

Colish, Marcia L. *The Stoic Tradition from Antiquity to the Early Middle Ages*, vol. 1: *Stoicism in Classical Latin Literature*. New York: E. J. Brill, 1990.

Cooper, John. "The Emotional Life of the Wise." Unpublished manuscript, 2004.

———. *Reason and Emotion: Essays on Ancient Moral Psychology and Ethical Theory*. Princeton: Princeton University Press, 1999 (1999a).

———. "Friendship and the Good in Aristotle." In *Aristotle's Ethics: Critical Essays*, edited by Nancy Sherman, 277–301. New York: Rowman and Littlefield, 1999 (1999b).

Crane, Stephen. *The Portable Stephen Crane*. Edited by Joseph Katz. New York: Penguin, 1969.

Darwall, Stephen. "Empathy, Sympathy, Care." *Philosophical Studies* 89, 3 (1998): 261–82.

Davidson, William. *The Stoic Creed*. New York: Arno Press, 1979.

de Becker, Gavin. *The Gift of Fear: Survival Signals That Protect Us from Violence*. New York: Little, Brown and Company, 1997.

De Sousa, Ronald. "Emotion and Self-Deception." In *Perspectives on Self-Deception*, edited by B. McLaughlin and A. O. Rorty. Berkeley, CA: University of California Press, 1988.

———. *The Rationality of Emotion*. Cambridge, MA: MIT Press, 1987.

de Waal, Francis. *Good Natured: The Origins of Right and Wrong in Humans and Other Animals*. Cambridge, MA: Harvard University Press, 1996.

De Lacy, Phillip, ed. *Galen: On the Doctrines of Hippocrates and Plato*. 3 vols. Berlin: Akademie-Verlag, 1984.

DeLancey, Craig. *Passionate Engines: What Emotions Reveal About Mind and Artificial Intelligence*. New York: Oxford University Press, 2002.

Desch, Michael C. *Civilian Control of the Military: The Changing Security Environment*. Baltimore, MD: Johns Hopkins University Press, 1999.

Dillon, John M. "Metriopatheia and Apatheia: Some Reflections on a Controversy in Later Greek Ethics." In *Essays in Ancient Greek Philosophy*, edited by John P. Anton and Anthony Preus, 508–17. Albany: State University of New York Press, 1971.

Dillon, Robin. "Self-Respect: Moral, Emotional, Political." *Ethics* 107 (1997): 226–49.

———, ed. *Dignity, Character and Self-Respect*. New York: Routledge, 1995.

Dominik, William J., ed. *Roman Eloquence: Rhetoric in Society and Literature*. New York: Routledge, 1997.

Driver, Julia. "Caesar's Wife: On the Moral Significance of Appearing Good." *The Journal of Philosophy* 89 (1992): 331–43.

Dudley, Donald R. *A History of Cynicism*. London: Methuen, 1937.

Dunn, Judy. *The Beginnings of Social Understanding*. Cambridge, MA: Harvard University Press, 1988.

Dworkin, Gerald. "The Concept of Autonomy." In *The Inner Citadel: Essays on Individual Autonomy*, edited by John Christman, 54–62. New York: Oxford University Press, 1989.

————. "Autonomy and Behavior Control." *Hastings Center Report* 6 (1976): 23–28.

Dyck, Andrew. *A Commentary on Cicero, De Officiis*. Ann Arbor: University of Michigan Press, 1996.

Earl, Donald. "The Moral and Political Tradition of Rome." In *Aspects of Greek and Roman Life*, edited by H. H. Scullard. Ithaca, NY: Cornell University Press, 1967.

Eisenberg, N., R. Faber, P. Miller, J. Futz, R. Shell, R. Mathy, and R. Remo. "Relation of Sympathy and Personal Distress to Prosocial Behavior: A Multimethod Study." *Journal of Personality and Social Psychology* 57, 1 (1989): 55–66.

Ekman, Paul. "Facial Expression and Emotion." *American Psychologist* 48 (1993): 384–92.

————. "Facial Expressions of Emotion: New Findings, New Questions." *Psychological Science* 3, 1 (1992): 34–38.

————. "Expression and the Nature of Emotion." In *Approaches to Emotion*, edited by K. R. Scherer and Paul Ekman. Hillsdale, NJ: Lawrence Erlbaum, 1984.

————, ed. *Emotion in the Human Face*. 2nd ed. Cambridge: Cambridge University Press, 1982.

Ellis, Albert. *Better, Deeper, and More Enduring Brief Therapy: The Rational Emotive Behavior Therapy Approach*. New York: Brunner/Mazel, 1995.

————. *How to Stubbornly Refuse to Make Yourself Miserable About Anything— Yes, Anything!* New York: Carol Publishing Group, 1993.

————. *Reason and Emotion in Psychotherapy*. Secaucus, NJ: Lyle Stuart, 1962.

Ellis, Anthony. "Offense and the Liberal Conception of the Law." *Philosophy and Public Affairs* 13 (1984): 3–23.

Emerson, Ralph Waldo. *The Selected Writings of Ralph Waldo Emerson*. Edited by Brooks Atkinson. New York: The Modern Library, 1950.

————. *Essays*. Author's copyright ed. London: Routledge.

Engberg-Pederson, Troels. "Marcus Aurelius on Emotions." In *The Emotions in Hellenistic Philosophy*, edited by Juha Sihvola and Troels Engberg-Pederson, 305–37. Dordrecht, Netherlands: Kluwer, 1998.

————. "The Stoic Theory of Oikeiōsis." In *Studies in Hellenistic Civilization*, edited by Per Bilde, Troels Engberg-Pederson, Lise Hannestad, and Jan Zahle. Aarhus: Aarhus University Press, 1990.

Englert, Walter. "Stoics and Epicureans on the Nature of Suicide." In *Proceedings of the Boston Area Colloquium on Ancient Philosophy*, edited by John J. Cleary and William Wians, 67–113. Lanham, MD: University Press of America, 1996.

Epictetus. *The Discourses as Reported by Arrian, the Manual, and Fragments.*
    Translated by W. A. Oldfather. 2 vols. Loeb Classical Library. Cambridge,
    MA: Harvard University Press, 1989.
————. *The Discourses of Epictetus.* Translated by Robin Hard. Edited by Chris-
    topher Gill. London: Everyman, 1995.
————. *Handbook of Epictetus.* Translated by Nicholas White. Indianapolis,
    IN: Hackett, 1983.
Erskine, Andrew. *The Hellenistic Stoa: Political Thought and Action.* Ithaca, NY:
    Cornell University Press, 1990.
Faludi, Susan. *Stiffed: The Betrayal of the American Man.* New York: William
    Morrow and Company, 1999.
Feaver, Peter D., and Richard H. Kohn, ed. *Soldiers and Civilians: The Civil-
    Military Gap and American Security.* Boston: MIT Press, 2001.
Feinberg, Joel. "Autonomy." In *The Inner Citadel: Essays on Individual Autonomy,*
    edited by John Christman, 27–53. New York: Oxford University Press, 1989.
————. *Offenses to Others.* New York: Oxford University Press, 1984.
Fenichel, Otto. *The Psychoanalytic Theory of Neurosis.* New York: Norton, 1945.
Fischer, John Martin, and Mark Ravizza, eds. *Perspectives on Moral Responsi-
    bility.* Ithaca, NY: Cornell University Press, 1993.
Fisher, Philip. *The Vehement Passions.* Princeton, NJ: Princeton University Press,
    2002.
Flower, Harriet I. *Ancestor Masks and Aristocratic Power in Roman Culture.* New
    York: Oxford University Press, 1996.
Foa, E. B., and B. O. Rothbaum. *Treating the Trauma of Rape: Cognitive-Behavioral
    Therapy for PTSD.* New York: Guilford Press, 1998.
Follette, Victoria, Josef Ruzek, and Frances Abueg. "A Contextual Analysis of
    Trauma: Theoretical Considerations." In *Cognitive Behavioral Therapies for
    Trauma,* edited by Victoria Follette, Josef Ruzek, and Frances Abueg. New
    York: Guilford Press, 2001.
Fortenbaugh, William, ed. *On Stoic and Peripatetic Ethics.* Vol. 1, Rutgers Se-
    ries in Classical Humanities. New Brunswick, NJ: Transaction, 1983.
Frankel, Nat, and Larry Smith. *Patton's Best: An Informal History of the 4th
    Armored Division.* New York: Hawthorne Books, 1978.
Frankfurt, Harry. "Identification and Wholeheartedness." In *The Importance
    of What We Care About,* edited by Harry Frankfurt. Cambridge: Cambridge
    University Press, 1988.
————. "Freedom of the Will and the Concept of a Person." *The Journal of
    Philosophy* 68, 1 (1971).
Frede, Michael. "The Stoic Notion of a *Lekton.*" In *Companion to Ancient
    Thought,* vol. 3: *Language,* edited by Stephen Everson. New York: Cambridge
    University Press, 1994.
Freud, Anna. *The Ego and the Mechanisms of Defense.* Madison, WI: Interna-
    tional Universities Press, 1966.

Freud, Sigmund. *The Standard Edition of the Complete Psychological Works of Sigmund Freud*. London: Hogarth Press, 1955.

Fridlund, Alan J. "The New Ethology of Human Facial Expressions." In *The Psychology of Facial Expression*, edited by James A. Russell and Jose Miguel Fernandez-Dols, 103–29. Cambridge, MA: Cambridge University Press, 1997.

Friedman, Matthew. "Acknowledging the Psychiatric Cost of War." *New England Journal of Medicine* 351 (2004).

———. "Post Traumatic Stress Disorder: An Overview." National Center for Post-Traumatic Stress Disorder Web site, www.ncptsd.org, May 14, 2003 (2003a).

———. "Epidemiological Facts About PTSD." National Center for Post-Traumatic Stress Disorder Web site, www.ncptsd.org, May 14, 2003 (2003b).

———. "Neurobiological Research on PTSD." *PTSD Research Quarterly* 6, 4 (1995).

Friedman, Matthew, Dennis Charney, and Ariel Deutch. "Key Questions and a Research Agenda for the Future." In *Neurobiological and Clinical Consequences of Stress: From Normal Adaptation to PTSD*, edited by Matthew Friedman, Dennis Charney, Ariel Deutch. Philadelphia: Lippincott-Raven, 1995.

Frijda, N. H. *The Emotions*. Cambridge: Cambridge University Press, 1986.

Furley, David. "Nothing to Us?" In *The Norms of Nature*, edited by Malcolm Scholfield and Gisela Striker, 75–91. New York: Cambridge University Press, 1986.

Fussell, Paul. *The Great War and Modern Memory*. Oxford: Oxford University Press, 1975.

Fussell, Samuel Wilson. *Muscle: Confessions of an Unlikely Bodybuilder*. New York: Avon Books, 1991.

Galen. *On the Doctrines of Hippocrates and Plato*. Translated by Phillip De Lacy. 3rd ed. 3 vols. Berlin: Akademie-Verlag, 1984.

———. *On the Passions and Errors of the Soul*. Translated by Paul W. Harkins. Columbus: Ohio State University Press, 1963.

Garber, Judy, and Kenneth A. Dodge, eds. *The Development of Emotion Regulation and Dysregulation*. New York: Cambridge University Press, 1991.

Garber, Judy, and Martin E. P. Seligman, eds. *Human Helplessness: Theory and Applications*. New York: Academic Press, 1980.

Garfield, Jay, and Geshe Nganang Samten. *Oceans of Reasons*. New York: Oxford University Press, forthcoming.

Gautier, Leon. *Chivalry*. New York: Barnes and Noble, 1965.

Gawande, Atul. "Crimson Tide." *The New Yorker*, Feb. 12, 2001, 50–57.

Gellius, Aulus. *The Attic Nights of Aulus Gellius*. Translated by John C. Rolfe. 3 vols. Loeb Classical Library. Cambridge, MA: Harvard University Press, 1927.

Gibson, James William. *Warrior Dreams: Paramilitary Culture in Post-Vietnam America*. New York: Farrar, Straus and Giroux, 1994.

Gill, Christopher. "Personhood and Personality: The Four-*Personae* Theory in Cicero, *De Officiis I*." In *Oxford Studies in Ancient Philosophy*, edited by Julia Annas, 169–200. Oxford: Oxford University Press, 1988.

Gill, Christopher, ed. *Virtue, Norms, and Objectivity: Issues in Ancient and Modern Ethics*. New York: Oxford University Press, 2005.

Gilligan, James. *Violence: Reflections on a National Epidemic*. New York: Vintage, 1996.

Gladwell, Malcolm. "The Naked Face." *The New Yorker*, August 5, 2002, 38–49.

Gleason, Maud W. *Making Men: Sophists and Self-Presentation in Ancient Rome*. Princeton, NJ: Princeton University Press, 1995.

Glenn, Russell W. *Reading Athena's Dance Card: Men Against Fire in Vietnam*. Annapolis, MD: Naval Institute Press, 2000.

Glover, Jonathan. *Humanity: A Moral History of the Twentieth Century*. New Haven, CT: Yale Nota Bene, 1999.

———. *Responsibility*. New York: Humanities Press, 1970.

Goffman, Erving. "The Nature of Deference and Demeanor." In *Interaction Ritual: Essays on Face-to-Face Behavior*, edited by Erving Goffman. New York: Anchor, 1967 (1967a).

———. "On Face-Work." In *Interaction Ritual: Essays on Face-to-Face Behavior*, edited by Erving Goffman. New York: Anchor, 1967 (1967b).

Goldie, Peter. *The Emotions: A Philosophical Exploration*. Oxford: Oxford University Press, 2000.

Goldsworthy, Adrian Keith. *The Roman Army at War 100 BC–AD 200*. Oxford: Clarendon Press, 1996.

Gorgemanns, Herwig. "*Oikeiosis* in Arius Didymus." In *On Stoic and Peripatetic Ethics: The Work of Arius Didymus*, edited by William W. Fortenbaugh. New Brunswick, NJ: Transaction Books, 1983.

Gould, Josiah B. *The Philosophy of Chrysippus*. Albany: State University of New York Press, 1970.

Gourevitch, Philip. *We Wish to Inform You That Tomorrow We Will Be Killed with Our Families: Stories from Rwanda*. New York: Picador, 1998.

Govier, Trudy. "Forgiveness and the Unforgivable." *American Philosophical Quarterly* 36 (1999): 59–75.

Graver, Margaret, "Philo of Alexandria and the Origins of the Stoic Propatheia." *Phronesis* 44, 4 (1999): 300–25.

Green, Peter. "Philosophers, Kings, and Democracy, or, How Political Was the Stoa." *Ancient Philosophy* 14 (1994): 147–56.

Greene, Bob. *Duty: A Father, His Son, and the Man Who Won the War*. New York: HarperCollins, 1985.

Greenspan, Stanley. *The Development of the Ego*. Guilford, CT: International Universities Press, 1989.

Griffin, Miriam. "From Aristotle to Atticus: Cicero and Matius on Friendship." In *Philosophia Togata II: Plato and Aristotle at Rome*, edited by Jonathan

Barnes and Miriam Griffin, 86–109. New York: Oxford University Press, 1997.

———. "Roman Suicide." In *Medicine and Moral Reasoning*, edited by K. W. M. Fulford, G. Gillett, and J. M. Soskice, 106–30. New York: Cambridge University Press, 1994.

———. *Seneca: A Philosopher in Politics*. Oxford: Clarendon Press, 1992.

———. *Nero: The End of a Dynasty*. New Haven, CT: Yale University Press, 1984.

———. "The Paedagogic Strategy of *De Beneficiis*." Unpublished ms.

Grossman, Dave. *On Killing: The Psychological Cost of Learning to Kill in War and Society*. Boston: Little, Brown and Company, 1995.

Grotstein, James. *Splitting and Projective Identification*. Northvale and London: Jason Aronson, 1995.

Guenther, Herbert. *Tibetan Buddhism in Western Perspective*. Berkeley, CA: Dharma Publishing, 1991.

Haase, Wolfgang, and Hildegard Temporini, eds. *Aufstieg und Niedergang der Romischen Welt*. Vol. 36.3. New York: Walter de Gruyter, 1989.

———. *Aufstieg und Niedergang der Romischen Welt*. Vol. 32.2. New York: Walter de Gruyter, 1985.

Habinek, Thomas. "Seneca's Renown: *Gloria, Claritudo*, and the Replication of the Roman Elite." *Classical Antiquity* 19, 2 (2000): 264–303.

Hadley, Arthur T. *The Straw Giant: Triumph and Failure: America's Armed Forces*. New York: Random House, 1986.

Halbfinger, David M. "Hearing Starts in Bombing Error That Killed 4." *New York Times*, January 15, 2003 (2003a), A1.

———. "Pilots Ignored Rules on When to Attack, Commander Says." *New York Times*, January 16, 2003 (2003b), A1.

Hallett, Judith P., and Marilyn B. Skinner, ed. *Roman Sexualities*. Princeton, NJ: Princeton University Press, 1997.

Hanson, Victor Davis. *The Western Way of War: Infantry Battle in Classical Greece*. New York: Knopf, 1989.

Harris, George W. *Dignity and Vulnerability: Strength and Quality of Character*. Berkeley: University of California Press, 1997.

Harris, William. *Restraining Rage: The Ideology of Anger Control in Classical Antiquity*. Cambridge, MA: Harvard University Press, 2001.

Hayden, John O., ed. *William Wordsworth: The Poems—Volume One*. New Haven: Yale University Press, 1989.

Heichelheim, Fritz M., Cedric A. Yeo, and Allen Ward. *A History of the Roman People*. 4th ed. Upper Saddle River, NJ: Prentice Hall, 2003.

Herman, Judith Lewis. *Trauma and Recovery*. New York: Basic, 1992.

Hersey, John. *Of Men and War*. New York: Scholastic, 1991.

Hersh, Seymour. *Chain of Command: The Road from 9/11 to Abu Ghraib*. New York: HarperCollins, 2004.

Hill, Thomas E., Jr. "The Kantian Conception of Autonomy." In *The Inner Cita-del: Essays on Individual Autonomy*, edited by John Christman, 91–108. New York: Oxford University Press, 1989.

Hoge, Charles, Carl Castro, et al. "Combat Duty in Iraq and Afghanistan, Mental Health Problems, and Barriers to Care." *New England Journal of Medicine* 351 (2004).

Holland, Francis. *Seneca*. Freeport, NY: Books for Libraries Press, 1969.

Holmes, Richard. *Acts of War: The Behavior of Men in Battle*. New York: The Free Press, 1985.

Homer. *The Iliad*. Translated by Robert Fagles. New York: Penguin, 1999.

Honderich, Ted. *After the Terror*. Edinburgh: Edinburgh University Press, 2002.

Hopkins, Keith. *Death and Renewal: Sociological Studies in Roman History*, vol. 2. New York: Cambridge University Press, 1983.

Hughes, Paul. "Moral Anger, Forgiving, and Condoning." *Journal of Social Philosophy* 25 (1995): 103–18.

Hume, David. *Essays, Moral, Political, and Literary*. Edited by Eugene F. Miller. Indianapolis, IN: Liberty Classics, 1987.

———. *A Treatise of Human Nature*. Edited by L. A. Selby-Bigg. New York: Oxford University Press, 1968.

Ierodiakonou, Katerina, ed. *Topics in Stoic Philosophy*. Oxford: Clarendon Press, 1999.

Ignatieff, Michael. *The Lesser Evil*. Princeton, NJ: Princeton University Press, 2004.

Inwood, Brad. "Politics and Paradox in Seneca's *De Beneficiis*." In *Justice and Generosity: Studies in Hellenistic Social and Political Philosophy*, edited by Andre Laks and Malcolm Schofield. New York: Cambridge University Press, 1995 (1995a).

———. "Seneca in His Philosophical Milieu." *Harvard Studies in Classical Philology* 97 (1995): 63–76 (1995b).

———. "Goal and Target in Stoicism." *The Journal of Philosophy* 83, 10 (1986): 547–56.

———. *Ethics and Human Action in Early Stoicism*. Oxford: Clarendon Press, 1985.

Inwood, Brad, and L. P. Gerson, eds. *Hellenistic Philosophy: Introductory Readings*. 2nd ed. Indianapolis: Hackett, 1997.

Inwood, Brad, and Fred D. Miller Jr. "Law in Roman Philosophy." In *Treatise of Legal Philosophy and General Jurisprudence*, vol. 6, edited by Fred D. Miller Jr. Dordrecht: Kluwer, forthcoming.

Irwin, T. H. "Socratic Paradox and Stoic Theory." In *Companion to Ancient Thought*, vol. 4: *Ethics*, edited by Stephen Everson, 151–92. New York: Cambridge University Press, 1998.

———. "Virtue, Praise and Success: Stoic Responses to Aristotle." *Monist* 73, 1 (1990): 59–79.

————. "Stoic and Aristotelian Conceptions of Happiness." In *The Norms of Nature*, edited by Malcolm Schofield and Gisela Striker, 205–44. New York: Cambridge University Press, 1986.

Izard, Carroll E. *The Face of Emotion*. New York: Meredith, 1971.

Jacoby, Susan. *Wild Justice: The Evolution of Revenge*. New York: Harper and Row, 1983.

Jakobs, E., A. S. R. Manstead, and A. Fischer. "Social Motives, Emotional Feelings, and Smiling." *Cognition and Emotion* 13, 4 (1999): 321–45.

James, Susan. *Passion and Action: The Emotions in Seventeenth-Century Philosophy*. Oxford: Oxford University Press, 1997.

James, William. *The Moral Equivalent of War and Other Essays*. Edited by John K. Roth. New York: Harper Torchbooks, 1971.

Jamison, Kay Redfield. *An Unquiet Mind: A Memoir of Moods and Madness*. New York: Random House, 1995.

Jaycox, L., L. Zoellner, and E. Foa. "Cognitive-Behavior Therapy for PTSD in Rape Survivors." *Journal of Clinical Psychology/In Session: Psychotherapy in Practice* 58, 8 (2002): 891–906.

Johnson, James Turner. *Morality and Contemporary Warfare*. New Haven, CT: Yale University Press, 1999.

Josephson, Michael S., and Wes Hanson, eds. *The Power of Character*. San Francisco: Jossey-Bass, Inc., 1998.

Kant, Immanuel. *Anthropology from a Pragmatic Point of View*. Translated by Mary J. Gregor. The Hague: Martinus Nijhoff, 1974.

————. *The Doctrine of Virtue*. Translated by Mary J. Gregor. Philadelphia: University of Pennsylvania Press, 1964.

————. *Groundwork of the Metaphysic of Morals*. Edited by H. J. Paton. New York: Harper Torchbooks, 1956.

————. *Lectures on Ethics*. Translated by Louis Infield. Indianapolis: Hackett, 1930.

————. *The Metaphysical Elements of Justice*. Translated by John Ladd. New York: Macmillan, 1965.

————. *Religion within the Limits of Reason Alone*. Translated by Theodore Greene and Hoyt Hudson. New York: Harper and Brothers, 1960.

Katz, Joseph, ed. *The Portable Stephen Crane*. New York: Penguin Books, 1969.

Keegan, John, ed. *The Book of War: 25 Centuries of Great War Writing*. New York: Penguin, 1999.

————. *A History of Warfare*. New York: Vintage Books, 1993.

————. *The Face of Battle*. New York: Viking, 1976.

Keegan, John, and Richard Holmes. *Soldiers: A History of Men in Battle*. New York: Viking, 1986.

Kekes, John. "The Great Guide of Human Life." *Philosophy and Literature* 8 (1984): 236–49.

Kelsay, John, and James Turner Johnson, eds. *Just War and Jihad: Historical and Theoretical Perspectives on War and Peace in Western and Islamic Traditions*. New York: Greenwood Press, 1991.

Kerr, Douglas. *Wilfred Owen's Voices: Language and Community*. New York: Oxford University Press, 1993.

Kessler, Ronald, et al. "Posttraumatic Stress Disorder in the National Comorbidity Survey." *Archives of General Psychiatry* 52, 12 (1995): 1048–60.

Kilner, Peter. "Military Leaders' Obligations to Justify Killing in War." Command and General Staff College, 2002.

Kimmel, Michael. *Manhood in America: A Cultural History*. New York: The Free Press, 1996.

Kimmel, Michael S., and Michael A. Messner. *Men's Lives*. 2nd ed. New York: Macmillan, 1992.

Kindlon, Dan, and Michael Thompson. *Raising Cain: Protecting the Emotional Life of Boys*. New York: Ballantine, 1999.

Kingwell, Mark. "Is It Rational to Be Polite." *The Journal of Philosophy* 90, 8 (1993): 387–404.

Kipnis, Laura. *Bound and Gagged: Pornography and the Politics of Fantasy in America*. Durham, NC: Duke University Press, 1999.

Klein, Melanie. "Envy and Gratitude and Other Works, 1946–1963." New York: Dell, 1975.

Klinnert, M. D., J. J. Campos, F. J. Sorce, R. N. Emde, and M. J. Svejda. "Social Referencing: Emotional Expressions as Behavior Regulators." In *Emotion: Theory, Research, and Experience, Vol. 2.: Emotions in Early Development*, edited by Robert Plutchik and Henry Kellerman, 57–86. Burlington, MA: Academic Press, 1983.

Kluger, Ruth. *Still Alive: A Holocaust Girlhood Remembered*. New York: Feminist Press at CUNY, 2001.

Krause, Sharon R. *Liberalism with Honor*. Cambridge, MA: Harvard University Press, 2002.

Kübler-Ross, Elisabeth. *On Death and Dying*. New York: Macmillan Publishing Company, 1969.

Kukla, Richard, et al. *Trauma and the Vietnam War Generation: Report of Findings from the National Vietnam Veterans Readjustment Study*. New York: Brunner/Mazel, 1990.

Laertius, Diogenes. *Lives of Eminent Philosophers*. Translated by R.D. Hicks. 2 vols. Cambridge, MA: Harvard University Press, 1972.

Laks, Andre and Malcolm Schofield, ed. *Justice and Generosity: Studies in Hellenistic Social and Political Philosophy*. New York: Cambridge University Press, 1995.

Lazarus, R. S. "On the Primacy of Cognition." *American Psychologist* 39 (1984): 124–29.

LeDoux, Joseph. *The Emotional Brain*. New York: Touchstone, 1996.

Leslie, Alan M. "Pretense and Representation: The Origins of 'Theory of Mind.'" *Psychological Review* 94, 4 (1987): 412–26.

Lesses, Glenn. "Content, Cause, and Stoic Impressions." *Phronesis* 43, 1 (1998): 1–25.

———. "Virtue and the Goods of Fortune in Stoic Moral Theory." In *Oxford Studies in Ancient Philosophy*, vol. VII, edited by Julia Annas, 95–127. New York: Oxford University Press, 1989.

Levi, Primo. *Survival in Auschwitz*. New York: Simon and Schuster, 1996.

Lipsky, David. *Absolutely American: Four Years at West Point*. New York: Houghton Mifflin Co., 2003.

Long, A. A. *Epictetus: A Stoic and Socratic Guide to Life*. Oxford: Oxford University Press, 2002.

———. *Stoic Studies*. Cambridge: Cambridge University Press, 1996.

———. "Hellenistic Ethics and Philosophical Power." In *Hellenistic History and Culture*, edited by Peter Green, 138–67. Berkeley: University of California Press, 1993.

———. "The Harmonics of Stoic Virtue." In *Oxford Studies in Ancient Philosophy: Supp. Volume, Aristotle and the Later Tradition*, edited by Henry Blumenthal and Howard Robinson. New York: Oxford University Press, 1991.

———. "Epictetus and Marcus Aurelius." In *Ancient Writers*, edited by J. Luce. New York: Scribner, 1982.

———. *Hellenistic Philosophy*. London: Duckworth, 1974.

———, ed. *Problems in Stoicism*. London: Athlone Press, 1971.

Long, A. A., and D. N. Sedley. *The Hellenistic Philosophers*, vol. 1: *Translations of the Principal Sources, with Philosophical Commentary*. Cambridge: Cambridge University Press, 1987 (1987a).

———. *The Hellenistic Philosophers*, vol. 2: *Greek and Latin Texts with Notes and Bibliography*. Cambridge: Cambridge University Press, 1987 (1987b).

Lord, F. A. *Civil War Collector's Encyclopedia*. Harrisburg: Stackpole Co., 1976.

Lorenz, Konrad. *On Aggression*. New York: Harcourt Brace, 1966.

Luban, David. "The War on Terrorism and the End of Human Rights." In *War After September 11*, edited by Verna V. Gehring. Lanham, MD: Rowman and Littlefield, 2002.

Lucanus, Marcus Annaeus. *Civil War*. Translated by Andrew Saunders. (forthcoming)

Lucian. *Lucian IV*. Translated by A. M. Harmon. Loeb Classical Library. New York: G. P. Putnam's Sons, 1925.

———. *Lucian VII*. Translated by M. D. Macleod. Loeb Classical Library. New York: G. P. Putnam's Sons, 1961.

Maass, Peter. "A Bulletproof Mind." *New York Times Magazine*, November 10, 2002.

———. *Love Thy Neighbor: A Story of War*. New York: Knopf, 1996.

Maher, Brendan A. *A Passage to Sword Beach: Minesweeping in the Royal Navy.* Annapolis, MD: Naval Institute Press, 1996.

Malatesta, Carol. "Human Infant: Emotion Expression Development." In *The Development of Expressive Behavior,* edited by Gail Zivin. Burlington, MA: Academic Press, 1985.

Marshall, S. L. A. *Men Against Fire: The Problem of Battle Command in Future War.* Gloucester, MA: Peter Smith, 1978.

Matsakis, Aphrodite. *Vietnam Wives: Women and Children Surviving Life with Veterans Suffering Post Traumatic Stress Disorder:* Woodbine House, 1988.

Matthews, Lloyd J., ed. *The Future of the Military Profession.* Boston: McGraw Hill, 2002.

May, Larry, Shari Collins-Chobanian and Kai Wong, ed. *Applied Ethics: A Multicultural Approach.* 3rd ed. Upper Saddle River, NJ: Prentice Hall, 2002.

Mayes, Linda C., and Donald J. Cohen. "Children's Developing Theory of Mind." *Journal of the American Psychoanalytic Association* 44, 1 (1996): 117–42.

———. "The Development of a Capacity for Imagination in Early Childhood." *Psychoanalytic Studies of the Child* 47 (1992): 23–47.

Mayo, James. *War Memorials and Political Landscape.* New York: Praeger, 1988.

McMahan, Jeff. "The Ethics of Killing in War." *Ethics* 14 (2004): 693–733.

Meyer, Ben, and E. P. Sanders, eds. *Jewish and Christian Self-Definition: Self-Definition in the Greco-Roman World.* Vol. 3. Philadelphia: Fortress Press, 1982.

Meyer, Susan Sauve. "Fate, Fatalism, and Agency in Stoicism." *Social Philosophy and Policy* 16, 2 (1999): 250–73.

Milgram, Stanley. *Obedience to Authority.* New York: Harper and Row, 1974.

———. "Some Conditions of Obedience and Disobedience to Authority." *Human Relations* 18, 1 (1965): 57–76.

———."Behavioral Study of Obedience." *Journal of Abnormal and Social Psychology* 67, 4 (1963): 371–78.

Miller, William Ian. *Faking It.* New York: Cambridge University Press, 2003.

———. *The Mystery of Courage.* Cambridge, MA: Harvard University Press, 2000.

———. *The Anatomy of Disgust.* Cambridge, MA: Harvard University Press, 1997.

Minow, Martha. *Between Vengeance and Forgiveness: Facing History after Genocide and Mass Violence.* Boston: Beacon Press, 1998.

Montor, Karel, ed. *Ethics for the Junior Officer.* Annapolis: Naval Institute Press, 1994.

Moore, Michael. "The Moral Worth of Retribution." In *Punishment and Rehabilitation,* edited by Jeffrie G. Murphy. Belmont, CA: Wadsworth, 1995.

Moran, Charles. *Anatomy of Courage.* London, 1945.

Moran, Richard. *Authority and Estrangement: An Essay on Self-Knowledge.* Princeton, NJ: Princeton University Press, 2001.

Morris, Herbert. "A Paternalistic Theory of Punishment." In *Punishment and Rehabilitation*, edited by Jeffrie G. Murphy. Belmont, CA: Wadsworth, 1995 (1995a).

————. "Persons and Punishment." In *Punishment and Rehabilitation*, edited by Jeffrie G. Murphy. Belmont, CA: Wadsworth, 1995 (1995b).

————. "Guilt and Shame." In *On Guilt and Innocence*, 59–63. Berkeley: University of California Press, 1976.

Murphy, Jeffrie G., ed. *Punishment and Rehabilitation*. Belmont, CA: Wadsworth, 1995 (1995a).

————. "Getting Even: The Role of the Victim." In *Punishment and Rehabilitation*, edited by Jeffrie G. Murphy. Belmont, CA: Wadsworth, 1995 (1995b).

————. *Retribution Reconsidered: More Essays in the Philosophy of Law.* Dordrecht, Netherlands: Kluwer, 1992.

————. *Retribution, Justice, and Therapy: Essays in the Philosophy of Law.* Dordrecht, Netherlands: D. Reidel, 1979.

Murphy, Jeffrie G., and Jean Hampton. *Forgiveness and Mercy.* Cambridge: Cambridge University Press, 1988.

Nardin, Terry, ed. *The Ethics of War and Peace: Religious and Secular Perspectives.* Princeton, NJ: Princeton University Press, 1996.

Nelson, Hilde. "Identities Damaged to Order." In *Damaged Identities, Narrative Repair*, 106–49. Ithaca: Cornell University Press, 2001.

————. "Narrative Repair: Reclaiming Moral Agency." In *Damaged Identities, Narrative Repair*, 1–35. Ithaca: Cornell University Press, 2001.

Newman, Robert P. *Truman and the Hiroshima Cult.* East Lansing, MI: Michigan State University Press, 1995.

Nordenfelt, Lennart. "The Stoic Conception of Mental Disorder: *The Case of Cicero.*" *Philosophy, Psychiatry, and Psychology* 4, 4 (1997): 285–91.

Norman, Richard. *Ethics, Killing and War.* Cambridge: Cambridge University Press, 1995.

Nussbaum, Martha. "Compassion and Terror." *Daedalus* 132, 1 (2003): 10–26.

————. *Upheavals of Thought: The Intelligence of Emotions.* Cambridge: Cambridge University Press, 2002.

————. *Women and Human Development: The Capabilities Approach.* New York: Cambridge University Press, 2000.

————. "Comments on Englert's 'Stoics and Epicureans on the Nature of Suicide.'" In *Proceedings of the Boston Area Colloquium in Ancient Philosophy*, edited by John J. Cleary and William Wians. Lanham, MD: University Press of America, 1996.

————. "Equity and Mercy." In *Punishment and Rehabilitation*, edited by Jeffrie G. Murphy. Belmont, CA: Wadsworth, 1995.

————. *The Therapy of Desire, Chapter 11: Seneca on Anger in Public Life.* Princeton, NJ: Princeton University Press, 1994.

Nussbaum, Martha, and Juha Sihvola, ed. *The Sleep of Reason: Erotic Experience and Sexual Ethics in Ancient Greece and Rome*. Chicago: University of Chicago Press, 2002.

Oatley, Keith. *Best Laid Schemes: The Psychology of Emotions*. Cambridge: Cambridge University Press, 1992.

Orwin, Clifford. "Civility." *American Scholar* 60 (1991): 553–64.

Owen, Wilfred. *The Complete Poems and Fragments*, vol. 1. Edited by Jon Stallworthy. New York: Norton, 1984.

———. *The Collected Poems of Wilfred Owen*. Edited by C. Day Lewis. London: Chatto and Windus, 1974.

Parrott, W. Gerrod, ed. *Emotions in Social Psychology*. Philadelphia: Psychology Press, 2001.

Peters, R. S., and C. A. Mace. "Emotions and the Category of Passivity." Paper presented at the Meeting of the Aristotelian Society, London, January 29, 1962.

Peterson, Christopher, Steven F. Maier, and Martin E. P. Seligman. *Learned Helplessness: A Theory for the Age of Personal Control*. New York: Oxford University Press, 1993.

Pettit, Philip. *A Theory of Freedom: From the Psychology to the Politics of Agency*. New York: Oxford University Press, 2001.

Philpott, Tom. "Can Mike Boorda Salvage the Navy?" *Washingtonian*, February 1995, 52–55, 98–100.

Plato. *The Republic*. Translated by G. M. A. Grube. Indianapolis: Hackett, 1974.

Plutarch. *Moralia*, vol. 1. Translated by W. C. Helmbold. Cambridge, MA: Harvard University Press, 2000.

Pollack, William. *Real Boys*. New York: Holt, 1998.

Pomeroy, Arthur, ed. *Arius Didymus: Epitome of Stoic Ethics*. Atlanta: Society of Biblical Literature, 1999.

Pope, Harrison, Katherine Phillips, and Roberto Olivardia. *The Adonis Complex*. New York: Touchstone, 2000.

Posidonius. *Posidonius*, vol. I: *The Fragments*. Edited by I. G. Kidd and L. Edelstein. New York: Cambridge University Press, 1989.

———. *Posidonius*, vol. II: *The Commentary*, part 1: *Testimonia and Fragments 1–149*. Edited by I. G. Kidd. New York: Cambridge University Press, 1989.

———. *Posidonius*, vol. II: *The Commentary*, part 2: *Testimonia and Fragments 150–293*. Edited by I. G. Kidd. New York: Cambridge University Press, 1989.

———. *Posidonius*, vol. III: *The Translation of the Fragments*. Edited by I. G. Kidd. New York: Cambridge University Press, 1999.

Powell, Colin, with Joseph Persico. *My American Journey*. New York: Random House, 1995.

Powell, J.G.F., ed. *Cicero the Philosopher*. Oxford: Clarendon Press, 1995.

Power, Samantha. *A Problem from Hell: America and the Age of Genocide*. New York: Basic, 2002.

Puryear, Edgar Jr. *Nineteen Stars: A Study in Military Character and Leadership*. Novato, CA: Presidio, 1971.

Rawls, John. *A Theory of Justice*. Cambridge, MA: The Belknap Press of Harvard University Press, 1971.

Rawson, Elizabeth. *Roman Culture and Society: Collected Papers*. Oxford: Clarendon Press, 1991.

———. *Intellectual Life in the Late Roman Republic*. Baltimore: Johns Hopkins University Press, 1985.

———. *Cicero: A Portrait*. Ithaca, NY: Cornell University Press, 1983.

Reddy, William M. *The Navigation of Feeling: A Framework for the History of Emotions*. New York: Cambridge University Press, 2001.

Reed, Henry. *Collected Poems*. Oxford: Oxford University Press, 1991.

Reesor, Margaret. *The Nature of Man in Early Stoic Philosophy*. New York: St. Martin's Press, 1989.

Remarque, Erich Maria. *The Road Back*. Translated by A. W. Wheen. Boston: Little, Brown, and Company, 1931.

Richardson, Henry. "Institutionally Divided Moral Responsibility." *Social Philosophy and Policy* 16 (1999): 218–49.

Richlin, Amy. "Gender and Rhetoric: Producing Manhood in the Schools." In *Roman Eloquence: Rhetoric in Society and Literature*, edited by William J. Dominik. London: Routledge, 1996.

Ricks, Thomas E. *A Soldier's Duty*. New York: Random House, 2001.

———. *Making the Corps*. New York: Touchstone, 1997.

Rist, John M. "Are You a Stoic? The Case of Marcus Aurelius." In *Jewish and Christian Self-Definition, Volume III: Self-Definition in the Greco-Roman World*, edited by Ben and E. P. Sanders Meyer, 23–45. Philadelphia: Fortress Press, 1982.

———. *Stoic Philosophy*. London: Cambridge University Press, 1969.

Rivers, W. H. R. "The Repression of War Experience." *The Lancet* (1918).

Roberts, Wess. *Leadership Secrets of Attila the Hun*. New York: Warner Books, 1987.

Rodin, David. *War and Self-Defense*. New York: Oxford University Press, 2002.

Rorty, Amelie Oksenberg. *Mind in Action: Essays in the Philosophy of Mind*. Boston: Beacon Press, 1988.

Rosenbaum, Stephen E. "Epicurus on Pleasure and the Complete Life." *Monist* 73, 1 (1990): 21–41.

Sabini, John. *Social Psychology* (1992): 55–61.

Sankowski, Edward. "Responsibility of Persons for Their Emotions." *Canadian Journal of Philosophy* 7, 4 (1977): 829–40.

Sassoon, Siegfried. *Siegfried Sassoon's Long Journey: Selections from the Sherston Memoirs*. Edited by Paul Fussell. New York: The K. S. Giniger Company, 1983.

———. *Selected Poems*. London: Faber and Faber, 1968.

———. *Sherston's Progress*. New York: Book League of America, 1936.

———. *Vigils*. New York: Viking, 1936.

———. *Counter-Attack and Other Poems*. New York: Dutton, 1918.

Schachter, S., and J. Singer. "Cognitive, Social, and Psychological Determinants of Emotional State." *Psychological Review* 69 (1962): 379–99.

Scherer, K. R. "Studying the Emotion-Antecedent Appraisal Process: An Expert System Approach." *Cognition and Emotion* 3/4 (1993): 325–55.

Schneewind, J. B. *The Invention of Autonomy*. New York: Cambridge University Press, 1998.

Schoeman, Ferdinand, ed. *Responsibility, Character, and the Emotions: New Essays in Moral Psychology*. Cambridge: Cambridge University Press, 1987.

Schofield, Malcolm. *The Stoic Idea of the City*. Chicago: University of Chicago Press, 1991.

Schofield, Malcolm, and Gisela Striker, eds. *The Norms of Nature*. New York: Cambridge University Press, 1986.

Schulhofer, Stephen J. *Unwanted Sex: The Culture of Intimidation and the Failure of Law*. Cambridge, MA: Harvard University Press, 1998.

Sedley, David, ed. *The Cambridge Companion to Greek and Roman Philosophy*. New York: Cambridge University Press, 2003.

———, ed. *Oxford Studies in Ancient Philosophy*. Vol. 22. Oxford: Oxford University Press, 2002.

———. "The Stoic-Platonist Debate on *Kathekonta*." In *Topics in Stoic Philosophy*, edited by Katerina Ierodiakonou. New York: Oxford University Press, 1999.

Seidler, Michael J. "Kant and the Stoics on the Emotional Life." *Philosophy Research Archives* 7 (1981): 1093–150.

Seneca. *Epistulae Morales*. Translated by Richard Gummere. 3 vols. Loeb Classical Library. Cambridge, MA: Harvard University Press, 1989.

———. *Moral and Political Essays*. Translated by John M. Cooper and J. F. Procopé. New York: Cambridge University Press, 1995.

———. *Moral Essays*. Translated by John W. Basore. 3 vols. Loeb Classical Library edition. Cambridge, MA: Harvard University Press, 1989.

Shay, Jonathan. *Odysseus in America: Combat Trauma and the Trials of Homecoming*. New York: Scribner, 2002.

———. *Achilles in Vietnam: Combat Trauma and the Undoing of Character*. New York: Touchstone, 1994.

Shephard, Ben. *A War of Nerves: Soldiers and Psychiatrist in the Twentieth Century*. Cambridge, MA: Harvard University Press, 2001.

Sher, George. *Desert*. Princeton, NJ: Princeton University Press, 1987.

Sherman, Nancy. "Changing Places in Fancy." In *Philosophie Morale: Amitié*, edited by Jean-Christophe Merle and Bernard Schumacher. Paris: Presses Universitaires de France, forthcoming.

————. "The Look and Feel of Virtue." In *Norms, Virtue, and Objectivity: Issues in Ancient and Modern Ethics*, edited by Christopher Gill. New York: Oxford University Press, 2005 (2005a).

————. "Virtue and a Warrior's Anger." In *Working Virtue: Virtue Ethics and Contemporary Moral Problems*, edited by R. L. Walker and P. J. Ivanhoe. New York: Oxford University Press, 2005 (2005b).

————. "Virtue and Emotional Demeanor." In *Feelings and Emotions: Interdisciplinary Explorations*, edited by Nico Frijda Anthony Manstead, and Agneta Fischer. New York: Cambridge University Press, 2004 (2004a).

————. "Empathy and the Family." *Acta Philosophica* 13 (2004) (2004b).

————. "The Analyst as Stoic Sage." Paper given at the APA Pacific Division annual conference, April 2004 (2004c).

————. "Stoic Meditations and the Shaping of Character: The Case of Educating the Military." In *Spirituality, Philosophy, and Education*, edited by D. Carr and J. Haldane. New York: Routledge, 2003.

————. "Educating the Stoic Warrior." In *Bringing in a New Era in Character Education*, edited by William Damon. Stanford, CA: Hoover Institution, 2002 (2002a).

————. "Emotions." In *Encyclopedia of Bioethics*, 3rd ed., edited by Warren Reich. New York: Macmillan, 2002 (2002b).

————. "Emotional Agents." In *The Analytic Freud: Philosophy and Psychoanalysis*, edited by Michael P. Levine. London: Routledge, 2000 (2000a).

————. "Wise Emotions." In *Understanding Wisdom*, edited by Warren Brown, 319–39. Radnor, PA: Templeton Foundation Press, 2000 (2000b).

————. "Is the Ghost of Aristotle Haunting Freud's House?" In *Proceedings of the Boston Area Colloquium in Ancient Philosophy*, edited by Gary Gurtler and John Cleary. Leiden: Brill, 2000 (2000c).

————, ed. *Critical Essays on the Classics: Aristotle's Ethics*. New York: Rowman and Littlefield, 1999 (1999a).

————. "Taking Responsibility for Our Emotions." *Social Philosophy and Policy* 16, 2 (1999): 294–323; also in *Responsibility*, edited by Ellen Frankel Paul, Fred D. Miller Jr., and Jeffrey Paul. Cambridge: Cambridge University Press, 1999 (1999b).

————. "Character Development and Aristotelian Virtue." In *Virtue Theory and Moral Education*, edited by D. Carr and J. Steutel, 35–48. New York: Routledge, 1999 (1999c).

————. "Concrete Kantian Respect." *Social Philosophy and Policy* 1998; also in *Virtue and Vice*, edited by F. Miller E. Paul, and J. Paul, 119–48. New York: Cambridge University Press, 1998 (1998a).

————. "Empathy and Imagination." *Philosophy of Emotions, Midwest Studies in Philosophy* 22 (1998): 82–119 (1998b).

————. "Empathy, Respect, and Humanitarian Intervention." *Ethics and International Affairs* 12 (1998): 103–19 (1998c).

————. "Aristotles og Kant om Folelsenes Nodvendighet." In *Dydsetikk*, edited by A. J. Vetlesen, 126–50. Oslo, Norway: Humanist Forlag, 1998 (1998d).

————. *Making a Necessity of Virtue*. Cambridge: Cambridge University Press, 1997 (1997a).

————. "Kantian Virtue: Priggish or Passional." In *Reclaiming the History of Ethics: Essays for John Rawls*, edited by C. Korsgaard B. Herman, and A. Reath, 270–96. New York: Cambridge University Press, 1997 (1997b).

————. "Kant on Sentimentalism and Stoic Apathy." *Proceedings of the Eighth International Kant Congress* 1 (1995): 705–11 (1995a).

————. "The Moral Perspective and the Psychoanalytic Quest." *The Journal of the American Academy of Psychoanalysis* 23, 2 (1995): 223–41 (1995b).

————. "The Role of Emotions in Aristotelian Virtue." *Proceedings of the Boston Area Colloquium in Ancient Philosophy* 9 (1994): 1–33 (1994a).

————. "The Heart's Knowledge." *Internationale Zeitschrift fur Philosophie* 2 (1994): 204–19 (1994b).

————. "Wise Maxims/Wise Judging." *Monist* 76, 1 (1993): 41–65 (1993a).

————. "The Virtues of Common Pursuit." *Philosophy and Phenomenological Research* 53, 2 (1993): 277–99 (1993b).

————. "Virtue and Hamartia." In *Essays on Aristotle's Poetics*, edited by A. O. Rorty, 177–96. Princeton, NJ: Princeton University Press, 1992.

————. "The Place of Emotions in Kantian Morality." In *Character, Psychology and Morality*, edited by O. Flanagan and A. O. Rorty, 158–70. Cambridge, MA: MIT Press, 1990.

————. *The Fabric of Character*. New York: Oxford University Press, 1989.

————. "Common Sense and Uncommon Virtue." *Midwest Studies in Philosophy*, 1988: 97–114.

————. "Aristotle on Friendship and the Shared Life." *Philosophy and Phenomenological Research* 47, 4 (1987): 589–613.

————. "Commentary on T. Irwin's 'Aristotle's Conception of Morality.'" In *Proceedings of the Boston Area Colloquium in Ancient Philosophy*, edited by J. Cleary, 144–50. Lanham, MD: University Press of America, 1986.

————. "Character, Planning and Choice in Aristotle." *Review of Metaphysics* 39, 1 (1985): 83–106.

Sherman, Nancy, A. Donovan, D. Johnson, G. Lucas Jr., and P. Roush, ed. *Ethics for Military Leaders*. 2 vols. New York: American Heritage Custom Publishing, 1997.

Sherman, Nancy, and Heath White. "Intellectual Virtue, Luck, and the Ancients." In *Intellectual Virtue*, edited by M. DePaul and L. Zagzebski. New York: Oxford University Press, 2003.

Sides, Hampton. *Ghost Soldiers: The Forgotten Epic Story of World War II's Most Dramatic Mission*. New York: Doubleday, 2001.

Sihvola, Juha, and Troels Engberg-Pederson, eds. *The Emotions in Hellenistic Philosophy*. Dordrecht, Netherlands: Kluwer, 1998.

Singer, P. W. *Children at War.* New York: Pantheon, 2005.

————. *Corporate Warriors: The Rise of the Privatized Military Industry.* Ithaca, NY: Cornell University Press, 2003.

Sinopoli, Richard C. "Thick-Skinned Liberalism: Redefining Civility." *American Political Science Review* 89, 3 (1995): 612–20.

Slavin, M. O., and D. Kriegman. *The Adaptive Design of the Human Psyche.* New York: Guilford, 1992.

Sledge, E. B. *With the Old Breed at Peleliu and Okinawa.* Novato, CA: Presidio Press, 1981.

Solomon, Robert C. "Emotions and Choice." *Review of Metaphysics* 27 (1973): 20–41.

Sonnenberg, Stephen M., Arthur S. Blank Jr., and John A. Talbott, eds. *The Trauma of War: Stress and Recovery in Viet Nam Veterans.* Washington, DC: American Psychiatric Press, 1985.

Sorabji, Richard. *Emotion and Peace of Mind: From Stoic Agitation to Christian Temptation.* Oxford: Oxford University Press, 2000.

————. "Perceptual Content in the Stoics." *Phronesis* 35, 3 (1990): 307–14.

Spiller, Roger. "S. L. A. Marshall and the Ratio of Fire." *RUSI Journal,* winter (1988): 63–71.

Stanton, Doug. *In Harm's Way.* New York: Owl Books, 2001.

Stanton, G. R. "The Cosmopolitan Ideas of Epictetus and Marcus Aurelius." *Phronesis* 13, 2 (1968): 183–95.

Statman, Daniel. "Hypocrisy and Self-Deception." *Philosophical Psychology* 10, 1 (1997): 57–75.

————. "Modesty, Pride and Realistic Self-Assessment." *The Philosophical Quarterly* 42, 169 (1992): 420–38.

Sterba, James P., ed. *Terrorism and International Justice.* New York: Oxford University Press, 2003.

Stewart, Nora Kinzer. *Mates and Muchachos: Unit Cohesion in the Falklands/Malvinas War.* Washington: Brassey's, 1991.

Stobaeus, John. *Anthology.* Vol. 2: Apud Weidmannos, 1884.

Stockdale, James. "Stockdale on Stoicism II: Master of My Fate." Center for the Study of Professional Military Ethics, U.S. Naval Academy, 2001.

————. *Thoughts of a Philosophical Fighter Pilot.* Stanford, CA: Hoover Institution Press, 1995.

————. *Courage Under Fire: Testing Epictetus's Doctrines in a Lab of Human Behavior.* Stanford, CA: Hoover Institution Press, 1994.

Stocker, Michael. *Valuing Emotions.* Cambridge: Cambridge University Press, 1996.

Strack, Fritz, Leonard L. Martin, and Sabine Stepper. "Inhibiting and Facilitating Conditions of the Human Smile: A Nonobtrusive Test of the Facial Feedback Hypothesis." *Journal of Personality and Social Psychology* 54, 5 (1988): 768–77.

Strawson, Peter. "Freedom and Resentment." In *Free Will*, edited by Gary Watson, 72–93. Oxford: Oxford University Press, 2003.

Striker, Gisela. "Plato's Socrates and the Stoics." In *The Socratic Movement*, edited by Paul Vander Waerdt, 241–51. Ithaca, NY: Cornell University Press, 1994.

———. "Following Nature: A Study in Stoic Ethics." In *Oxford Studies in Ancient Philosophy*, edited by Julia Annas, 1–73. New York: Oxford University Press, 1991.

———. "Antipater, or the Art of Living." In *The Norms of Nature*, edited by Gisela Striker, 185–203. New York: Cambridge University Press, 1986.

Swofford, Anthony. *Jarhead: A Marine's Chronicle of the Gulf War and Other Battles*. New York: Scribner, 2003.

Tacitus. *The Annals of Imperial Rome*. Translated by Michael Grant. New York: Penguin Books, 1977.

Thera, Hyanaponika, and Bikkhu Bodhi. *The Vision of Dhamma*. Boston: Weiser Books, 1986.

Theweleit, Klaus. *Male Fantasies*. 2 vols. Minneapolis, MN: University of Minnesota Press, 1989.

Thomas, Evan. "A Matter of Honor." *Newsweek*, May 27, 1996, 25–29.

Thurman, Robert. *Essential Tibetan Buddhism*. New York: HarperCollins, 1995.

Timberg, Robert. *The Nightingale's Song*. New York: Simon and Schuster, Inc., 1995.

Tomkins, Silvan S. *Affect, Imagery, Consciousness*. 2 vols. New York: Springer, 1962.

Toynbee, J.M.C. *Death and Burial in the Roman World*. Ithaca, NY: Cornell University Press, 1971.

Tzu, Sun. *The Art of War*. Translated by Thomas Cleary. Boston: Shambhala, 1988.

———. *The Art of War*. Translated by Samuel B. Griffith. New York: Oxford University Press, 1971.

Van Wees, Hans. *Status Warriors: War, Violence and Society in Homer and History*. Amsterdam: J. C. Gieben, 1992.

———, ed. *War and Violence in Ancient Greece*. London: Duckworth, 2000.

Vander Waerdt, Paul A. "Politics and Philosophy in Stoicism." In *Oxford Studies in Ancient Philosophy*, vol. IX, edited by Julia Annas. New York: Oxford University Press, 1991.

Vandergriff, Donald. *The Path to Victory: America's Army and the Revolution in Human Affairs*. Novato, CA: Presidio Press, 2002.

Velleman, David. "Don't Worry, Feel Guilty." In *Philosophy and the Emotions*, edited by Anthony Hatzimoysis, 235–48. Cambridge: Cambridge University Press, 2003.

———. "Identification and Identity." In *Contours of Agency: A Festschrift for Harry Frankfurt*, edited by Sarah Buss, and Lee Overton. Cambridge, MA: MIT Press, 2002.

————. "A Rational Superego." *Philosophical Review* 108 (1999): 529–58.

Veyne, Paul. *Bread and Circuses: Historical Sociology and Political Pluralism.* London: Penguin, 1990.

Vistica, Gregory L. "What Happened in Thanh Phong." *New York Times Magazine*, April 29, 2001.

Von Armin, H., ed. *Stoicorum Veterum Fragmente.* Leipzig: Reprint Library, 1924.

Wakin, Malham M., ed. *War, Morality, and the Military Profession.* Boulder, CO: Westview Press, 1979.

Waller, Willard. *On the Family, Education, and War.* Chicago: University of Chicago Press, 1970.

Walzer, Michael. *Arguing About War.* New Haven, CT: Yale University Press, 2004.

————. *Just and Unjust Wars.* New York: Penguin, 1977.

Watson, Gerard. *The Stoic Theory of Knowledge.* Belfast: The Queen's University, 1966.

Weiss, Roslyn. "The Moral and Social Dimensions of Gratitude." *The Southern Journal of Philosophy* 23, 4 (1985): 491–501.

White, Nick. "Stoic Values." *Monist* 73, 1 (1990): 42–58.

White, Stephen A. "Cicero and the Therapists." In *Cicero the Philosopher*, edited by J.G.F. Powell. Oxford: Clarendon Press, 1995.

Wieseltier, Leon. *Kaddish.* New York: Alfred A. Knopf, 1998.

Wiesenthal, Simon. *The Sunflower: On the Possibilities and Limit of Forgiveness.* New York: Schocken, 1997.

Williams, Bernard. *Shame and Necessity.* Berkeley: University of California Press, 1993.

Williams, Craig A. *Roman Homosexuality: Ideologies of Masculinity in Classical Antiquity.* Oxford: Oxford University Press, 1999.

Wilson, Marcus. "The Subjugation of Grief in Seneca's 'Epistles.'" In *The Passions in Roman Thought and Literature*, edited by Susanna Morton Braund and Christopher Gill. Cambridge: Cambridge University Press, 1997.

Wolfe, Tom. *A Man in Full.* New York: Bantam, 1999.

Wood, David. "Abuses Damaging in a War Cast as Moral Struggle, Say Officers, Ethicists." *Newhouse News Service*, May 4 2004.

Woolf, Virginia. *Mrs. Dalloway.* New York: Harcourt, Inc., 1981.

Zajonc, R. B. "On the Primacy of Affect." *American Psychologist* 39 (1984): 117–23.

Ziegler, Philip. *Soldiers: Fighting Men's Lives, 1901–2001.* New York: Knopf, 2002.

Zimbardo, P. G. "Pathology of Imprisonment." *Society* (1972): 4–8.

Zimbardo, P. G., C. Haney, and W. C. Banks. "Interpersonal Dynamics in a Simulated Prison." *International Journal of Criminology and Penology* 1, 1 (1973): 69–97.

Photograph Credits and Permissions

All other photos are from the collection of Nancy Sherman or are in the public domain.

Index

Note: Page numbers in *italics* refer to illustrations; page numbers in **bold** refer to chapters.

ML

7/05